Key Concepts in International Relations

Series Editor: Paul Wilkinson

3

International Cultural Relations

D0961737

Key Concepts in International Relations

Series Editor: Paul Wilkinson

International Cultural Relations

J. M. Mitchell

London
ALLEN & UNWIN
Boston   Sydney

Published in association with
THE BRITISH COUNCIL

Allen & Unwin (Publishers) Ltd,
40 Museum Street, London WC1A 1LU, UK

Allen & Unwin (Publishers) Ltd,
Park Lane, Hemel Hempstead, Herts HP2 4TE, UK

Allen & Unwin, Inc.,
8 Winchester Place, Winchester, Mass. 01890, USA

Allen & Unwin (Australia) Ltd,
8 Napier Street, North Sydney, NSW 2060, Australia

First published in 1986

British Library Cataloguing in Publication Data

Mitchell, J. M.
    International cultural relations—(Key concepts in international
    relations; 3)
1. Cultural relations
I. Title   II. Series
303.4'82   HM101
ISBN 0-04-327082-4
ISBN 0-04-327083-2 Pbk

Library of Congress Cataloging-in-Publication Data

Mitchell, J. M., 1925–
    International cultural relations.
    (Key concepts in international relations; 3)
Bibliography: p.
Includes index.
1. Cultural policy.   2. International relations and culture.
I. Title.   II. Series.
K3712.M58   1986   344'.09   86-3425
                        342.49
ISBN 0-04-327082-4 (alk. paper)
ISBN 0-04-327083-2 (pbk.: alk. paper)

Set in 10 on 11 point Times by Fotographics (Bedford) Ltd,
and printed in Great Britain by Billing and Son Ltd,
London and Worcester

Contents

Acknowledgement

The publishers are grateful to the Public Record Office for permission to reproduce material which is in Crown copyright.

The views expressed in this book are those of the author and not necessarily of the British Council.

General Editor's Introduction

The word 'concept' is derived from a Latin root meaning literally gathering or bundling together. In any organized body of knowledge the major concepts developed and deployed by scholars are the vital instruments for organizing information and ideas; they are as indispensable for the tasks of gathering classification and typology as they are in the more ambitious work of model and theory-building. And in any study of human history and society these key concepts inevitably constitute weapons and battlefields in the conflict of normative theories, ideologies and moral judgements. Every major concept of international relations has a very different connotation depending on the philosophical beliefs, ideology, or attitude of the beholder. Take the terms 'imperialism' and 'revolution': although liberal and Marxist writers frequently use these words the precise meanings and significance they attach to them will vary enormously, and even if a single author is perfectly consistent in usage in a single book, he may alter his usage, either consciously or unwittingly, over time. None of us is immune against this process of continual redefinition and reevaluation. This is one of the reasons why it is so important for us all, whether laymen or specialists to become more aware, vigilant and critical of the problems and pitfalls of conceptualization both for ourselves and others. The review and clarification should not be left to a small coterie of professional philosophers and linguistic analysts. It should be a regular part of our own mental preparation for study, reflection, writing, and the practical burdens of communicating and participating in a democratic society. Careful and informed use of the full range of major concepts developed in any field of knowledge, with due attention to clarity and consistency and the interrelatedness of concepts is also obviously a vital heuristic tool, a prerequisite for good scientific research. More than this, the refinement, modification and reevaluation involved in operationalizing well-tried concepts often lead to the introduction of new concepts, fresh building-blocks in the development of knowledge, discovery and fuller under-standing, whether of the physical universe, human history and society, or the nature and development of the individual human spirit, personality, and imagination.

If one examines the standard range of introductory texts on inter-national relations used by universities in America and Western Europe, one is struck by three features of their conceptual apparatus, aspects which are now so widespread that they can be said to typify the stock-in-trade of the discipline. First, there is the astonishingly wide consensus on the basic checklist of key organizing concepts in the subject, almost invariably reflected in the contents outline: international system, nation–state, sovereignty, power, balance of power, diplomacy, military strategy, nuclear deterrence, alliances, foreign policy-making, international law, international organization, trade, aid, and development. These are the almost ubiquitous repertoires. Other themes such as human rights, conflict resolution, ideology, and propaganda find inclusion in a minority of contents pages; almost invariably in the modern texts they will be mentioned only briefly at some point in the introductory survey course.

A second recurrent feature is the lack of attention to the origin and development of the concepts themselves. This characterizes nearly all the well-known texts. It is almost as if the text-book writers wish to leave the student in innocence of the major historical developments of their subject. How many of the introductory texts, for example, even bother to mention such seminal contributions as those of Grotius in international law, Clausewitz in military strategy, or Mitrany in the field of international organization? Only rarely is attention given to problems of definition, to conflicting theories and approaches, and to the problems of conceptual obsolescence and innovation.

The third major weakness, in the editor's view, is the failure to adequately relate the key concepts of international relations to the real world thinking and activities of statesmen, officials, political parties, media, public, and other key participants in the international system. Yet the language of international relations we use as academic teachers, researchers, and students, is not the esoteric product of a research laboratory or seminar room: our major concepts are the very stuff of international diplomacy, foreign policy, and intercourse. True, on occasion, as in the case of the key concepts of nuclear deterrence and functionalist and neo-functionalist theories of integration, academicians and scientists serving or advising governments have also played a key role in developing new concepts. Yet the plain fact is that many of our newer concepts – in, for example, military strategy, economic development and international organization – have been originated, modified, developed and debated mainly among politicians, diplomatists, civil servants, service chiefs, guerrilla leaders, and even journalists. And because we need to be closely in touch with the nuances and subtleties of the constant evolution of ideas and assumptions of the main participants in the international system, narrowly-based surveys of conceptual usage and development in the scholarly literature would also be inadequate and distorting.

It is to remedy these grave deficiencies that this new series of individual monographs, each devoted to a thorough review of a major international relations concept, has been devised. The editor and publishers hope that the series will educate and illuminate at both the undergraduate and post-graduate teaching levels in all universities and colleges that offer courses in international relations. It is also hoped that the volumes will provide valuable background, sources, and stimulus to teachers and researchers, many of whom have long complained about the absence of such guides. Finally, the series should also be of value to officials, politicians, industrial executives and others whose professional work involves some degree of participation in, and understanding of, international developments, trends, policy-making and problems. The series should also be of interest and value to students and specialists in cognate disciplines, such as history, economics, political science, and sociology.

It may help to recapitulate the brief given to each contributor in the series. It is intended that each volume will deal thoroughly with the following aspects: The origins and evolution of the concept, including significant variations and changes in usage, and in relation to changes in the international system and in the political systems of major powers; an attempt at an authoritative definition of the concept in order that it may be employed as a more effective tool in the analysis and theory of international relations; the identification of any important sub-concepts and typologies; a critical review of the ways in which the concept is utilized in major theories, models and approaches in the contemporary study of international relations; the relationship between the concept and the contemporary practice of international relations; the relationship between the concept and policy-making in international relations; the future of the concept in international relations.

It should hardly be necessary to add that the publishers and the series academic editor should have chosen the individual authors commissioned to review each concept, with considerable care, taking into account not only their previous record of scholarly work in the field, but also their experience as teachers and expositors. We hope and believe that the completed series will provide a boon to international relations teaching and research world-wide. We welcome suggestions, responses and even practical proposals for additional contributions to the series. Please correspond in the first instance with Gordon Smith of Allen & Unwin at the address printed on the reverse of the title page.

*   *   *

In addition to dealing with the key concepts traditionally included in any university syllabus on international relations, it is one of the tasks of this series to re-examine neglected or undervalued concepts and even to pioneer the analysis of those totally omitted from the conventional general textbooks on the subject. *International Cultural Relations* clearly falls into the latter category. Yet when one considers the historical role and importance of cultural developments, changes in cultural influences and patterns of dominance, and the often seminal role of cultural attitudes and differences in triggering and sustaining international conflicts and determining their outcomes, this omission is clearly indefensible. The reasons why the concepts of cultural relations, culture-clash, cultural imperialism, and cultural diplomacy are missing from the contents of our standard textbooks on international relations have nothing to do with their relative importance in the international system: rather they are a reflection of the uneven and incomplete development of the subject and, in particular, our contemporary preoccupations with the short-term shifts in the balance of power, alliances, and foreign policy. In the 1950s and 1960s the huge burgeoning of strategic studies, stimulated by the development of nuclear weapons, led to a diversion of considerable energy and resources in these aspects of the subject. This preoccupation is of course largely explained by the insatiable demands of the policymakers for conceptual, analytical and theoretical tools to help them deal with the complex problems raised by the revolution in weapons technology. Substantial grants by government agencies to promote such studies in research institutes and university departments in the United States and Western Europe have fuelled this rush to strategic studies to such an extent that there are clear signs of over-commitment and exhaustion, with much duplication and inferior work being sustained often simply because there is no money for research on other aspects of international relations. Since the oil crisis of 1973 there has been a new fashionable preoccupation with the study of international economic relations. Considering the severity of the problems of lack of economic development, poverty and famine in the Third World, the debt crisis, and the strong reemergence of protectionist pressures in the international economy, this impetus in international economic research is to be greatly welcomed. Thus far it has hardly received a fraction of the government support lavished on strategic studies. At least it is increasingly recognized as a key focus for further concerted research efforts.

Alas there has been no serious effort to sponsor research in the field of cultural relations. Because governments and other major bodies concerned with funding cannot see any obvious application or 'payoffs' for such investigations, they simply have not been carried out. In policy terms this is mirrored in the miserly grants made to cultural and educational agencies such as the British Council. But it is not our job as academics to pander and adjust to the fashions and prejudices of our political masters. There *is* an overwhelming intellectual case for the study of international cultural relations as an area of basic research. For if we take the long-term view of international relations we find that cultural changes are the most pervasive and irreversible elements in human history. To take a famous and striking example, the influence of Latin and of Roman ideas of law, governance, civic and architectural design, military strategy and organization, agriculture and trade was seminal in moulding the history of Europe from Byzantium in the East to Britain in the West. Long after the fall of the Roman Empire in the West, this cultural experience provided a framework, a series of models and a source of knowledge which could be constantly rediscovered, modified and applied by later societies in different conditions. Like the Hellenic civilization that preceded Roman culture it was to become a kind of master 'data bank' for the development of future civilizations.

Yet perhaps the most vivid demonstration of the tenacity of cultural imprints on history is the way in which the cultures of small and politically and militarily powerless societies can survive for centuries, even under conditions of rapacious colonial domination and subjection by more powerful civilizations. This is strikingly illustrated in the dogged survival of the languages and arts and crafts of the indigenous Indian peoples of North and South America.

Ranging between the imperialism of temporarily dominant cultures and the almost 'underground' survival of the weak and vulnerable ones there is a whole fascinating field for investigation in the processes and effects of cultural intermixing and interaction and the political, social, economic and religious relations of multi-ethnic societies. This has been the subject of some superb pioneering work by social historians such as Oscar Handlin in the case of the USA. But the international interactions, for example between Francophone and indigenous Black culture in West Africa, or between British and Indian culture in the sub-continent are still little understood.

A careful reading of John Mitchell's exciting and pioneering study of international cultural relations in the contemporary international system shows how little we really know about the underlying processes of cultural influence, growth and decay. Why is it that some cultures appear to leave profound and lasting influences on the societies which have experienced contact with them while others disappear almost without trace? Are some languages more suited than others to cultural 'transplantation'? Why is it that some cultures appear more resistant than others to the assimilation of externally derived technology and scientific knowledge? John Mitchell does not pretend to have simple answers to any of these questions. But, drawing on his long personal experience as a senior official of the British Council and a formidable erudition in the modern history of cultural relations, he provides a thought-provoking analysis of the problems of international cultural relations and poses some crucial questions about their future development. With a fascinating blend of historical comparison and professional insight he explores the crucial distinction between cultural relations and the much narrower field of formal cultural diplomacy. He critically examines the role of the national cultural agencies of the leading powers and assesses their limitations, resource problems, and relative effectiveness.

John Mitchell has a striking and iconoclastic view of the role of the professional expert in cultural relations. In his view he should not be seen as a servant of national power politics or economic enrichment. He sees culture as a vehicle for more fundamental purposes than manipulation or the purchase of influence. To him the ideal exponent of international cultural relations is dedicated to the task of helping different cultures to understand each other and to learn from each other. It is a noble aspiration of 'nation speaking unto nation', totally free from machination, pressure or coercion. In this task, the author argues, higher education, the arts and sciences, and the broadcasting media all have a key part to play. In all these activities successful conduct of international relations calls for endless reserves of patience, a dedicated pursuit of greater knowledge of other languages and cultures, enormous sensitivity, and total integrity. In addition it requires all the skills of the educator and expositor.

The author does not for one minute pretend that the successful conduct of cultural relations is easily achieved. He constantly emphasises the formidable constraints. Unlike some of the more superficial commentators on international relations, he never underestimates the degree to which language differences can pose barriers to understanding and communication. By this he does not, of course, simply refer to the contacts of government leaders and officials with their universal paraphernalia of interpreters. He means that the people of one language group will only be able to acquire a thorough and profound understanding of another if it is able to converse in a language both can understand. Hence his considerable, and in my view totally justified, emphasis on the activities of language training as the cornerstone of a cultural relations policy. Secondly, John Mitchell never attempts to avoid the problem of instinctive suspicion towards foreign or alien ideas. In so many of the so-called cosmopolitan societies of the industrialized West there are ample signs of an ugly latent xenophobia in many sectors of society. Such feelings are often partly the result of bitter conflicts and wars in living memory. They are also often whipped up by unscrupulous politicians pandering to populist instincts.

Last but not least, Dr Mitchell is profoundly aware of the deep and lasting effect of socialization, the formal education process and the dominant political and religious culture. But as a dedicated exponent of international cultural relations he views all these inherent difficulties as an exciting challenge. He has the abiding faith of the true liberal internationalist that they can be overcome. Not for him the music of doom and despair. His argument is always as beautifully calm and lucid as it is crisp and incisive. Teachers and students of international relations everywhere will do well to depend on this magisterial guide to this important but little understood branch of international relations.

Paul Wilkinson
Professor of International Relations
University of Aberdeen

Foreword

One balmy evening in Cairo, when I was a junior member of the British Council, I got into conversation at a cocktail party with a sophisticated Egyptian freshly returned from taking a higher degree in English Literature at Oxford. On discovering my profession, he languidly asked, 'Don't you find it slightly absurd to be representing your country's culture abroad?' This was in the early 1950s when the campaign against the British Council in the Beaverbrook press was at its height; it was also the time when the British presence in the Suez Canal Zone was the object of constant attack from the Nasser régime, and one did not feel by any means *persona grata* in all company. 'No', I replied, 'not at all.' And feeling that this response required some elaboration, I added, 'At least, no more absurd than anything else.' Shadows of Albert Camus hung between us. The Egyptian nodded in acknowledgement that I had made a point, and changed the subject.

The incident is significant not because this book is meant to be a more adequate reply thirty years too late – that would be a frivolous beginning – but because the question, so typical then, would hardly be asked today. We have progressed. If my interlocutor and I could take up our conversation now, conscious of the afflictions of the intervening years, I imagine we would both agree that if relations between our two countries had been conducted with more understanding decades ago a great deal of waste could have been avoided, and I have no doubt he would agree that a greater investment in cultural relations would have been a means towards that understanding.

Having declared I now disavow my national interest. This book is an attempt to set cultural relations in a wide context, to take a world-wide conspectus of this aspect of international affairs. The task would be inconceivable in a volume of this size if it meant compiling a gazetteer. My treatment will be thematic rather than synoptic. This will in any case be appropriate to the thesis that the book serves to demonstrate: that cultural relations have become an intrinsic part of the way governments and nations relate to one another, and of the way institutions and peoples form an understanding of one another across frontiers. I hope the book will prompt further research into some of the themes I expose.

To provide a focus on the main issues, special attention has been paid to five countries which are valuable references: France, Italy and the Federal Republic of Germany as long-established practitioners, the United States as an inescapable giant, and Japan as a country whose external cultural role is evolving to match her prosperity and riches. In addition, information supplied by British Council colleagues in some eighty countries has been drawn upon. My own thirty-five years' experience of working at home and abroad with the British Council inevitably, and I hope helpfully, informs my own perceptions. Within the time at my disposal to collect material and visit the five analogue countries, it has not been possible to consult archives anywhere but in Britain. My primary sources are therefore for the most part British or found in Britain.

Translations from French, German and Italian are, except where otherwise indicated in the bibliography, my own. Terminology presents something of a problem, especially in regard to more basic concepts (culture, civilization, etc.), which do not have the same connotation in every language. Some of the terms used in this book are rehearsed in Chapter 9. They are not always satisfactory from the semantic or aesthetic point of view, but the aim has been to achieve intelligibility rather than to revolutionize the vocabulary. The work by Albert Salon, *Vocabulaire critique des relations internationales dans les domaines culturel, scientifique et de la coopération technique* contains a comparative index of terms in French, German and English.

In order to standardize at least the name of one basic institution, the phrase 'foreign ministry' is used throughout for various countries' ministries of external or foreign affairs. The English terms of Foreign (and Commonwealth) Office and State Department are used, however, in respect of Britain and the United States. The word 'foreign' itself deserves a come-back in the English language. Out of apology for latent xenophobia, 'foreign' has in recent years been slowly supplanted by 'overseas' ('overseas students', etc.). In a book on cultural relations, foreigners do not require euphemistic handling. The neutral use of 'foreign' in this book may help to make them seem less foreign.

The book is in three parts. First, the nature and development of international cultural relations; second, their organization and management; third, the various activities whereby they are practised. Since not all readers will be familiar with documentation on this subject the following Appendices are included:

A   Cultural Convention between Great Britain and France.
B   Cultural Agreement between Great Britain and the Soviet Union.
C   External Broadcasting: programme hours.
D   Budgets of Britain and Analogue Countries.

Author's Acknowledgements

The groundwork for this book was accomplished in the last year of my service with the British Council, after I had spent the three and a half decades since 1949 in a variety of overseas and home posts. The last of these was as Assistant Director-General 1981–4.

I am grateful to Sir John Burgh, Director-General of the British Council, for accepting my proposal that I should be released from duties in the Council's headquarters for the year 1984–5 to work on this book. I am particularly indebted to Rayner Unwin of George Allen and Unwin for his counsel when I first broached the project of producing a book on this subject, and for his enthusiasm and encouragement thereafter. I also record my gratitude to Council colleagues and members of the Diplomatic Service in the five analogue countries for their helpfulness and welcome, and to colleagues elsewhere who gave useful answers to the questionnaire I distributed to Council representatives. Among those in the Council's London office to whom I am indebted I would particularly mention Trevor Rutter, Sandy Edington, Harriet Harvey Wood, Sandra Cromey, Teresa Spurgeon and Cilla Rohacz; also Marion Robinson of Central Typing Services, Bournemouth.

My thanks go to Roland Hindmarsh, ex-Council officer and now language adviser, for his advice on language questions; to Henry Croom-Johnson, Kenneth Walsh and David Dilks for the loan of materials from their personal collections; to Francis King and Albert Sloman for their interest; also to members of the Foreign and Commonwealth Office, the Department of Education and Science, the BBC, the Royal Society, Chatham House, the Public Record Office, the Committee of Vice-Chancellors and Principals, PEN, and the Central Bureau for Educational Visits and Exchanges who supplied information. I am grateful also to those cultural representatives of their countries based in London who gave me their assistance, and to all those people I visited abroad, who were invariably informative and welcoming. In particular, I wish to thank Delia Lennie for her advice on Italian translations of English literature and David Rundle, Director of the British Institute of Florence.

Finally, I acknowledge with gratitude the permission kindly given by Lady Leeper to quote from the correspondence of her late husband, Sir Reginald Leeper. Any account of the development of cultural relations in Britain must be a tribute to his grasp of affairs and far-sightedness.

In tribute to those who have devoted their best efforts to the promotion of understanding between nations and to the reduction of mental frontiers.

1

Beyond Diplomacy

The heading *Beyond Diplomacy* suggests further horizons. In the often quoted definition by Sir Ernest Satow, 'Diplomacy is the application of intelligence and tact to the conduct of official relations between the governments of independent states' (Gore-Booth, 1979, p. 3). One is struck by the constraints implied in this form of words. Official relations do not directly touch the lives of most people, not even of elites, though everyone may be disastrously affected when they go wrong. Governments, whether elected or not, are executors of a political will determined by present necessities and burdened by the past. And governments are preoccupied with short-term policies to meet immediate crises.

Politics as a mechanism for bridging the gap between national interest and the compulsive forces at work in the world at large does not score obvious successes. Diplomacy is, however skilfully conducted, the instrument of the political will. Ours is hardly a visionary age. Its technological wonders often exacerbate rather than resolve its fundamental problems. But one unsensational progression has been achieved that brings a degree of international convergence of thought. This is the spread of education, the propagation of the written word, information across frontiers, and the availability of cultural goods in people's lives. It is in this area that cultural relations work is done. The time is opportune to capitalize on the potential it yields for world stability. If, as is often said, the golden age of diplomacy is past, then beyond diplomacy lie alternative forms of international relations.

That cultural relations are of great importance is not today generally in dispute. It is accepted in many countries that they are an essential third dimension in relations between states: third, because they accompany politics and trade (for some American writers, they come fourth after politics, trade and defence). It was Willy Brandt, when he was German Foreign Minister in 1966, who first gave currency to the term 'third pillar of foreign policy'. Senator Fulbright, after whom one of the most imaginative exchange schemes is named (see pp. 54, 57 and 157), wrote in his Foreword to *The Fourth Dimension of Foreign Policy*: 'Foreign policy cannot be based on military posture and diplomatic activities alone in today's world. The shape of the world a generation from now will be influenced far more by how well we communicate the values of our society to others than by our military or diplomatic superiority' (Coombs, 1964, p. ix). The French, who pioneered the whole business, consider the representation of their culture abroad almost a sacred mission and spend half their budget for foreign relations on fulfilling it. But whereas the French government has traditionally identified this work closely with French interests and foreign policy, the general tendency in other democracies since 1945 has, as Doka (1956, p. 33) points out, been to distance it from government direction. The idea of people communicating with each other across national boundaries has been frequently invoked. Indeed, some expressions of the idea have gone further than can altogether be sustained. Writing in a period of postwar idealism, the American author Archibald MacLeish, who was then Assistant Secretary in charge of public and cultural affairs in the State Department, went so far as to say, 'Foreign Offices are no longer offices to speak for one people to another; the people can speak now for themselves. Foreign Offices are offices of international understanding, the principal duty of which is the duty to make the understanding of peoples whole and intelligible and complete' (McMurry and Lee, 1947, p. x). This seems today to carry to extremes the Open Door and New Deal approach, but the desirability that communication between nations should not be inhibited by political barriers remains fundamental and has steadily gained in recognition.

Cultural Relations and Cultural Diplomacy

These two terms are often used as though they were synonymous. In fact, the differences between them are fundamental, but also complex and fairly subtle. Both apply to the practice followed by modern states of interrelating through their cultures. Both have acquired greater currency with the recognition that culture is an expression of national identity and therefore a factor in international affairs. Culture lends impetus to the quest for convergence between conflicting national interests; it has a particular part in overcoming conventional barriers that separate peoples, by promoting understanding between them. Culture represents a dimension in international attitudes where alienation between nations yields to familiarity and feelings of common humanity.

This evolution has had important consequences, which have not been fully appraised and described. The underlying concepts, therefore, remain ambiguous. The term cultural relations itself is neutrally descriptive and throws up little semantic difficulty. It has a wide reference going beyond the actions of governments and their agencies. Cultural relations can be conducted on the initiative of private as well as public institutions. Cultural diplomacy is narrower in scope because it is essentially the business of governments. But cultural diplomacy has two levels of meaning. The first-order meaning applies to the agreements, whether bilateral or multilateral, which are made between governments to permit, facilitate or prescribe cultural exchanges. The inter-governmental negotiation of cultural treaties, conventions, agreements and exchange programmes is cultural diplomacy. Two examples of these are shown in Appendices A and B (see pp. 233 and 235). Likewise the inclusion of cultural clauses in major international agreements, such as the Final Act of the Conference on Security and Co-operation, signed in Helsinki in 1975, is cultural diplomacy. The creation of the United Nations Educational, Scientific and Cultural Organization (UNESCO) in 1946 was an act of cultural diplomacy. The same applies to the cultural aspects of international organizations that are primarily political or economic; for instance, the Organization of Economic Co-operation and Development (OECD), the European Community (although the Treaty of Rome, 1957, makes no mention of culture), the Council of Europe (whose members signed a European Cultural Convention in 1954), the Association of South-East Asian Nations (ASEAN), and the Nordic Council.

The Tindemans Report (1976, p. 28) proposed the creation of a European Foundation 'to promote, either directly or by assisting existing bodies, anything which could help towards greater understanding among our peoples by placing the emphasis on human contact'. The aim in fact was to further wide-scale cultural relations by an act which in itself rates as cultural diplomacy. The examples Tindemans gives of this human contact – 'youth activities, university exchanges, scientific debates and symposia, meetings between the socio-professional categories, cultural and information activities' – clearly go beyond governmental or governmentally inspired activity; they illustrate the way agreements under the heading of cultural diplomacy can facilitate, by collective resolution and budgetary obligation, a wider range of operations involving the institutions of member states. Yet the motive force of diplomacy is clear, as in the sentence: 'This Foundation will also have a role to play in presenting abroad the image of a United Europe' (p. 28). This is a political purpose, but it requires the backing of cultural relations for its implementation. Political agreement or decree involving individuals and institutions would be tenuous without some expectation of their support; there must therefore be a basis in the popular will, and this basis rests upon cultural attitudes.

An outstanding example of multilateral cultural diplomacy is seen in the Helsinki Agreement of 1975. A major section of this, known as Basket III, is concerned with 'Co-operation in Humanitarian and Other Fields'. There are important elements in this which represent concessions made by the Warsaw Pact countries, in return for the recognition of the status quo of Central and Eastern European frontiers, to the demand by the Western democracies for greater freedom of contact and for human rights. Although these concessions have by no means been fully honoured, they provide a text, the product of long diplomatic negotiation and the object of protracted subsequent debate, which can be invoked in the cause of those relations between people that contribute to international security through access and exchanges. Basket III comprises Human Contacts, Information, Co-operation and Exchanges in the Field of Culture and Co-operation in the Field of Education. Under Culture, the participating states:

Declare that they jointly set themselves the following objectives:

(a)   to develop the mutual exchange of information with a view to a better knowledge of respective cultural achievements,
(b)   to improve the facilities for the exchange and for the dissemination of cultural property,
(c)   to promote access by all to respective cultural achievements,
(d)   to develop contacts and co-operation among persons active in the field of culture,
(e)   to seek new fields and forms of cultural co-operation.

(Conference on Security and Co-operation in Europe, 1975, p. 40)

The first-order meaning of cultural diplomacy is apparent enough, then, as one of the areas of international affairs governed by negotiations and agreements between governments. The second-order meaning is less determinate. Essentially, the execution of these agreements and the conduct of cultural relations flowing from them may be seen either as the extended responsibility of governments or as something delegated by governments to agencies and cultural institutions. The former is cultural diplomacy of the second order. As an aspect of diplomacy it is normally carried out abroad by diplomatic staff. It is closely aligned to official policy and national interest. Its ulterior purpose is political or economic. This may or may not be perceptible to its foreign clients, depending on the tact and restraint with which it is executed. Cultural diplomacy seeks to impress, to present a favourable image, so that diplomatic operations as a whole are facilitated. Typically, though with a touch of exaggeration, it would be cultural diplomacy for a government to dispatch its national opera company, with a galaxy of international stars, to perform at a prestigious foreign festival before a cosmopolitan audience, or to mount a series of image-building lectures in a foreign capital, followed by lavish diplomatic receptions, for an invited audience of the great and the good. Both activities would be designed to redound to the credit of the sending country; they might even be timed to further some particular diplomatic end. Now, there is nothing wrong with this. Much activity that rates as cultural diplomacy is defensible and desirable. This might well be true of the examples above. It could undoubtedly be true of national participation in gala occasions, such as arts festivals, to which national representation cannot be denied without offence to the host country or without a significant and damaging forfeit of presence. The manner and cost of representation will of course need careful thought, as we shall see in later chapters, but the compulsion to be included, not to default on an occasion of international offerings, is a worthy reaction not only of diplomacy in general but also of cultural diplomacy. No government and no people wishes to fade into oblivion. Flying the flag is a common manifestation of national identity. Of the colours to be hoisted at the masthead, those that unfurl a nation's cultural achievement are in many modern situations the most appealing. And it is, of course, part of cultural diplomacy to appeal.

Cultural relations on the other hand, are more neutral and comprehensive. In a sense, they embrace the methods of cultural diplomacy, for they employ the resources granted by governments and the benefits resulting from international agreements. The difference is, in practice, one of mode. The purpose of cultural relations is not necessarily, and in advanced thinking hardly at all, to seek one-sided advantage. At their most effective, their purpose is to achieve understanding and co-operation between national societies for their mutual benefit. Cultural relations proceed ideally by the accretion of open professional exchanges rather than by selective self-projection. They purvey an honest picture of each country rather than a beautified one. They do not conceal but neither need they make a show of national problems. They neither pretend that warts are not there nor do they parade them to the repugnance of others.

Obviously, it would make for easier intelligibility if the term cultural diplomacy were reserved for its first-order meaning, and if cultural relations were applied generally to the execution and to the craft. The second-order meaning of cultural diplomacy could then be abandoned to the archives, where it figures prominently in documented history. In effect, this is the tendency that is at work. But to postulate its fulfilment at present would be to presume too far on the intention of all modern states to handle their cultural representation objectively and not to link it inexorably with national interest. After all, cultural diplomacy is probably still the only realizable mode for countries that have not been able to evolve beyond a high degree of government control.

The boycott belongs to cultural diplomacy. It is an expression of political animus. For instance, the cultural boycott placed by Western democracies on the Soviet Union after its invasion of Afghanistan in 1979 and on Poland after its imposition of military rule in 1980 is a short-term political response. It is based on the calculation that a greater effect will be achieved in the boycotted country, and before world opinion, by restriction than by the maintenance of normal cultural relations as a projection of alternative and presumably superior values. Normally, boycotts of this kind involve the suspension of major cultural events rather than the cessation of routine exchange programmes; they are therefore more declamatory than fundamental, the equivalent of the withdrawal of ambassadors rather than the rupture of diplomatic relations. The desirability and efficacy of boycotts can be debated from various points of view. But it is clear that the political motivation, however justified in its own terms, is alien to the spirit of cultural relations, since these operate on a longer time-scale and different wavelength. Admittedly, it might be the case, though it usually is not, that society at large in the sending country would not tolerate more than a minimal level of cultural activity towards a state that has offended against international law or the accepted code of conduct. Then it would be appropriate to cultural relations for more than obligatory activities to be frozen. Indeed, the executors, whether artists or whatever, might refuse their services for reasons of conscience. But in general the cultural boycott is politically motivated and unwelcome to the executors, who as members of elite groups value professional contacts abroad and do not wish them to go by default. For just as cultural relations can continue through non-governmental agencies in countries with which diplomatic relations have been broken off, so they can remain a vehicle for longer-term understanding between peoples, even when hostility between their governments finds its natural political expression in the way in which diplomacy and trade are restricted. Indeed, the citizens of the offending state may use their response to visiting cultural events as a means of indirectly expressing their own condemnation of their government's actions. The acclamation that artists from the free world receive in totalitarian countries is often fuelled by protest.

This book is concerned with cultural relations. Cultural diplomacy of both the first and the second order takes due place, but the progressive and exciting aspects of the actual work lie beyond government direction. Already, democratic countries with open societies subscribe to the idea of two-way benefit, of mutuality. Admittedly, some governments even in open democratic countries look for a return on the investment of funds in cultural relations in terms of immediate national advantage, whereas the real return is in long-term relationships, which produce and propagate understanding and encourage co-operation. It is because these relationships can flourish only if they are not subject to politics that cultural relations work is best done by organizations that enjoy an appropriate degree of independence of the state machinery. Sometimes, for instance in some major countries with traditions in this direction, such organizations are constitutionally independent; elsewhere, they are formally responsible to a ministry, usually the foreign ministry, but are encouraged by the home authority and by the ambassador to exercise a considerable measure of autonomy. Indeed, today the concept of the cultural attaché slavishly scoring points for his political masters, the very antithesis of right-minded cultural relations, is probably out of date even in the embassies of totalitarian states. If such a person still exists, he inhabits a world of his own, unblessed by ideals, untouched by modern communications and the cynicism of his clients – and of himself.

Meaning of Culture

This book, then, is about cultural relations. The component parts comprise the arts, libraries and information services, literature, language teaching, science and technology, social structure, the exchange of persons, links between communities and institutions, and educational aid and training in the developing world. But what of culture itself, that undefined concept at the very heart of the matter? Fortunately, this is not the place to attempt a comprehensive definition: if T. S. Eliot (1948, p. 22) in his *Notes towards the Definition of Culture* was prepared to settle for 'Culture may even be described simply as that which makes life worth living', we need not plague ourselves over abstractions. All that matters here is to establish what we mean by culture in cultural relations (or cultural diplomacy). This is rendered more difficult, however, because culture means different things in different languages. In German, for instance *Kultur* is a more elemental word than 'culture' in English, where it tends to have associations of preciosity. In England, the idea of culture has never moved the man on the Clapham omnibus, as the ordinary citizen has been styled, and yet he himself incorporates a very distinctive culture in the sense of a set of values. When at the 1982 World Conference on Cultural Policies the opening address by the Mexican Minister of Education included the sentence, 'Culture is man's capacity for reflection on himself' (UNESCO, 1982, p. 179), no doubt everyone thought it a fine phrase but few could have distilled from it the pure lymph of meaning. It would hardly have lent speed to the man on the Clapham omnibus.

These two examples demonstrate the range of meaning in culture. It embraces a narrower sense, which is concerned with the intellect and the arts, and a broader sense, which extends to a way of life and the values that this manifests. Both meanings are the business of cultural relations; each is a necessary complement to the other. The purpose should be not only to present learned and artistic accomplishment (high culture) but to represent the vital substance of a nation. Past glories are a powerful ingredient, but over-concentration on them would lead to a heritage obsession. The living element would be missing. It is now generally agreed, though practised in varying degrees, that the cultures to be related to one another should be conceived comprehensively.

It is also generally agreed that culture has become an indispensable form of communication within societies and between societies. Cultural conventions and agreements between states are now a common feature of their relations, and one that more obviously leads to convergence than do the inherent divisiveness of politics or the competitiveness of trade. This is why in recent decades, and particularly since the outbreak of the Cold War, multilateral forums such as UNESCO (of which more later) and the Committee for Cultural Co-operation of the Council of Europe have attracted some of the universalist idealism that previously found a more political expression in the League of Nations and the early United Nations. Indeed, the Conferences of European Ministers with responsibility for Cultural Affairs (held in Oslo, 1976; Athens, 1978; Luxembourg, 1981; Berlin, 1984), organized by the Council of Europe, are a sounding-board for this thinking. At the Luxembourg conference, for instance, the host minister, Pierre Werner, spoke about the concept of development in European societies in these words:

In short, the centre of gravity of the concept of development has shifted away from the economic towards the social and now towards the cultural. One is tempted to take this evolution of concepts to what should be its natural, logical conclusion, namely that the cultural aspect should be not just one factor to be taken into account, but indeed the supreme element of development. (Werner, 1981, p. 15)

Policy at Home and Abroad

The motive force behind international cultural relations work, whether of the responsible ministry or of non-governmental organizations, is expressed in external cultural policy. This calls for clear formulations, no less than any other aspects of public expenditure. In Chapters 9 and 12 we shall consider how policies should be determined and the issues of which they should take account. Clearly, external cultural policy cannot be practised in abstraction: its validity will depend on the vitality of the domestic scene, on internal cultural policy. The two should ideally interlock. This happens most obviously in countries where both are the responsibility of one ministry, such as a ministry of culture. This is often the case in Eastern Europe.

There is also a connection between internal and external cultural policies in domestic matters such as the treatment of minorities: it would hardly make sense to present an image of tolerance abroad while maintaining a stance towards minorities at home that is contrary to this. This is a factor that affects work in the Third World and educational aid. Culture very much includes education. Education is conceived by governments in national rather than international terms. Yet it contains elements, such as the teaching of languages, which constitute a link with other countries, at least potentially. One of the services rendered by cultural relations is to facilitate the opening-up of international dimensions in national education systems. To quote Senator Fulbright again (Coombs, 1964, p. x), 'Education is in reality one of the basic factors in international relations – quite as important as diplomacy and military power in its implications for war or peace'.

Terminology would be simplified if the word 'propaganda' could be used. But it is too severely discredited by abuse to be reinstated as a term for cultural diffusion. Its final demise, as an objective definition, came as a result of the Second World War. Earlier, we find the phrase 'cultural propaganda' used with little reservation. The British Council's most celebrated chairman, Lord Lloyd of Dolobran, in speaking at the opening of the British Institute in Rome in December 1939, was using the phrase in a neutral sense when he said (British

Council, 1939), 'Italy, indeed, with its great Dante Alighieri Society has shown its understanding and appreciation of the importance of cultural propaganda long before we in England had woken up to it'. Yet not long afterwards, in the introductory pages to the British Council's annual report for 1942/43, there is reference to 'that double horror of a phrase – cultural propaganda' (British Council, 1943a, p. 1). Horror or not, the expression is immediately intelligible, even today. And one notes with amusement the horrific reputation of the word 'cultural'.

Propaganda, for all the innocence of the word's derivation, has acquired the connotation of forcing lies down people's throats. And yet the essence of propaganda is making people believe a message, perhaps quite reputable, that you want them to believe. On the home front, propaganda is familiar enough – in anti-smoking campaigns, in road safety, and in commercial advertisements; in democracies, it is only in projection across frontiers for purposes of national advantage that propaganda is in disgrace. And yet it remains an element, implicit rather than explicit, in much cultural diplomacy. The desire to influence gives a dynamic to various cultural activities. Cultural work of all kinds, at home or abroad, is often fed by missionary zeal. Although the missionary, let alone the propagandist, would not make a good cultural representative – because he would not be content to let his national culture and its exponents speak for themselves – the desire to convince, to bestow benefits, and bring about beneficent change, is a cogent form of motivation. As for explicit propaganda, one can only hope it has in any case become self-defeating.

It may be objected that cultural relations and external cultural policy are as old as the hills. What of ancient Greece and Rome – did they not know a thing or two about spreading their cultures? Rome did not need a Ciceronian Institute for the Cultivation of the Latin Tongue, nor Greece an Athenian Council for Relations with Other States; yet each stood high and their cultural legacy has survived. Well, there is a distinction between the cultural influence exercised by dominant states or empires and the deliberate invocation of culture as an instrument of international affairs. The cultural influence exercised today by the United States, for instance, is not always consistent with its external cultural policy. Influence is not easily directed or controlled. Or, to take another example, the high degree of multiplier effect achieved by individual *savants*, such as Diderot at the court of Catherine II of Russia and Voltaire at the Prussian court of Frederick II, does not constitute an argument against maintaining cultural attachés at embassies abroad in our own day. The incidental achievements of the past should not inhibit more conscious endeavour in our own time. The equivalent of the politely imitative foreign court for the cultural representative of today is the raucous lecture-hall in a crowded university, the overrun library, the film show under the stars, the meeting of minds over a recondite subject at a symposium, the enraptured response to guest performances, the opening of a bizarre exhibition where the micro-phone does not work.

2

The Uses of Cultural Relations

Cultural relations work is bound to depend to a large extent on the public purse. However much money may be raised from the activities themselves or from collaborators or sponsors, it can do no more than make up a proportion of the total cost. The proportion will vary according to each agency's policy and management, and it will be determined by the attractiveness of what is on offer – artistically, scientifically, linguistically, educationally – but it can be no more than a proportion.

The reason for this is partly that many forms of cultural activity are subsidized and this is the accepted style of our age, partly that maintaining personnel, premises and material in other countries is expensive. Governments are therefore called upon to make grants. They must be able to justify these to taxpayers. If governments are to be persuaded to go on paying up at a time of recession, a convincing rationale is needed concerning the good done by cultural relations, not just to their participants and beneficiaries but to national interests at large. The principal arguments in their support will follow.

As an Instrument of Peace

One could hardly countenance any dissent from the proposition expounded by the Aspen Institute in its pamphlet *Managing East–West Conflict*: 'Preventing war between East and West is the first duty of statesmen on both sides' (Aspen, 1984, p. 27). Among the prominent politicians who lent their name to it were Edward Heath, Helmut Schmidt, Pierre Trudeau and Bruno Kreisky. Presumably, present world leaders would have been prepared to join these signatories. It is a patent fact that Clausewitz's pronouncement of 1827, 'War is the continuation of politics by other means', has long outlived its validity. When wars happen they are as far as possible contained and seen as sad, wasteful affairs. The heroics of war have been swamped by the realization that there are pressing world needs for the resources that war squanders. Mussolini's 'War is to the man what maternity is to the woman' would hardly appeal nowadays even to the most macho and unenlightened.

Yet, although there is a consensus about the avoidance of war, there is little in the way of a concerted policy to promote peace. Few universities have departments of peace studies, peace is rarely a school subject and, however fervently ordinary citizens desire peace, they find little scope for action on its behalf. When such action is attempted it easily gets channelled into political campaigns such as unilateral nuclear disarmament. One of the reasons for this is that the cause received a setback in Stalin's peace campaign of the late 1940s. The World Peace Council allegedly collected 550 million signatures. Probably a majority of the signatories genuinely wanted peace based on mutual respect for differing political systems. But as the Cold War between East and West grew more pronounced it became manifest that, as Barghoorn (1960, p. 13) wrote, 'Soviet communists, like all communists, use words in unusual ways. It is well known, for example, that the word "peace" in Soviet usage means, as Lindley Fraser observes, "the state of affairs inside a communist country" '.

Although international interests may occasionally converge and provide opportunities for agreements (like the Final Act of the Helsinki Conference of 1975), the process is laborious and uncertain in its consequences: agreements that are painfully extracted from bargaining lead only too easily to suspicion about the other side's keeping the terms of the bargain (after Helsinki, the disharmonies of Belgrade and Madrid). Nevertheless, Basket III of the Helsinki Agreement (the section concerned with access to information and humanitarian, cultural and educational provisions) had been included at the instance of the Western democracies for sound reasons. They recognized that one of the principal threats to peace in Europe since 1945 has been the possibility of a civic explosion in Eastern Europe. It is an all too convincing scenario for conditions that could lead to the Third World War: that is, the people in one of the Warsaw Pact countries rise up against their communist oppressors; public reaction in the West instigates popular support; this provokes Soviet counter-attack, which in turn involves the armed forces of the West in an escalating conflict. There have been several incidents that might hypothetically have produced this result: for instance, in East Germany in 1953, in Hungary and Poland in 1956, in Czechoslovakia in 1968, and in Poland again in 1970 and 1980. Richard Davy states the underlying intention at Helsinki in these words:

> Bring to Eastern Europe a basket full of human rights, human contacts, and economic benefits, it was argued, and the governments of the area would become more popular, more secure, and less dependent on the presence of Soviet troops. Tension would then be lowered and security increased. (Davy, 1975, p. 351)

Basket III, therefore, provides an example of a major intergovernmental agreement using cultural diplomacy in the cause of peace. Admittedly, the effects have been limited by the reluctance of the Soviet Union to accept any real modification of the power it exercises through satellite governments and the party apparatus.

How then can cultural relations be invoked to advance the cause of peace? First, we must remind ourselves of the long-term nature of cultural relations work. Culture is not a quick wonder-cure for trouble-spots. But, as part of the pattern of relationships between states, cultural relations create an atmosphere that is favourable to peace. This they do by their natural emphasis on 'that which makes life worth living', and therefore not to be destroyed, by the transfer of valuable skills and experience, by the reduction of negative images, by revealing people to one another as they are rather than as stereotypes. This is not a matter of woolly idealism but of practical commonsense, of sound investment. The British government's statement about the British Council's future, written under the stress of the concluding phase of the war, said of the reasons for recommending to Parliament continued expenditure on the Council's work, 'The most general and remote of these aims is a peace of understanding between the peoples of the world' (Foreign Office, 1944, p. 4).

The Federal Republic of Germany, having borne the consequences of war more than other Western European countries, gives particular prominence to peace in its cultural relations: 'Our foreign cultural policy is essentially international cooperation in the cultural sector. It is part of our foreign policy, a policy designed to promote the safeguarding of world peace' (German Federal Foreign Office, 1978, p. 7). And, in an interview on the subject of Germany's cultural relations, its State Minister at the foreign ministry said:

> Our foreign cultural policy is not only in the service of the preservation of peace – and opposed to all wars; it is also in the service of shaping peace and opposed to all forms of constriction. Here, our foreign cultural policy enjoys an important place: it does not dissipate its energy in the portrayal of our cultural achievements in other countries. It is aimed at cultural exchange on the basis of partner-like collaboration. (*Bildung und Wissenschaft*, 1984, p. 72).

President Eisenhower, in launching his People to People Programme in 1956, told a Washington conference of business and other leaders that the way to exploit the general desire for peace was to persuade people 'to lead their governments – if necessary to evade governments' (Coombs, 1964, p. 42). In cold war terms, this notion was reasonable enough: if other governments control information to the extent that the truth is obscured, how does a campaign for peace get through to their peoples except over the heads of governments? He had the mass of the population in mind. The work of cultural relations is, of course, much more directed at particular groups, at targets appropriate to the activity, at elites. Its bearing on the promotion of peace is through them and through the multiplication which they provide in their capacity as writers, teachers, artists and people of influence in their social milieu. Pendergast (1973) makes the original and striking point in writing about the way cultural relations reduce the feeling of threat:

> They constitute an alternative channel of information and impressions and relieve mass insecurities by symbols of hope and understanding. In this sense, cultural relations act as a mechanism of social adjustment which is necessary for social and elite dominance. (Pendergast, 1973, p. 696)

The contribution then that cultural relations make to peace is a cumulative one and is achieved through promoting understanding. *Si vis pacem para pacem.*

As a Support for Conventional Diplomacy

Activities arranged by cultural agencies create a favourable impression on foreigners in leading positions, either directly as with high culture, or indirectly through the reputation built up by more routine operations in their countries such as language classes, libraries, etc. These activities speak for the concern of the sending country to maintain relations at more than a formal level, and demonstrate that it understands the language of culture. It is also true, as Ninkovich (1981, p. 2) says, that, 'Although cultural relations are a minor form of diplomacy, at the same time the entire foreign policy process is itself subordinate to larger cultural dynamics'. The reason why ambassadors support their countries' cultural presence – and fight against its reduction – is that they have no doubt about the favourable effect it has on bilateral relations in general.

Willy Brandt's use in 1966 of the expression 'third pillar' in reference to cultural relations was echoed by the Commission of

Inquiry of the German Bundestag, which reported on the Federal Republic's external cultural policy in 1975, and in much subsequent literature. The same point had been made less conspicuously in a British Foreign Office memorandum of 1938:

> Of the three main elements which go to make up British influence – political, economic and culture – the first two had long been recognised as fundamental and both our political and our commercial influence had been carefully promoted and protected. The third element, our cultural influence, was regarded either as something vaguely creditable but of little practical use or, alternatively, as something so far above worldly considerations that it ought never to be degraded to political ends. (Foreign Office, 1938, p. 7)

Sometimes cultural relations achieve a topical, dramatic effect in breaking down barriers between countries. For instance, the United Kingdom's support for the Bolivar bicentenary of 1983 in Venezuela did much to restore friendly feelings after the strain that followed the Falklands campaign of the previous year.

Since sport, in its non-commercial form, is regarded as coming within the broad definition of cultural relations, we should remember the greatest break-through of all, the ping-pong diplomacy of 1971. An American table-tennis team on an Asian tour got on well with a competing team from China, who invited them to visit. The Americans were received by Chou En-lai, who made a speech in terms of friendship going beyond ping-pong. This led to Henry Kissinger's exploratory visit to Peking, and subsequently to President Nixon's. A positive change of relations followed. Kissinger (1979, p. 710) commented, 'One of the most remarkable gifts of the Chinese is to make the meticulously planned appear spontaneous'.

The French have traditionally been highly conscious of the diplomatic benefits from the projection of their culture: Talleyrand as foreign minister used to dismiss French ambassadors going to take up their posts with the words, 'Make them love France' ('*Faites aimer la France*'). The realization has become general among enlightened governments that, in the words of the Canadian Department of External Affairs, 'Today the development of international cultural relations is an essential dimension of our diplomacy' (Applebaum and Hébert, 1982, p. 317).

This applies no less to North–South relations. Cultural programmes can create a more constructive basis for political and economic relations with Third World countries, especially when they are executed in partnership with local institutions so that any implication of cultural imperialism is avoided. When a colony becomes independent, the political act is rapidly accomplished; economic independence takes longer but, given reasonable conditions, also follows; what takes longest of all is cultural independence – the assertion of cultural identity.

Help is needed in this, especially when the metropolitan country has bequeathed its institutions and thought patterns. The work of cultural agencies, through the resources they have to offer and through their collaboration in developing local cultural expression, can have a stabilizing political function. National identity is reinforced by cultural identity. The cultural dimension of the aid relationship is also a human dimension.

Finally a quotation from the remarkably unstuffy introduction written by the then German ambassador in London, Karl-Günther von Hase, to a book on town twinning:

> It has been suggested that ambassadors have been degraded to messenger boys in international politics. I do not think that is true, but if it were I should not mind as long as the message we carry is worthwhile and well-understood – it is friendship of the people, by the people and for the people. (Breitenstein, 1974, p. 5)

As a Vehicle for International Understanding

Although one agrees with Herr von Hase, one would not necessarily venture to postulate friendship as the inevitable fruit of cultural relations. It is too unpredictable a quality. Understanding is the essential purpose. Admittedly, understanding is not only a matter of the head but also of the heart, but one cannot assume that liking, or feelings of friendship, will accompany understanding. To make naïve assumptions on this score is to fall into the trap of loose thinking. Understanding is the aim. Affection is a bonus, and fragile unless based on a true appreciation.

Stereotypes are one barrier to understanding. They are often deep-seated and unconscious. Those that attach to foreigners are particularly pernicious, because it is from them that hostility is bred. Stereotyping the alien is an ancient by-product of tribalism. The alien is reduced to manageable shape by simplification or ridicule. St Paul set a bad example in his *Epistle to Titus*, and showed how to play on prejudice:

> One of themselves, even a prophet of their own, said, the Cretans are always liars, evil beasts, slow bellies. This witness is true. Wherefore rebuke them sharply, that they may be sound in the faith. (Epistle of Paul to Titus, ch. 1, vv. 12, 13)

The best way to combat stereotypes is by contrary evidence. This is one of the reasons why cultural programmes should avoid embellishment or falsification. If one should succeed in putting over a picture that is better than reality it would be seen through sooner or later, with damaging consequences. The exchange of persons – sending people in both directions to see for themselves – in an open cultural policy is both the best witness, and the best guarantee of objectivity.

There is a particular point in eliminating stereotypes in materials for the education of the young. For instance, the Georg Eckert Institut in Brunswick has as its aim the improvement of knowledge and understanding between nations; it concentrates on history, politics and geography in textbooks and co-operates with UNESCO and the Council of Europe. In Japan, the International Society for Educational Information exercises its vigilance over what is written in foreign books, especially textbooks, about Japan. (Japan itself has come in for criticism from Korea and Hong Kong for making too light of its wartime activities in textbooks.) Sometimes it is rather a matter of semantics, of avoiding words that are negatively emotive. The British and the French have come to be amused by their reciprocal badinage: for instance, the fact that 'to take French leave' and *filer a l'anglaise* both mean to abscond furtively and both make it seem a characteristic of the other side of the Channel. But there are many countries where custom has not brought this degree of tolerance.

Cultural representations abroad operate those programmes that further positive understanding in accordance with the subject requirements of the host country; this will best be accomplished in partnership with local institutions. The one-sided, the doctrinaire, the propagandist is unproductive. The editor of the periodical, *Zeitschrift für Kulturaustausch*, Michael Rehs, in a number devoted to the problem of stereotypes, sums it up:

> Ideologies of whatever sort represent the greatest obstacle to the sincere combating of stereotypes. Ideologies are in general nothing but prejudices refined as a system for influence and ultimately for domination. (Rehs, 1973, p. 6)

The exchange of persons is probably the most enduring means of increasing understanding: that is the reason why it rightly takes up a large part of the resources of cultural agencies. Mostly, it is directed at key persons in priority areas. The careful identification of target groups is essential; so are tact and restraint. Frankel (1966, p. 85) is surely right in saying: 'International "goodwill" and "understanding" appear to have the same relationship to human effort that happiness does. They are rarely achieved by direct assault. They are more usually by-products of activities in which men work together for other reasons that seem to them good and sufficient in themselves.' It is by doing things together – by co-operation, in fact – that understanding is won, whether between compatriots or peoples of different nations, rather than by protestation.

As a Lubricant for Trade

The conviction that trade benefits flow from cultural relations is more strongly argued in Britain than elsewhere: it was one of the prime reasons for the creation of the British Council in 1934 and for the financial support it received from industry. Lord D'Abernon wrote in his report on the trade mission he led to South America in 1929: 'to those who say that this extension (of cultural influence) has no connection with commerce, we reply that they are totally wrong; the reaction of trade to the more deliberate inculcation of our own culture which we advocate is definitely certain and will be swift' (Foreign Office, 1935a, p. 2).

Several official reports subsequently have emphasized the trade benefits from British Council work. Drogheda (1954, p. 33) said, 'although the method all through is strictly non-political, at the end of the process a considerable political and commercial benefit is likely to be received'. Duncan (1969), with a more trade-related brief, went so far as to say:

> We are in no doubt that the British Council will become an increasingly important medium through which Britain will project her interests and her new approach to international relations . . .
> As Britain turns from politico-military relations towards other ways of making her presence known to other countries, especially outside Western Europe and the North Atlantic area, it will be necessary to develop more fully the other forms of contact with governments and peoples . . . the British Council (and the BBC) will enable Britain to make direct contact with overseas peoples, and to present herself to them as a future trading and cultural partner of major importance, rather than in the role of a leading world power. (Duncan, 1969, pp. 106–7)

In his British Council Fiftieth Anniversary lecture, Sir Anthony Parsons put it thus:

> If you are thoroughly familiar with someone else's language and literature, if you know and love his country, its cities, its arts, its people, you will be instinctively disposed, all other things being equal or nearly equal, to buy goods from him rather than from a less

well known and well liked source, to support him actively when you consider him to be right and to avoid punishing him too fiercely when you regard him as being in the wrong. (Parsons, 1984, p. 11)

He goes on to refer to 'these simple truths'. Most people would share this belief. Perhaps it is because they are 'simple truths' that they are so difficult to prove. It is seldom possible to demonstrate a direct causal connection between someone's exposure to another country's culture (as in study at one of its universities) and, for instance, the subsequent ordering of equipment from that country. There are any number of obstacles which may prevent the person in question from placing the order, however great his gratitude, piety or pre-disposition, when he eventually reaches a position of seniority. When a positive case can be substantiated it is all the more gratifying and may be taken to speak for many that cannot. The Director-General of the British Council, Sir John Burgh, gave this impressive example in a speech at Newcastle University:

Some years ago Indian mining engineers studied British mining technology at Bates and Wearmouth collieries in the North East. This has been followed by the introduction of Long Wall mining equipment into India, a training package for up to 46 trainees and a contract worth about £100 million for further equipment. (Burgh, 1984)

But the argument grows more complicated when it takes in contrary examples. The most obvious one is Japan. After 1945, Japan was heavily disadvantaged. The country was devastated, discredited and without natural resources. Its language was little understood, even in the countries that made up its erstwhile Greater East Asian Co-Prosperity Sphere. And yet without the benefit of a favourable image or cultural support Japan performed the economic miracle that results in its accounting for some 10 per cent of the gross national product of the world. Clearly, the industrial product, and the management and salesmanship behind it, are more powerful determinants for the placer of orders than sentiment. Nowadays, Japan is directing her cultural work overseas – which is small in proportion to her wealth – more at correcting the materialistic image she has acquired than at reinforcing it.

If this contrary evidence complicates the argument, it does not disprove it. Favourable circumstances and a high standing, such as Britain had, comparatively, after the Second World War, will not of themselves bring victory over competitors; but without them the situation might have been worse. And there are direct cultural exports, such as books (of which Britain exports about one-third of its annual production), the arts and, of course, the English language, the greatest export of the lot. These are indisputably furthered by cultural relations. Tourism is a burgeoning industry, which several countries in the developed and the developing world deliberately further by their cultural representations. Knowledge of a country's cultural attractions is a prime attraction for tourists. Culture serves as an 'invisible export'.

We have examined the case for funding cultural relations under four aspects: peace, diplomacy, understanding and trade. A rationale is clearly needed. Treasuries look for returns that justify expenditure. The most telling justification emerges from what has been said above: that cultural relations have become an integral part of the interaction of states and peoples in our time, and that they present the best hope we have of transmuting traditional prejudices into attitudes of understanding and co-operation. Culture has the advantage of being a possession in common for all people. One can speak more meaningfully today than ever before of a 'world culture'. Accessible by virtue of its shared humanity, it can be transmitted in its diversity beyond political frontiers by modern vehicles of diffusion. The Secretary-General of the Danish Institute (*Det Danske Selskab*), Per Himmelstrup, recently wrote (Himmelstrup, 1985): 'It is through constant interaction, positive or negative, with other people and nations that social and cultural development is able to take place. Every culture needs constant challenges in order to avoid fossilization and decadence'.

3

Origins and Early Evolution

The distinction between cultural diplomacy and cultural relations consists in the greater attachment of the former to the purposes and style of conventional diplomacy. Cultural relations are a refinement that is more appropriate to open societies in an age of rapid communication and universal education. They are less dependent on the mechanisms of the state and operate through reciprocal activity and mutual understanding. Although this mode has been practised among advanced countries (for instance, between their learned societies) for centuries, it was not in this spirit that the nineteenth-century nation state first spoke beyond its own boundaries. The beginnings lie in cultural diplomacy, closely allied to the traditional interests of the state.

These beginnings contain elements of proselytizing, of propaganda, that go back much earlier, to the religious missions and the propagation of the faith. It used to be easier than it is now for intelligent Europeans to believe that their culture enjoyed such a superiority that its propagation was an obligation hardly less undeniable than that of the good book. Even within living memory there have been cultural representatives who looked on the ability of foreign students to learn their language and mentality as a sign of grace: those students who could not progress so far were dismissed to outer darkness.

No one disputes France's primacy in this cultural enterprise. The two great expansionist kings, Louis XIII (1610–43) and Louis XIV (1643–1715), encouraged missionary work and saw their culture diffused throughout Europe and in Canada and the Levant. By the end of the eighteenth century French was the common language of monarchs and nobles, ambassadors and men of learning: the French governess was that age's equivalent of today's itinerant English teacher. This dominance continued into the nineteenth century, but gradually the confusions of the political scene and the spread of nationalism destabilized France's cultural ascendancy. It was after her defeat in the war against Prussia (1870–1) that France, invoking her cultural patrimony as a means of rehabilitation, founded the Alliance Française (for teaching French in the colonies and elsewhere) in 1883, the Lay Mission (for non-religious teaching overseas) in 1902 and the *Office national* (for school and university exchanges) in 1910. In 1910 also a Bureau for Schools and French Foundations Abroad (*Bureau des écoles et des oeuvres françaises a l'étranger*) was set up in the foreign ministry.

This last was the first creation of an administrative unit for the co-ordination of the work of various operators in the field; by its location, the French government identified this essentially educational work abroad with the interests of foreign policy. The connection was natural enough and probably the most expedient; but what is of particular interest is that this French example has been followed by most other countries. So it came about that the projection of culture was seen to support diplomacy and to find its justification in the extent to which it did so. Indeed, until recently there have hardly been other arguable criteria. We shall see later that this model poses some structural problems so far as the requirements of mutuality, or two-way traffic, are concerned: for the model makes the main responsibility one of export, while the importing responsibility (that is, helping other countries to serve up their cultural products) goes to the ministry of culture or education, or to fragmented organs of local government and artistic enterprise. This division of responsibility runs through the way institutional budgets are allocated and costs are apportioned. One of the tasks facing administrators in this field is to overcome the resultant dichotomy between inward and outward flows.

Large-scale emigration from countries such as France, Germany and Italy, in the nineteenth and twentieth centuries, created a particular need for the provision of schools so that children could be brought up in loyalty to the mother country and in the parents' linguistic tradition. McMurry and Lee (1947, p. 14) tell us that by 1913 the French government, through the foreign ministry, was subsidizing schools in Europe alone to the tune of 138,000 francs as against 3,000 francs in 1906, and that, 'The Ministry had made it a policy to subsidise all schools existing abroad where there was an important French colony, so that the children of French parents might have a French education and preserve their French nationality'.

French state policy gradually extended beyond schools, to bringing French culture and cultural ideas to the influential classes in its empire, but the schools were the mainstay. Increasingly, their role was widened to take in the education of indigenous children as well as French; they became a network with a uniformly high standard, and with trained teachers seconded from France, throughout much of the world. They were reinforced by the work of the Alliance Française in teaching the language to adults and providing focal points of French culture in a growing number of countries, and by the more intellectual services of French institutes, which were set up first in major European centres (Madrid, St Petersburg, Florence) under the direction of individual French universities.

Germany was, like France, in the period up to 1914, concerned with the education of its subjects abroad. German unification in 1871, after the Franco-Prussian War, put a new emphasis on Germanism, and the industrial expansion that followed gave Germany a larger role to sustain. By the end of the nineteenth century, Germany commanded much international respect for her example of a balanced, modern educational curriculum; several countries welcomed German help in bringing their education systems up to date in the rapidly changing conditions of industrialization. This happened in South America, China, Turkey and Japan. Even today, Japanese high school students still wear the black tunics, with a row of shiny buttons up to the neck, which were modelled on German school uniforms of a hundred years ago and solved the problem of reconciling Japanese dress to the physical and social demands of the classroom. German religious missions ran schools and hospitals; scientific and archaeological institutes were celebrated for their scholarship. However, all this was more the product of private than official initiative. The organization that promoted schools abroad, the *Allgemeine Deutsche Schulverein zur Erhaltung des Deutschtums im Auslande* (the German Schools Association for the Preservation of Germanism Abroad) was private. When it was necessary to appeal for official support, the request was more often directed to the Prussian ministry of culture, because of its known interest, than to the foreign ministry of the new German Empire (Twardowski, 1970, p. 9). Germany as a country had no state policy and organization comparable to the French. It supported German schools abroad, however, through a budget voted to the foreign ministry. This was the *Reichsschulfonds*, which amounted to 1.5 million marks in 1913 (McMurry and Lee, 1947, p. 46). Germany came to attach more and more importance to Germanism abroad (*Deutschtum im Ausland*), especially with the crumbling of the Austro-Hungarian Empire.

The question of Germany's need for an external cultural policy is brought out in an exchange of letters in 1913 between the Reich Chancellor, von Bethmann Hollweg, and the historian, Professor Karl Lamprecht of Leipzig. Lamprecht wrote to Bethmann Hollweg to point out the inadequacy of Germany's policy, starting with the example of Germany's standing in Russia and generalizing to take in other civilized countries. He said, 'A positive, creative external cultural policy is still in its very beginnings so far as we are concerned; in Western Europe this has become one of the most important instruments of foreign policy altogether, as I have been able to discover regarding England from a recent visit to London and regarding France from searching conversations and correspondence . . .' He went on to suggest various learned men who might advise, and appealed to the Chancellor to seize the favourable moment ('the immediate danger of war has passed') and invoke a new idealism to meet national and international demands. Bethmann Hollweg replied courteously, agreeing with the thesis. He said, 'I fully appreciate the advantages which France's politics and economy derive from this cultural propaganda, and the role which British cultural policy plays for preservation of the British Empire'. But he thought Germany had not reached this stage. 'We are not yet sufficiently sure and conscious of our culture, our inner being, our national ideal. It is a characteristic of our really rather individualistic culture, with its lack of equilibrium still, that it does not possess the same suggestive force as the British and French, that not every German abroad represents his fatherland in his person, as the Frenchman does Paris and the Englishman the British Isles'. He then throws the ball back in his correspondent's court by saying that the government must lean on the initiative of the educated classes in waking the people to the requirements of the situation (Kuhn and Rossbach, 1980, Annexes).

Bethmann Hollweg remained Chancellor through most of the First World War that broke out a year later; he was forced to resign in 1917 by pressure from General Ludendorff because, being a man of moderate inclination, as his letter suggests, he was thought to be too conciliatory in his attitude to the Allies' likely conditions for peace. There are several curious features in his letter to Lamprecht. The tone seems surprisingly idealistic in retrospect, and reminds us that the common conception of Germany before 1914 was much more of a land of dreamy romantics than of ruthless militarists. Another surprise is the statement that Germany was behind Britain as well as France. But one peculiarity of cultural relations is that those involved tend to believe that their country has fallen behind its rivals. Sometimes this is a line taken to induce Treasuries to part with more money and reflects the contingent nature of the funding of such work;

sometimes it discloses deep-lying fears of being outmanoeuvred by subtle foreigners.

Britain before the First World War could, in the terms by which we judge such matters today, hardly have qualified as a country with an active external cultural policy. There was no budget for this, no responsible government department and, apart from Victoria College in Alexandria, founded in 1902, there was no encouragement of schools abroad: nothing in fact on a scale approaching Germany's activities, let alone France's.

Much later, two years after the inauguration of the British Council, its Chairman, Lord Eustace Percy, wrote in the *Sunday Times* of 21 March 1937, 'except to a small extent recently in Egypt, no penny of public money has gone to the schools maintained by British communities abroad'. And a Foreign Office memorandum of 1936, *British Cultural Propaganda in the Mediterranean Area* says:

> It is scarcely an exaggeration to say that, except for the foundation of Victoria College at Alexandria in 1902 as an institution on public school lines for boys of all nationalities, nothing was done between the British occupation of Egypt in 1882 and Lord Lloyd's period as High Commissioner in 1925–29 to make Great Britain the chief educational and cultural, as well as the chief political, force in that country. (Foreign Office, 1936, p. 13)

Bethmann Hollweg and Lamprecht were obviously assessing Britain's cultural standing in the world from a different standpoint; also, they were talking about *Kultur*, that fundamental concept of a nation's soul, rather than 'culture'. They saw the way the British Empire had established its values and its language and the way it had spread its power and commerce over a quarter of the globe; and they naturally saw the whole as a grand design to imprint British *Kultur* on the world by the export of British stock and the imposition of British institutions. The British themselves thought quite differently. Of course, there was a cultural element, even in terms recognizable to the British at the turn of the century, but it found its expression more obliquely, with irony and self-mockery:

> Take up the White Man's burden –
> Send forth the best ye breed –
> Go bind your sons to exile
> To serve your captive's need . . .

When Kipling wrote that in 1899 he was speaking for the Empire rather than for Britain (in fact, the immediate occasion was the United States' involvement in the Philippines). The enlargement of the cultural concept to match the Victorian idea of Empire would have seemed to continental observers a triumph of deliberate national policy, whereas it was in fact a vaguer, more romantic expression of kinship in diversity and backed by little official support.

Italy had a special reason to be concerned about the loyalty of her emigrants, for from the latter part of the nineteenth century they went in large numbers, prompted mainly by unemployment and over-population. In one year alone, 1913, more than 800,000 Italians took themselves off to the New World. Italian schools abroad, both state and private (including religious) existed, but many people thought, at a time when nationalist feelings were strong in Italy following unification, that an organization of cultural diffusion was required for emigrants of all ages. The Italian consul-general in Alexandria wrote a letter to the Prime Minister, Cavour, pointing out the need to provide Italian education abroad. Slightly later, in November 1888, a leading citizen of Trieste wrote to the Italian nationalist poet Carducci about preserving the spirit of nationhood better at home as a result of caring for its preservation abroad: the idea of *Italia irredenta* – those parts of Italy such as Trieste and Trento which were not yet included in the new kingdom – was strong, and Carducci not only embraced the cause of spreading language and culture but lent it the dignity of the name of Dante Alighieri. A manifesto was signed in 1889 by cultural and political figures of all persuasions. It was said by Italians themselves to be one of the few occasions when they were able to overcome their divisions and factions. The Dante Alighieri Society followed the model of the Alliance Française with autonomous committees at home and abroad providing language instruction and cultural activities under the co-ordination of a head-quarters in the home capital. Apart from the Fascist period, indeed, the Dante received no support from the state until 1960. For much of its existence, it has been a private, voluntary organization.

These networks of schools and associations came into existence to provide the service of maintaining contacts with the home country. They were welcomed by the emigrants. They found less appeal in the English-speaking world, especially the United States, where people were more content to be culturally assimilated. Once established, however, these networks afforded a means of competing for the attention and allegiance of locals as well as nationals. They were a ready instrument to be used in the propaganda battle of the nineteen-thirties.

4

Propaganda

Propaganda is a word that has declined in respectability. We saw in the first chapter that there is something regrettable about its loss of innocence. The word is well born. Pope Gregory XV in 1622 founded the *congregatio de propaganda fide*, the college for the propagation of the faith, a committee of cardinals with oversight of teaching missions. Then, by extension, the word came to mean, in a sense first recorded in 1842 by the Oxford English Dictionary, 'Any association, systematic scheme, or concerted movement for the propagation of a particular doctrine or practice'. From this interim stage the word evolved to take on the modern meaning of the diffusion of ideology. Evil connotations cling to propaganda because of the abuse of its techniques for purposes of distortion and domination by aggressive states. As McMurry and Lee (1947, p. 244) put it, 'The Axis Powers gave fanatical devotion to a doctrine of world supremacy which they attempted to force upon other nations first through their powerful propaganda machine and then through armed force. The USSR, operating within an ideological framework, has sought to win sympathisers to the Soviet cause through an intensive propaganda programme'. But 'propaganda' still retains something of its more neutral meaning: it is not totally banished. Although the term 'cultural propaganda' would probably be used today only by its critics (at least in English), it nevertheless has a relevance to our subject.

Cultural propaganda is at one end of a scale that passes through cultural diplomacy to cultural relations at the other end; the progression is from the use of culture as a force to advance national ends, through the association of culture with current diplomatic aims, to an open collaborative relationship. But at any point on the scale there may be an element, greater or smaller, of propaganda. Even in the most enlightened policies there may, for perfectly good reasons, be the desire to convince partner institutions in the other country: it may be a matter of persuading them to accept an exhibition by an unknown painter, or of overcoming their reluctance to introduce new methodology in teaching one's language. To seek improvement is intrinsic to commitment in cultural relations. Personal conviction is a motivating and dynamic force. Cultural representatives without it would be shadowy middlemen. A belief in the quality of their own country's culture should be part of their make-up. A controlled patriotism is in order.

Nowhere has propaganda acquired more negative associations than in Britain, and yet the British have proved more imaginative than most in the way they have made use of it in war. Adolf Hitler devoted the sixth chapter of the first volume of *Mein Kampf* to war propaganda (Hitler, 1944). This and the succeeding chapter, where he writes of his experiences on the Western front, display more observation than bombast. He thought the British were superior to the Germans in the arts of propaganda because they understood it should appeal to the simple feelings of the masses and not to the minds of intellectuals. He describes the effect on the morale of German troops of enemy leaflets dropped behind the lines, how he was wounded in 1916 and gassed in 1918, how in his convalescence he witnessed the collapse of Germany and resolved to become a politician.

The Department of Propaganda in Enemy Countries (based in Crewe House in London) scattered leaflets among Austro–Hungarian forces, appealing to their national aspirations, encouraging them to desert and, among German forces, persuading them of the futility of prolonging the war (Stuart, 1920, pp. 10–79). Both Hindenburg and General von Stein, the Minister of War, testified to the demoralizing effects of this campaign. Another success of First World War propaganda was in helping to bring the United States into the conflict. America was 'fundamentally neutral' to what seemed a very distant affair at the outbreak of war:

> in the late autumn of 1914 a prominent American weekly magazine printed the results of a questionnaire sent to three hundred and sixty-seven American newspaper proprietors in which the question was asked: Which side in the European struggle has your sympathies? The results showed that 105 editors favored the Allied side; 20 sympathized with the Central Powers; while 242, or almost exactly two-thirds of the total, expressed no particular preference. (Squires, 1935, pp. 42–3)

The propaganda bureau in Wellington House in London distributed pamphlets and books in the United States. Whereas German propagandists made no secret of their propaganda activities and therefore roused opposition, the British were more covert and effective (Squires, 1935, pp. 45–9). Propaganda was only one cause among several for the United States entering the First World War, but it was a potent one. As Squires says:

> British propaganda was a real force in winning the World War. It kept the home masses docilely patriotic. It gained, or mightily helped to gain, powerful allies. It was of prime importance in bringing about disintegration of civilian and military morale in Germany. (Squires, 1935, p. 82)

Clearly there is a generic difference between military propaganda and cultural propaganda, though there have been points of intersection in both World Wars. The importance of these quotations here is that they reveal the power of propaganda, which was to have even greater potential in the coming age of mass communication and radio. Also, these quotations partly explain the repugnance felt by most British people, and generally in the Anglo-Saxon world, for propaganda and anything that smacks of it. Indeed, many who had been in the know felt remorse. In a debate in the House of Commons in 1938 on the supply of British news abroad, Harold Nicolson, who before entering Parliament was a well-connected diplomat, said that in the Great War Britain had lied 'damnably'. He continued:

> Therefore, we must not be self-righteous and say we could never practise propaganda by such untruthful and dirty methods – because we can. But that was in time of war. In peace, the ordinary Englishman does not like telling lies and that is one reason why the whole thing is uncongenial. (Hansard, 1938, cols 1929–30)

Rex Leeper, the Foreign Office official who was more responsible than any other single person for establishing cultural diplomacy between the wars and eventually for the creation of the British Council, wrote:

> Many people are suspicious of the word propaganda, which they connect with the control and manufacture of information for political and military purposes during the war. Certainly the word itself suggests the diffusion rather of what is wished that others shall believe than of unbiased fact. (Leeper, 1935, p. 203)

Britain was remarkably slow to respond to hostile cultural propaganda between the wars. The reluctance of the Treasury to find money was always an obstacle. In a series of Nazi propaganda publications devoted to the *British Empire in World Politics*, one pamphlet on *English Cultural Imperialism* (Thierfelder, 1940, p. 10) presents the following theory: 'It had previously belonged to the ideal of the gentleman never to bring the value of his way of life into question and so he had to deny himself any defence or propaganda'.

But the overriding deterrent to responding in kind was the disrepute attaching to all forms of propaganda and the ignorance of an alternative concept, of cultural relations in fact. The problem was partly semantic too. The French, who were still the leaders in external cultural policy, continued to use the word 'propaganda' in something closer to its original curial sense: when they spoke of cultural propaganda they meant intellectual influence, whereas to the English ear there were more sinister connotations.

In Italy the Fascist Party quickly took control of the news media. By 1925 journalism was restricted to state-licensed writers, and the Government Press Bureau issued instructions as to what should be published. Similarly, a state monopoly was established in the cinema; external broadcasting from Radio Bari to the Arab world took on a strident tone after the invasion of Abyssinia. F. C. Bartlett (1942, p. 42) says of Italian propaganda: 'There is in it all a spirit of daring and audacity, a brilliant inventiveness, both of phrase and of manner, a kind of realism in the midst of its most sweeping generalisations, which keep it moving and alive'. Fascist anti-British propaganda was so fanciful and sometimes absurd that it probably impeded rather than helped the cause. It was certainly persistent. One well-known newspaper editor, Virgilio Gayda of *Giornale d'Italia*, took every opportunity of attacking Britain after it led the policy of sanctions over Abyssinia. The stereotyped vilification of the British in the Italian press was echoed by Radio Bari, which spread the idea in the Middle East that Britain was effete and incapable of waging war. Mack Smith (1973, pp. 87–117) gives an entertaining synopsis in an article 'Anti-British propaganda in Fascist Italy'. The general line was that the British lacked culture and intelligence; moreover, except for the feudal aristocracy, they were either bourgeois and self-indulgent or proletarian and starving; British sexual mores and birth control had disastrous consequences; the people were unmilitary and cowardly. One medical writer attributed the poor fighting qualities of British troops to tonsillectomy:

The man with no tonsils is easily frightened and confused. Not for him the motto 'live or die'. Not for him the fascist precept 'better live one day as a lion than a hundred years as a sheep'. In many ways he is worse than a eunuch, since eunuchs have at least provided some statesmen in history.

Mack Smith says: 'Propaganda was not only the method by which fascist leaders deceived the population in general, but also the way in which they deceived one another and the Duce himself'.

According to the British ambassador's despatch from Rome of 16

July 1935 (Foreign Office, 1935b), the Italian government was spending the equivalent of more than £1 million on her propaganda abroad with half of it going to Italian schools, with a total of 50,000 pupils; furthermore, the Italian government 'exercised a measure of supervision over more than 200 privately owned schools and institutes, with a total of about 200,000 pupils'. The Directorate-General of the Italians Abroad, an offshoot of the foreign ministry, promoted the teaching of Italian, while 'Fascist organisations had encouraged Italians living abroad to continue to use their mother tongue and to teach it to their children; Italian lessons for adults and children had been followed with great enthusiasm' (Foreign Office, 1935c). The Foreign Office memorandum *British Cultural Propaganda in the Mediterranean Area* (Foreign Office, 1936) said that Italy spent more annually in Egypt than the British Council budget for the whole world. And the Italian government was offering every inducement to foreign students to follow higher education in Italy. 'In Palestine, for instance, the Italians are offering a complete education in Italy for £2 a year, all other expenses being paid for by the Italian Government' (Foreign Office, 1938, p. 7).

As the propaganda campaigns of the Axis powers became more vehement, British diplomats expressed their mounting concern. The Foreign Office sent out a memorandum on 19 February 1937 in which it confirmed that the governments of Germany, France and Italy were spending about £1 million each on cultural propaganda annually. It outlined the strategy followed by the Axis powers:

Education is the basis of all organised cultural propaganda, and a special feature of its modern development is its determination to secure a hold on the education of foreign children at as early an age as the Government of the foreign country concerned will allow. In this respect it may be said that the totalitarian State, abroad as well as at home, is following the example of the Church, though with a very different set of principles in view. In its full development, the organisation of German or Italian cultural propaganda in a foreign country begins with the schools. Very often pupils will be attracted to a German or Italian elementary school by the offer of education at a nominal fee or even gratis; thereafter they will proceed to a State school, in the curriculum of which every effort has been made to secure a privileged position for the teaching of German or Italian. There follows a course either at a local university (at which there will always be a professor of German or Italian language and civilisation), accompanied by generous facilities (scholarships, free journeys, etc.) for travel or study in Germany or Italy, or else at a German or Italian university. Finally, for the former student or for others who may be interested, there is usually a club or institute with every social and intellectual amenity through which contact can be maintained with what should, by now, have become the student's spiritual home. To this may be added such further influence as may be exerted by the visits of prominent statesmen, artists or men of learning, the visits of theatrical companies, the showing of German and Italian films and the energetic advertisement and sale of German or Italian products of all kinds. (Foreign Office, 1937)

Although they had certain agreed geographical spheres of interest, Nazi Germany and Fascist Italy had different styles. Italy posed as the friend of the Arabs and the defender of Islam; Germany was more aggressive in its harping on the repeated themes of Bolshevism, Judaism, the iniquities of Versailles, and German minority populations abroad. Goebbels took over the propaganda lessons that Hitler had learnt at the front: the message was one of assertion rather than argument. Goebbels sought more power for his Reich Ministry for Popular Enlightenment and Propaganda, and succeeded in taking over some responsibilities from the Cultural Department of the Foreign Ministry and from the Education Ministry, though not as much as he sought. One of the main operations of the Nazi state towards German minorities was through the Foreign Organisation (*Auslandsorganisation*), which was run by Gauleiter Bohle with the aim of mustering German communities abroad to support Nazi policies. Here there was another conflict of departmental competence with the youth movement led by von Schirach, which had its own foreign division. This was one of the ways in which the Nazi state lacked co-ordination. But there were advantages in the freebooting enjoyed by different organizations. For instance, if the ramifications of Nazi activity perturbed foreign governments, there could appear to be doubt as to where responsibility lay and reference could always be made to a decree by Hitler of 1937 whereby party members 'must follow the law of the land in which they were living and have nothing to do with its internal politics' (McMurry and Lee, 1947, p. 71).

What gave potency to German and Italian propaganda was the stirring of dynamic force behind it. Both countries, for instance, kept up a lively momentum in their Arabic broadcasts, which made those of the BBC, when they started in 1938, seem staid and coldly objective. In a comparison of German and Italian policies in cultural propaganda, Italy had a more attractive line to follow, for she invoked the virtues of classical Rome but also made more imaginative use of her own modernity, whereas the Nazi suppression of the creative elements of Weimar culture, especially those associated with Jews, alienated foreign intellectuals. After Hitler's references to cultural policy in his speech at the party rally at Nuremberg in 1937, the foreign minister, von Neurath, wrote to German diplomatic missions, enjoining special care not to stray from Nazi doctrine.

The kinds of propaganda we have been considering were phenomena of national expansionism at a time of mass literacy and the early years of external broadcasting. Cultural propaganda emerged as a recognized force in the penetration of target societies, in planting seeds of discontent and disruption at sensitive points, especially among the youth, and in exploiting the allegiance of emigrés for political ends. Until the second half of the 1930s, the only country that maintained a significant cultural service which might counteract these incursions was France.

5

The Example of France

Britain and France offer alternative approaches in so many aspects of human affairs that it is hardly surprising they should differ in their attitudes to something so essentially characteristic as their national cultures. The difference was writ large in the period between the wars in the importance they ascribed to the use of their cultures for purposes of international influence. Whereas France pursued a conscious and successful policy of cultural diplomacy, building on the lead it had established at the end of the nineteenth century on earlier foundations, Britain made no deliberate entry into the field until the second half of the 1930s, and then not so much for reasons of intrinsic policy as out of the compulsion to counter the hostile propaganda that was undermining its position in crucial areas of the world, and to protect export markets.

The French idea of bearing a civilizing mission (*mission civilisatrice*) is of long standing and the French themselves use the term *messianisme français*. Any notion that Britain had a sacred duty to spread its culture (as distinct from its order or its justice) would have found favour with few of its subjects. For one thing, culture was not a concept that attracted enthusiasm within Britain: the component parts of culture – literature, language, the arts, architecture, horticulture, sport – all had their exponents and advocates, but Britain did not, like France, possess the intellectual tradition of seeing them collectively as an expression of nationhood and certainly not as something that should be transmitted to others.

The difference was apparent in the colonial policies of the two countries. While France diffused her language through a network of schools with seconded teachers, and bestowed recognizably French attitudes of thought with it, Britain built upon autochthonous practices and left much English education to the mission schools. Matthew Arnold might have called the British neglect of cultural projection philistine; Napoleon might have applied his quip 'England is a nation of shopkeepers' to its eventual motivation to follow in France's footsteps. H. V. Routh (1941) wrote of the French:

Under the *Ancien Régime* they were the recognized leaders in humanism and intellectual refinement. Even after the reversals of 1870–1 they refused to accept defeat. The Sorbonne could still boast of the most cosmopolitan attendance in the world; their authors were the most discussed; their actors and actresses the most admired; their capital was recognized as the natural home of disinterested study and artistic enthusiasms. Many a Frenchman might despair of the French Empire ... but no Frenchman despaired of French humanism ... they clung with astonishing tenacity to their position as the leading influence in civilisation. (Routh, 1941, p. 7)

These expressions of national cultural pride were backed by government finance. A British diplomatic memorandum examines the estimates of the French Budget Commission for the foreign services:

Almost the whole of the 'Introduction', in which the past and future activities of the French foreign services are reviewed, is, however, devoted to that sphere of activity which should, in the opinion of the Commission, dominate all others, namely, the 'policy of national expansion', or more briefly, propaganda in all its forms. (Foreign Office, 1920b)

The memorandum collates the various organizations involved in this work: the 'voluntary societies concerned chiefly with educational propaganda both in France and abroad'; 'the propaganda departments of different Ministries' and the department of the French foreign ministry, *Service des oeuvres françaises a l'étranger*, concerned with propaganda abroad, which was until January 1920 more humbly known as the *Bureau des écoles et des oeuvres françaises a l'étranger* and was thus referred to in the previous chapter. The Budget Commission said, 'Our universities and schools abroad are real focal points of pro-French propaganda; they constitute a weapon in the hands of our public authorities'. The memorandum concludes:

Thus on educational propaganda and press services – but chiefly on the former – throughout the world the French are spending 25,014,000 fr., to which must be added 850,000 fr. to be authorised under a special Bill for the purchase of a central building in Rome, making a total of 25,864,000 fr. On examining details of this expenditure it will be found that the money is divided among objects precisely similar to those on which the expenditure of public funds by His Majesty's Government has been repeatedly recommended either by the Foreign Office Committee on British

Communities Abroad or by the different departments of the Foreign Office, in almost every case without success.

It will generally be admitted that, while the general financial condition of France is inferior to that of the British Empire, the French occupy, in the estimation of foreigners, the leading position in the realms of art and literature, and that foreigners know more about the intellectual, commercial and industrial development of France than of this country. Yet the French are devoting an increased sum of money – which they can presumably afford less well than we can – to the extension of French intellectual supremacy abroad . . .

It is only by such means that in the opinion of the French Budget Commission, France can hope to maintain her political importance and arise equal to the counter-propaganda which is already being started by Germany; they hold strongly that trade will follow the extension of French intellectual prestige, and that a more intimate acquaintance on the part of foreign peoples with the culture of France is the surest and most abiding form of economic and political propaganda. It is only by these means that the French can make up for the lack of young men to send forth to extend French commercial enterprise.

If France, in her impoverished condition, considers it worthwhile to pursue such a policy of intellectual and commercial penetration throughout the world . . . can this country under the stress of the severe competition which has followed the conclusion of peace neglect the use of similar means? (Foreign Office, 1920b)

At the same time as the French government was allocating this sum of over 25 million francs (the equivalent of roughly £475,000) the attitude of the British government is summarized in the Foreign Office memorandum *British Cultural Propaganda from 1919 to the Formation of the British Council*:

In the course of a letter from His Majesty's Treasury to Lord Curzon, His Majesty's Principal Secretary of State for Foreign Affairs, on the 31st May, 1919, reference was made to the Foreign Office estimate for propaganda expenditure 1919–20. The Lords Commissioners of His Majesty's Treasury stated that they recognised that it was not practicable at the moment to terminate altogether the existing system of propaganda and the expenditure involved, but they trusted that any particular type of propaganda would be discontinued as soon as experience showed that it was not productive of valuable results. They warned against the danger of 'a general desire to spread British culture throughout the world', and stated that it would not 'be possible to defend in Parliament or in its Committees expenditure on such a purpose', and a general ruling was laid down that the News Department of the Foreign Office should not venture upon any form of cultural propaganda. (Foreign Office, 1935a)

British Attempts to Follow Suit

The transition from the wartime operations of the Ministry of Information and the Office of Propaganda in Enemy Countries in Crewe House to peacetime conditions was accomplished by draconian reductions. There were several prominent politicians and officials who believed that an appropriate form and degree of propaganda should be maintained beyond the aftermath of war; Philip Taylor (1981) adduces the opinion of Victor Wellesley, who was to become one of the Foreign Office's most senior officials, that there should be three categories of British overseas propaganda: political, commercial and cultural. In elaboration of the last of these, Wellesley wrote, 'To render available to foreign countries all that is best in British life and education, using that term in the widest possible sense, so as to include book learning, art, literature, methods of training youth, athletics, etc. This in reality forms part of the economic policy.' (Taylor, 1981, p. 48)

Even in this more positive view there is an economic slant, which sets it apart from the French policies described above. Taylor quotes another official, S. A. Guest, who wrote:

> One of the chief lessons to be drawn from the experience of the war, and the events leading up to it, is that Diplomacy by itself is not enough for the maintenance of satisfactory international relations ... The fault lies in our lack of foresight in having to provide something further than Diplomacy. Now that nations are taking a much larger share than hitherto in their own government and international relations are being influenced by interests other than those of dynasties, we should be living in a Fools' Paradise if we were to expect that we should be able to maintain international equilibrium by means of a service which was originally designed to work under conditions which no longer exist. (Taylor, 1981, p. 50)

But such views did not prevail. Responsibility for propaganda in general was formally declared to lie with the Foreign Office, whose News Department was to be headed by Sir William Tyrell, subsequently ambassador to France and eventually, as Lord Tyrell, first chairman of the British Council. The News Department's budget was reduced to a level that precluded the possibility of its financing cultural work abroad. The Foreign Office estimate of £100,000 for the year 1919/20 (itself a massive reduction on the £2 million spent on all forms of propaganda during the last year of the war) was docked by the Treasury of the £20,000 which might have been used for small-scale propaganda activity abroad. The News Department was mainly confined to working through the British and foreign press. The Treasury expressed the assumption that, in view of the commercial rather than political purpose of propaganda in the future, the work would largely be transferred to the Department of Overseas Trade. On 19 May 1919, the Foreign Secretary, Lord Curzon, sent out a dispatch to all diplomatic missions, with the exception of Washington, saying that, 'British propaganda in Foreign Countries shall, in future, be regarded as part of the regular work of His Majesty's Missions Abroad'. But they were to have no additional money to do the job.

However, the pressure for a more active policy grew. The Foreign Office Committee on British Communities Abroad, which was set up by Lord Curzon to examine how the government could: '(1) foster a greater spirit of solidarity among British communities abroad, and (2) make British ideas more generally known, and appreciated by, foreign nations', had reported in 1920. The committee was chaired by Sir John Tilley, an Assistant Secretary at the Foreign Office and is usually known as the Tilley Committee. While acknowledging 'the deeply-rooted British spirit of independence' and stipulating, 'We do not advocate any form of political propaganda', the committee recommended, among other matters, that the government should aim at securing an English education for British children abroad, an English-speaking League should be set up on the lines of the Alliance Française, and that British books should be promoted. The government's moral and practical obligation on behalf of the education of British children abroad was stressed (Foreign Office, 1920a). These recommendations were rejected totally by the Treasury in July 1920.

The Treasury decision that commercial propaganda should become the responsibility of the Department of Overseas Trade meant that the Travel Association of Great Britain and Northern Ireland, formed in 1928, was concerned not only with attracting tourists but also, by virtue of a grant-in-aid of £5,000 on the DOT vote, was supposed 'To develop through travel a greater knowledge of, and interest in, British culture and British goods'. Accordingly, the Travel Association launched a publicity campaign in certain other countries, and established advisory committees in some foreign cities.

The Travel Association was important not only in itself as an indication of the weight the government had come to attach to national publicity (the word now preferred to propaganda) but also because, being under DOT auspices, it visibly represented a commercial stake in this publicity. Meanwhile other pressures were coming to bear. Lord D'Abernon led a trade mission to South America in 1929 and reported that Britain was letting its commercial advantages go to waste (D'Abernon, 1930, p. 6). The final chapter was called 'The commercial importance of cultural influence'. Lady Donaldson (1984, p. 18) says on this, 'The authors remark that it cannot be said "that we have sufficiently understood the direct relation between culture and trade", and they devote considerable space to the cultural influences of France, America, Germany and Italy'. Then at last the Treasury, confronted with the Foreign Secretary's request for £10,000 a year 'for the purpose of extending as far as possible a knowledge of this country and of its culture', conceded in 1930 that 'Parliament should henceforth be asked to provide an annual grant of £2,500 to be expended on books, lecturers, films and miscellaneous minor services' (Foreign Office, 1935a). Then this not altogether princely sum was suspended as a result of the financial crisis of 1931, though not before '£722 17s 5d had already been expended on talks for broadcasting; gifts of books, periodicals and newspapers; lecturers' fees and expenses; films, lantern slides, photographs, etc.' (Foreign Office, 1935a).

The grant was reinstated by a Treasury letter on 11 June 1932, but to the tune of £1,000; when the Foreign Office asked the Treasury to increase this to £1,500, pointing out the large sums spent by other governments on cultural propaganda, the Treasury approved 'the inclusion of £1,800 in the estimates to be submitted to Parliament . . . in 1933, for cultural publicity' (Foreign Office, 1935a). Whether the minor miracle of the uncovenanted £300 extra was due to a change of heart or a misreading is not clear.

It is sometimes supposed that the period between the wars in Britain was one of stability and complacency. In retrospect, from our own age, it may appear so; yet, at the time, people felt beset by financial and industrial problems, as well as by rapid social change. Increasingly, they felt menaced by the threat of war as the fuse burned slowly away to September 1939. There was an active social conscience, which prompted a variety of private initiatives such as the Peace Pledge Union, launched in 1934, and backed by 100,000 members by 1936, and the National Council for Civil Liberties (Mowat, 1955, pp. 525 and 538). One private enterprise that expressed the idealistic aspirations of the 1930s was the All Peoples Association. Since this to some extent made up the gap in official British provision for cultural relations and indeed almost played a more significant role as a channel for official funds when they belatedly began to flow, it merits some examination. For a time, it served as a focus for the endeavours of Reginald (later Sir Reginald) Leeper to secure a higher degree of cultural representation of Britain abroad.

The All Peoples Association (APA, as it was known to initiates) was founded in 1929 by Sir Evelyn Wrench (1882–1966). He occupied a position of influence as chairman and editor of *The Spectator* but left his mark in the annals as a philanthropic internationalist. He founded the Overseas League in 1910, the English-Speaking Union of the Commonwealth in 1918 and the English-Speaking Union of the United States in 1920. Much of his effort was directed at the Empire and the American connection; he had served in the wartime Ministry of Information in 1918 as Deputy Controller of the British Empire and USA Sections. But APA was completely international and completely independent. As an article in *The Spectator* of 1 February 1930, under the title 'APA – the new international society', explained:

All Peoples' Association seeks to make the peoples of the world better known to one another by personal contact, by printed word, by wireless, by correspondence, by the interchange of university professors, students and journalists, and by *making the foreigner feel at home wherever he may be.*

It was proposed to publish a magazine in English, French, German and Spanish, and 'to establish branches in every country in the world under the direction of local national committees of an entirely non-party and non-sectarian nature', while the British branch would set up a club and information bureau in London where the visitor from abroad could feel at home. Membership, the fee for which was fixed internationally at ten shillings per annum (equivalent to the present 50p), grew until, by the time of the demise of APA in 1936, there were 14 branches.

Reginald (Rex) Leeper became head of the Foreign Office News Department in 1935, after working there since 1929. He was in a key position for perceiving the mounting urgency in ambassadors' dispatches about the need for Britain to make itself better known and understood in other countries, particularly those where its opponents were undermining its standing. Leeper first sought a means of response to this challenge in Wrench's APA, which possessed the advantage of a network and also of meeting the Foreign Office desideratum that cultural propaganda should be conducted non-governmentally. Clearly, however, APA would have needed some remodelling. Leeper wrote to his father on 8 May 1934:

> I am convinced that with the present nationalism in Europe the only way that effective work can be done is through a series of national units. This is opposed by certain members of the International Governing Council in London who maintain that they should keep the control centralised and in their hands. In other words they want all the funds collected in this country to be used for general international purposes . . . (Leeper, 1934)

By this time there was clearly a need to co-ordinate the official and non-official organizations – 'such as the General Post Office Film Unit, the Travel Association, the Ibero-American Institute, the All People's Association, the Department of Overseas Trade, and the News Department of the Foreign Office – concerned with British publicity abroad, through the establishment of an unofficial Cultural Relations Committee' (Foreign Office, 1935a). The creation of such a body was in line with Stephen Tallents' remarkable pamphlet of 1932, *The Projection of England*, one of the most persuasive and certainly the most literary statements of Britain's propaganda (or publicity) requirements; it gave specific currency to the word 'projection'; Tallents wrote:

> We need, I suggest, to create in the borderland which lies between Government and private enterprise, a school of national projection. I see the members of this school as a small group, selected less on account of their existing affiliations than by reason of their diverse personal qualities. It must be their business to study professionally the art of national projection and to draw for the materials of that art upon all the resources of English life. (Tallents, 1932, p. 41)

So, at Leeper's instigation, the Committee of International Under-standing and Co-operation came into being in June 1934, with Sir Evelyn Wrench as its chairman. This committee had a short and uncelebrated life. Obviously discontented with its potential, Leeper convened another committee under Lord Tyrell, which had its first meeting on 5 December 1934 and christened itself 'The British Committee for Relations with Other Countries' (Donaldson, 1984, p. 26).

The British Council

From this Committee, the British Council evolved as a non-governmental organization, which could occupy the 'borderland' Tallents had described and bring together the various forms of endeavour struggling to survive on inadequate means. Wrench, who remained chairman of APA, was not best pleased; nor was the Travel Association, which did not relish a competitor in publicity work abroad. But Rex Leeper, with his often acclaimed sense of the manageable, had brought to fruition, and was going to nurse through its early years, the British Council as prototype of the publicly funded, but autonomous, cultural organization.

Why did it take so long for this consummation to be reached? Was it native modesty? This was frequently adduced as at least one reason, by Rex Leeper himself, for instance, in an article he wrote for the *Contemporary Review*: 'As for taking positive steps to explain our aims and achievements, that we regard as undignified and unnecessary. Good wine, we optimistically feel, needs no bush.' (Leeper, 1935, p. 201). It was true, then as now, that the British had inhibitions about blowing their own trumpet (though Leeper himself happened to be an Australian); and they lacked the repertoire to realize that a softer-toned instrument could be substituted – such as the French horn. We have seen in the previous chapter that Britain was not unversed in the arts of propaganda when under compulsion. But the traditional British style was to rely on diplomacy and the established forms of power, essentially the Empire and the Royal Navy, to secure stability, and to leave culture and propaganda to foreigners. Then, just as France turned to cultural projection as a compensation for her military defeat in 1870, so Britain began to pay attention to culture in her imperial standing when imperial power was seen to be under threat. That is why Egypt figured so often in statements made in the 1930s on this subject. Egypt was the strategic key to imperial communications; suddenly it transpired that Britain's previously assured position there lacked the vital component of cultural and educational capacity, and Britain's vulnerability was all the greater because of the intensity of Axis propaganda. *The Times* summed up the growing awareness on 8 February 1938:

A mixture of tolerance, laziness and indifference, and perhaps modesty has kept us from forcing our culture on others and from taking a self-conscious view of it ourselves. Positively, this attitude has expressed itself in a respect for the non-European civilizations of the Empire; negatively, it has led to such anomalies as that of our cultural position in Egypt, where after 50 years of British occupation we were still content to leave the educational and intellectual life of the country under foreign European influences.

The reason for the slowness to react to an obviously changing world situation lay also in a lack of imagination on the part of powerful elements of officialdom and in a deeply entrenched philistinism, clearly seen in the contrast with French policy. This was to dog the British Council for many years, and to find its most vociferous expression in the campaign assiduously run in his newspapers by Lord Beaverbrook, who is described by Frances Donaldson (1984, p. 63) as 'one of the few deliberately wicked men in British history'. Nevertheless, the British Council's first years saw a rapid expansion of activity. A. J. S. White (1965, p. 12) points out, 'The first eighteen months had shown how wide a variety of possible tasks awaited the Council ... the Council found itself engaged in work such as the organisation of hospitality for overseas students and the selection of teachers for schools overseas which was important but cost little'. Work on behalf of foreign students, which was to become a mainstay of the Council's operations, met the requirements of a committee, under the chairmanship of Sir Eugene Ramsden, on the Education and Training of Students from Overseas, which reported in 1933.

Although the British Council's budget grew from an initial £5,000 in 1935 to £60,000 in 1937/38, this was far too little if lost ground was to be made up. The voluntary principle was reasserted when anonymous donors gave £50,000 in 1937 for work in the Near East. The money came through Lord Lloyd, then chairman of the Council's Near East Advisory Committee. Later in 1937, Lord Lloyd became chairman of the British Council itself and brought to the task his incomparable drive and influence. He possessed the connections and standing of one who had been Governor of Bombay and High Commissioner in Egypt. A. J. S. White writes of him (1965, p. 20), 'By constant pressure on people in high places, many of whom were his personal friends, he secured the backing of Cabinet Ministers and others'. It was indicative that this key figure in the evolution of the British Council, and therefore of Britain's cultural relations, should have come from the top rank of imperial rule, even if at a certain remove in time. This again serves to illustrate the difference between the British and the French approach. Sir Stanley Unwin, the publisher (1960, p. 423), tells how, as a member of the Council's Executive Committee, he was at first aghast at the prospect of Lloyd's chairmanship. But he soon became a convert. He says of Lloyd, 'His driving power was magnificent, and under his guidance the work of the Council forged ahead. His dynamic personality was particularly needed'. Lloyd's biographer, Colin Forbes-Adam (1978, p. 284) speaks of 'the great personal kindness, the warmth of friendship, and the charm, as well as the exigence, the impatience, the overmastering determination to get results'. It was owing to Lord Lloyd that the Council avoided being absorbed by the Ministry of Information on the outbreak of war and received its Royal Charter in 1940.

Institutes

One point of similarity between France and Britain in their cultural work overseas is to be seen in the institutes that both countries maintained between the wars. The French effort was, of course, wider in scope and better funded, but the concept was much the same. The work of the British Council for the first twenty years or so of its existence was based on the institute model, that is, the subsidized teaching of language and literature, running a library, and providing a focus of cultural and social activity in a major city, usually a country's capital. The model was well established; indeed, it still gives structure to the cultural relations work of many countries, including France. We shall see later how it has yielded to alternative methodologies, which are more integrated with the institutions of the host country and less costly.

The origin of the French institutes was academic. The first one, at Florence, dating from 1908, was almost an outstation of the University of Grenoble. At the fiftieth anniversary celebrations, the rector of Grenoble University included these remarks in his address:

> The idea of founding a French institute at Florence is due to Julien Luchaire. In 1906–7, as a young don, he occupied the chair of Italian language and literature in the Faculty of Letters at the University of Grenoble. In a well-known work, *Confessions of an Average Frenchman*, he sets out the reasons which decided him: 'Our students of modern languages and literature', he says, 'were bound by the regulations to make long stays abroad. More than once I have seen my students return without having made the expected progress because they had been isolated, with no one to guide them, and had not been able to penetrate those areas where they would have learned to understand not only the language but the country itself'. (French Institute, Florence, 1962, p. 39)

The academic nature of the institute also gave it a reciprocal function. It brought France to Italy and was also a channel for greater understanding of Italy in France. The University of Grenoble was the first university in France to run special courses for foreign students, which it launched in 1896. The institute could draw on a supply of teachers from the parent university; it was well endowed, not only as a teaching institution but also as a centre for research which published its own studies, mainly on literary themes. Funds were provided by the foreign ministry. In its academic conception the institute had something in common with the archaeological schools which France, Germany and Britain set up on classical sites during the nineteenth century; these were also originally instituted on private initiative for the benefit of their own students and researchers, but they too came to exercise a wider cultural and more bilateral function. By 1914 there were four French institutes (Florence, London, Madrid and St Petersburg). By 1933 there were twenty-nine, with 7,000 students and 121 seconded teachers. Often the institute directors were also cultural attachés of their local embassies (Salon, 1981, p. 205).

The early British institutes were on a more modest scale. The earliest was the one in Paris. This, however, was founded in 1894 as the Franco-English Guild. The British Institute Fund acquired the Guild's assets in 1926 and the British Institute was attached to the University of Paris in 1927. This had a bilateral nature too, since it consisted of a Department of French for the benefit of British teachers and students of French as well as a Department of English for the benefit of Parisians. London University assumed responsibility for both departments in the 1960s. There were also British institutes in Brazil, which were brought into being through the work of the Ibero-American Institute. But it was the British Institute of Florence which was to be most influential in British thinking and which best typifies the problems resulting from inadequate official support.

This institute was founded in 1917, together with institutes in Rome and Milan that did not survive the end of the war. The Florence institute was not just a wartime propaganda measure: there were numerous British residents in Florence and the institute also served their needs; indeed, but for their support it too would not have survived the peace. The Department of Information in London (which became the Ministry of Information in 1918) wanted to step up propaganda in Italy in order to sustain that country's war effort. Lina Waterfield (1962, p. 168), who was honorary secretary of the institute, tells how by the year 1917 many Italians had little faith in the war or in Britain as their ally (this was the year when Austrian and German forces broke through the Italian lines at Caporetto) and how the opportunity was taken to relieve the gloom by implementing plans to form an Anglo–Italian Library on the lines of the French Institute. The British ambassador gave his support and the fully fledged institute received government subsidies of about £1,500 a year from 1918 to 1921.

Then the money dried up, when the British government refused to provide funds to continue wartime propaganda ventures or anything that in its perception looked like them. The fact that the institute survived to receive a Royal Charter in 1923 and flourishes today (though still with financial problems) is due to the same voluntary effort which, until 1934, made up for the absence of official British support to match the large sums spent by France, Germany and Italy.

Sir Walter Becker, a British shipowner resident in Turin, covered the institute's deficit for three years, the Serena Foundation weighed in with an annual grant, and there were individual benefactions. There had been no lack of approval from official quarters for the institute. The Tilley Report of 1920 said, 'We consider that His Majesty's Government should continue to subsidise this Institute until it becomes part of a centralised and self-supporting movement, and we hope that the Italian Government will look to this Institution for some at least of its teachers of English. The Committee regret that no other institute similar to that at Florence appears to exist' (Tilley, 1920). Certainly the institute introduced a great improvement in the teaching of English, which was not of high standard in Italy, but its longer-term future seemed questionable.

From 1923 to 1965, the institute was housed in the handsome Palazzo Antinori. The opportunity to buy the freehold, for £10,000 in 1937 and for £25,000 in 1952, and so to secure a permanent site, had to be passed over for lack of wherewithal (Greenlees, 1979, p. 7). It was in the courtyard of Antinori that there took place, according to legend, the celebrated incident when D. H. Lawrence, after visiting the British Institute's library, inveighed in a loud, incensed voice against the pro-Fascist tone of the establishment, saying, 'This is the *anti*-British Institute!' The Institute's director, 1922–39, Harold Goad, was a self-declared adherent of the 'New Italy' (he wrote a pamphlet on the corporate state) and followed policies that landed him in trouble with the embassy, especially when Britain championed the imposition of sanctions after Italy's invasion of Abyssinia (Ethiopia) in 1935. Yet it must be acknowledged that Goad's good standing with the Italian authorities probably prevented their closure of the institute.

When the British Council received its first official budget in 1935, this sum (£5,000) was too little for it to open up its own representations abroad. The money was used to support existing good causes which had been languishing for want of nourishment. One of these was the Florence Institute, which received regular subsidies from the Council. When the Council was able to apply an increased budget to run its own operations abroad, initially in Cairo, its principal model was the British Institute of Florence. Since this had itself been founded on the example of the French Institute, there is a direct line back to French precedent. This is another instance of the dominance that France enjoyed in cultural relations until the Second World War. Just as the French Institute ran two-way programmes, so the British Institute of Florence had a similar bilateral purpose and this was enshrined in its constitution of 1923. The British Council was founded for the sake of furthering British interests; its Royal Charter and financing accord with this purpose. Although in practice the Council observes the requirements of mutuality, it does not, like the British Institute of Florence (which naturally exists in this one place only), have this built into its constitution. The significance of this distinction will be considered in Chapter 9.

6

The War and the Unquiet Peace

Nothing could be more adverse to the spirit and purpose of cultural relations than war. The emotions that most effectively promote belligerency do not spring from understanding. Hitler's conclusion from the front in 1918 was that if you want the masses to hate the enemy the last thing you should do is to make them try to understand him. Hatred feeds on dehumanized stereotypes, not on objective perception. The perfect instrument for stereotyping and alienating is aggressive propaganda. Propaganda, including its cultural aspects, assumed a world-wide function in the Second World War. Zeman (1973, p. 86) quotes Rauschnigg's report of Hitler's remarks: 'The place of artillery preparation for frontal attack by the infantry in trench warfare will in future be taken by revolutionary propaganda to break down the enemy psychologically before the armies begin to function at all'.

Psychological warfare used propaganda to make the enemy doubt his cause and to undermine his willingness to fight. With neutral countries less strident propaganda was employed, supported by cultural appeal, to induce them to come in on one side rather than the other, or at least to maintain helpful relations. The style most likely to succeed was that of confidence and restraint. The stakes were high. Successful cultural penetration could be worth several army divisions if it turned the balance of national sympathy one way or the other. The British Council's representative in Turkey during the Second World War wrote to London on 26 July 1943 about the wide-scale publicity, especially on matters cultural, put out by Axis and satellite governments in the Balkans (British Council, 1943b):

The general conclusion from all this literature is that cultural propaganda is considered by the Axis as a very serious matter of first importance, as indeed would appear from the large number of high ranking cultural attachés distributed round Europe.

In Latin America, sometimes in rivalry with the more abundant efforts of the United States, the Council played a vital part also in a campaign to defend Britain's economic interests 'against United States as much as Axis encroachment ... And in this task cultural propaganda had a special and predominant role. Unable to match the United States in quantity, the Council hoped to win the hearts of the ruling classes in Latin America with the high quality and sophistication of British culture and political development and, by accident more than design, to appear as the foremost exponent of European culture and the counter-balance to the all-pervasiveness of "Yankee" culture' (Eastment, 1982, p. 180).

A memorandum on the British Council, issued by the Foreign Office towards the end of the war in March 1944, assessed the effort in neutral countries thus:

> The French sustained their influence in Egypt for many years by cultural means. Any contact with Frenchmen at the present time shows the importance they attach to the maintenance or recovery by France of her reputation as a seat of culture. In the years 1940–42, through the Council, the British gained considerable political profit by maintaining their cultural links with neutral countries. Many eloquent tributes were paid by Latin American statesmen to the fact that Britain could afford at that time to send abroad an exhibition of books or pictures. In short, the work is a valuable weapon in any time of political or economic difficulty. The same applies when a nation of its free will is giving up political power in a dependency overseas. Thus in Egypt the Council became an important means of keeping Egyptians and British in touch with one another after the departure of British officials from service with the Egyptian government. Similarly as constitutional ties with India are loosened, the Council's work there would become of great political value. (Foreign Office, 1944, p. 5)

The final part of this quotation implies an interesting parallel between cultural relations work in two situations of diminished political control: wartime and the emancipation of dependent territories.

During the war years, the annual budget of the British Council had enormously increased as part of the war effort: £130,000 in 1938/39 to £2,100,000 in 1944/45. The *Annual Report* for 1946/47 shows fifty-three institutes, seven in Egypt alone. In spite of the threat to Britain's existence, the Council's rapid expansion during the war was accomplished without surrender of its independence. This remarkable fact reflects the general understanding that the Council was not to be involved directly in propaganda. In the Introduction to the *Annual Report 1940/41*, it was stated:

the Council was prepared to let facts speak for themselves, to abstain from all political propaganda, and to encourage what demand might be met from foreign countries rather than, following the German method, to seek the imposition of ideas upon the outside world. Given the ultimate object to create friendship and understanding, the results have proved that this was the wise course. (British Council, 1941, p. 21)

The policy of giving clients what they want rather than what one feels should be served up to them is a basic distinction between propaganda and cultural relations. But the Council did have an important information role in support of the war effort. Its printed materials, photographic exhibitions and films had wide international circulation and showed the continuity of British life.

It produced various publications during the war. The best known was *Britain Today*, issued fortnightly from March 1935 and then, because of the paper shortage, monthly from 1942, with articles on subjects of general interest about Britain that might be expected to attract the foreign reader. Circulation peaked at 113,000; there were Spanish and Portuguese editions as well as English. Its success may be measured by the fact that 'Axis propagandists paid a compliment to the influence of *Britain Today* in Portugal by twice producing and circulating a replica' (British Council, 1943a, p. 75).

The Cold War

The Cold War that ensued after 1945 was a matter of posture and counter-posture. Aggression was ritualized not only in military gesture but also in the parading of ideologies. Competing political and economic systems defined the strategies but the cause was 'in the minds of men': victory was sought not only by asserting the merits of one's own side but also by undermining loyalties on the other side. It was not until the relative thaw of the late 1950s that the Cold War softened into peaceful co-existence. As the more blatant expressions of propaganda receded, there was a recognition that some effort at mutual understanding was desirable; cultural relations then came to occupy a more significant position between the power blocs.

To describe the postwar world in terms of the points of the compass, one could say that its dominant features were the East–West divide and the North–South dichotomy. The first conditioned international affairs from 1945, while the second set in more gradually with the spread of independence. The conventional starting date for the Cold War as a conscious phenomenon is Churchill's speech at

Fulton in March 1946 when he made famous the image of the 'iron curtain' (which many Americans at the time thought reactionary and which some historians today would consider a conditioning stereotype). The Berlin airlift of 1948, the communist seizure of power in Czechoslovakia in the same year, the Korean War of 1950, were the main incidents that reinforced the confrontation. It was the Korean War above all that roused the United States to the need to engage wholeheartedly in the propaganda battle. In the way of dictators, Stalin seems to have been as much a victim of Soviet propaganda as his followers in believing that, after the ruinous effects of the war, the West, and especially Europe, was faced with economic collapse followed by chaos and revolution. He therefore saw no reason to be anything but ruthless in pursuing communist advantage and preserving the single-mindedness of the Soviet camp. Barghoorn (1960) says on this period:

> Stalin, until 1951 or 1952 at least, adhered rigidly to the 'two camp' approach to international relations bluntly announced in his election speech of February 9, 1946, and later elaborated in a series of speeches by his lieutenant, Andrei A. Zhdanov. Stalin's address, together with Winston Churchill's reply a month later at Fulton, Missouri, clarified the issues of the East–West cold war. Stalin's policy required establishment and maintenance of monolithic controls throughout Moscow's domain and restriction to the barest minimum of contacts with all governments and political groups over which police control could not be established. (Barghoorn, 1960, p. 60)

Zhdanov it was who reimposed the controls on freedom of expression that had been a feature of Stalin's tyranny before the Soviet Union entered the war in 1941:

> In the early months of 1946 a new era began in Soviet cultural history: in a series of decrees affecting literature, music, the cinema, and eventually every aspect of cultural life, the intellectuals were told that with the passing of the immediate military crisis, the authorities regarded political indoctrination as a matter of top priority, and far stricter discipline would from now on be demanded. (Laqueur, 1970, p. 361)

Stalin's policies and the sequestered status forced upon the Soviet peoples as well as the populations of other communist countries, stirred the United States to action rather as Britain was stirred to action by Nazi and Fascist policies in the 1930s. The action was on an altogether grander scale. It had further-reaching consequences; it bred controversies that went to fashion America's self-awareness as the leading world power. One could speculate that if Soviet behaviour had been more conciliatory and open, and if the United States had thereupon reverted to isolationist attitudes, Western Europe would have been hard put to it to resist communist subversion. The left-wing inclinations of many European intellectuals, and the large communist parties of France and Italy in particular, yielded easy pickings in the decade after 1945.

The United States government did not engage in officially funded cultural relations until 1938. When the Prince of Wales said in his inaugural address as Patron of the British Council, on 2 July 1935, 'Of all the Great Powers this country is the last in the field in setting up a proper organisation to spread a knowledge and appreciation of its language, literature, art, science and education' (British Council, 1935, p. 5), he was being atypically Eurocentric. The initial US programme was confined to co-operation with 'the other American Republics' (where Nazi and Fascist propaganda was virulent) and to the creation of a Division of Cultural Relations in the Department of State. The Division was made responsible for official cultural relations work, 'embracing the exchange of professors, teachers, and students; co-operation in the field of music, art, literature and other intellectual and cultural attainments; the formulation and distribution of libraries of representative works of the United States and suitable translations thereof; the participation by this Government in international radio broadcasts; encouragement of a closer relationship between unofficial organizations of this and of foreign governments engaged in cultural and intellectual activities; and, generally, the dissemination abroad of the representative intellectual and cultural works of the United States and the improvement and broadening of the scope of our cultural relations with other countries.' (McMurry and Lee, 1947, pp. 208–9). The Department of State appointed Cultural Relations Officers to embassies and legations, first in the Americas, and then progressively in other countries until, by 1946, they 'had been appointed to diplomatic missions in each of the other American Republics and also in Belgium, China, England, France, Italy, the Netherlands, Portugal, Spain and Turkey' (McMurry and Lee, 1947, p. 215).

The United States also adopted the model of the cultural institute. Rather after the style of the British Institute of Florence, institutes had been founded jointly by American residents and local citizens in Latin American countries, with the main activity of teaching English to the local people and the native language to Americans. The number of these institutes expanded rapidly during the war. They provided some of the field experience that was to inform American language teaching theory after the war. Another arm of the Division of Cultural Relations was the books programme. By 1 July 1946 there were 27 cultural centres in the rest of the world (McMurry and Lee, 1947, p. 216). Also by July 1946 there were 300 American schools operating in other American Republics.

After the attack on Pearl Harbor in December 1941 the Department of State had co-operated with the Office of War Information to step up United States' broadcasting. Voice of America transmissions began in 1942. In 1946 Public Law 584, introduced by Senator Fulbright, was passed, authorizing the use of funds from the disposal of surplus war material to finance educational exchanges. This two-way programme proved to be an invaluable resource in America's cultural relations. Its imaginative conception was described by President Kennedy as 'beating swords into plough-shares'. Then the Smith–Mundt Act of 1948 provided for a peacetime overseas information programme.

The United States faced the Cold War, therefore, with a well-founded but relatively modest programme of cultural relations. The office of War Information had been scrapped in 1945. What America lacked was effective weapons in the battle of ideologies. The newly elected Senator from Massachusetts, William Benton, pleaded in his maiden speech in the Senate for a 'Marshall Plan in the field of ideas', and said the information gap was the channel through which communism spread (*New York Times*, 23 March 1950).

The Voice of America (VOA) was struggling on a budget which Congress was determined not to see substantially increased, and under a good deal of criticism, among others from Senator Benton (*New York Herald Tribune*, 5 February 1951). Then there were the two broadcasting services that were born of the Cold War itself, Radio Free Europe (RFE), created in 1950 for broadcasts to East Europe, and Radio Liberty (RL), created in 1953 for broadcasts to the various linguistic groups in the Soviet Union; both of them were based in Munich and both appeared for some years to be funded from private contributions. Later, it transpired that they received money from the Central Intelligence Agency. VOA, RFE and RL were all subjected to jamming, and various measures were proposed to overcome this. The most striking was the idea of using ships as floating transmitters in the Mediterranean, in order to outfox the jammers. This was called Operation Vagabond because of its mobility. A fleet of six ships was intended. President Truman went on board the first one on 3 March 1952 and *The Times* of 5 March reports him as saying, in the course of his broadcast to the world: 'There is a terrific struggle going on today to win the minds of people throughout the world. The rulers of the Kremlin are trying to make the whole world knuckle under to the godless totalitarian creed of Communism.'

Although radio was a vital means of getting through to the peoples behind the iron curtain, it did not satisfy the compulsion felt by millions of Americans to, in the words of President Truman in 1950 to the American Society of Newspaper Editors, 'make ourselves heard round the world in a great campaign of truth!' (*New York Times*, 23 March 1950). In the American tradition that retired commanders are often invited to lead popular movements (General Clay was in charge of the Crusade for Freedom), Admiral Kirk became Chairman in 1952 of the American Committee for the Liberation of the Peoples of Russia Inc. *The New York Times* of 11 February 1952 reports his words, 'If the Stalinist regime is our enemy, the peoples enslaved by them are our friends'. There were other organizations funded to similar ends, and millions of dollars were raised. The Common Council for American Unity operated through new immigrants, who were encouraged to include titbits of pro-American information in their letters to their countries of origin.

The most bizarre of the large-scale actions undertaken to break through the baffles of the communist world was the balloon campaign. The dropping of propaganda leaflets had been used extensively in the First World War: it remained a recognized if rather outmoded weapon of psychological warfare in the age of radio. Starting experimentally in 1951, the balloon campaign was in full swing by 1954. It gave straight news from the West and made revelations, based on intelligence reports, from the East. In the name of the Crusade for Freedom, balloons – by 1956 carrying 250 million copies of these leaflets – were launched over Czechoslovakia, Hungary and Poland. After two years of silence, the governments of those countries protested and even claimed that there had been damage to persons and to aircraft. *The Observer* remarked on 12 February 1956, 'Leaflet balloons are part of the price the Russians have to pay for refusing to agree to stop radio jamming'.

The balloon campaign came to an end after the 1956 uprisings in Hungary and Poland. It was thought to have fulfilled its purpose. Radio jamming was modified with the policy of peaceful co-existence under Khrushchev in the late 1950s. The United States had asserted the right to speak direct to suppressed peoples. *The New York Times* of 18 February 1959 reports the statement of George Allen, director of the United States Information Agency:

The new diplomacy finds governments aiming directly at the peoples of foreign lands. We do everything we can to reach them, in thirty-five languages, penetrating their living rooms, bedrooms, cellars, wherever the radio is kept. This has shocked some men in the State Department.

This 'new diplomacy' took its particular form because of the deliberate isolation of the Soviet bloc under Stalin. In the opposite direction, the Soviet Union operated, less visibly, through friendship societies and front organizations. The populations of Western countries had no reason to feel isolated from alternative sources of news. Soviet propaganda was not so direct, therefore; it rapidly lost credibility when it was seen – as with Stalin's peace campaign – to be so much at variance with Soviet actions. Moreover, in cultural and intellectual circles, people who were accustomed to openness of information soon detected the restrictive effect of ideology; even those who were Marxists came to realize that there was nothing actually new on offer. In the words of Barghoorn (1960, p. 28):

> Soviet Russia has offered to the world, or even demanded that the world adopt, its version of mass culture. This messianic approach challenges and threatens the established cultures of East and West, though the effectiveness of the challenge is limited by the failure of the Soviet leaders to create a really new and appealing Socialist culture.

Although the defence of its values against the threat from without strengthened conviction among Americans, another consequence of the Cold War was to undermine that same conviction from within. This was the phenomenon known as McCarthyism. Senator Joseph McCarthy rode the waves of disillusion in the wake of the Korean War. His thesis that communism had infiltrated government and other major institutions in the United States led to ferocious hearings of suspected individuals, which were also televised; it led as well to intervention in the practices of American cultural representations abroad. The most infamous form this took was the burning of books in American libraries written by authors who were thought to be left-wing, or who had failed to satisfy McCarthy's sub-committee (such as Howard Fast). *The New York Herald Tribune* of 14 June 1953 wrote: 'The burning of the books is now progressing merrily in all American diplomatic missions abroad for all to see. The State Department's book-burning program, undertaken in craven fear of Sen. Joseph R. McCarthy, even has certain amusing aspects – if one disregards the fact that it is making the US an object of derision all over the world.'

USIA

The United States Information Agency was set up on 1 August 1953. It was to be an independent agency reporting to the President through the National Security Council. The purpose was primarily, as the name implies, to consolidate information activities. Its remit excluded educational exchanges (e.g. Fulbright) and the 'overseas cultural presentations programs', which both remained the responsibility of the State Department. This separation was considered important for the sake of avoiding any possibility of carrying propaganda into educational and cultural work. There was a good deal of organizational chopping and changing before this compromise position was reached. When the publicist Edward Murrow became Director of USIA in 1961, he was reported in *The New York Times* of 11 August 1961 as having said of USIA, 'In the bare 20 years of its life it has had five titles and a dozen different directors'. He was referring to its antecedents as well as to USIA itself, including the Office of War Information created in 1942 (with its overseas component, the US Information Service) and the postwar Office of International Information and Education. The changing titles reflect the fluctuating competences. The debate concerning the advantages and disadvantages of combining responsibility for information with education and culture in one body was to continue; it will be followed in Chapter 13.

The infant USIA was badly mauled in the last stages of McCarthyism: the effects of this notorious campaign on USIA and the Voice of America (which was part of USIA responsibility) were severe. It became difficult to recruit competent staff for the broadcasting services. *The New York Herald Tribune* of 15 February 1954 reported the recommendation of Senator Hickenlooper, then chairman of the Senate Foreign Relations Sub-Committee, that USIA should be left in peace for a few years. And *The New York Times* (31 July 1954) records President Eisenhower quoting from Milton's *Areopagitica*, when he congratulated members of USIA for their achievements in their first year of existence: 'Let Truth and Falsehood Grapple; whoever knew Truth put to the worse in a free and open encounter?' He was not however, referring to the conflict of interests between USIA and the State Department.

7

Information and After in Europe

The Second World War left an 'information gap', which became a preoccupation of the Allies' official services during the postwar years. The need to fill this gap also conditioned the work of their cultural and educational services. The United States, Britain and France were concerned to purvey information to former enemy countries in order to strengthen the foundations of democracy. In Germany and Japan, particularly, information was disseminated not only on political questions, such as democracy, but also on social policies – education, trade unionism, individual rights. Here, and in other countries which had been isolated from the Western democracies by the war, there was also a need for cultural information to expound what had been happening in the arts, literature, and social developments. Cultural relations work assumed a characteristically informational style in order to meet this need. The background of the Cold War and the struggle for influence in Europe and in countries on the way to independence gave the whole strategy an urgency which attracted public support and official funds. In an article in *The Spectator* of 30 August 1946, Stephen King-Hall typified, and surpassed, current British attitudes when he wrote, 'I must declare a conviction which is that the spreading all over the world, and particularly in the USA and Russia, of full information about the British way of life should be one of the chief objects of our foreign policy; an object upon which I would spend £50,000,000 a year as a priority defence expenditure'. He went on to suggest that ten thousand copies of *Hansard* should be distributed to editors and publicists round the world.

Typical information activities in cultural relations work were lectures, documentary film shows, photographic displays of news and current affairs, lending libraries, presentation of books and periodicals (especially on 'life and institutions' subjects) and language teaching. These were based on the existing institute model.

Cultural representations offered activities to attract their members following language classes, who provided a faithful core of the audience, and also the general public. People could come in off the street to attend functions such as lectures and film shows, which were free of charge. There was accordingly little identification of targets or attempt at evaluation. The open-house policy in cultural relations is always vulnerable to invasion by less rewarding audiences. In war-torn Europe, for instance, where living quarters and heating were exiguous, a warm room was an attraction whatever was going on; for some, it was a strong enough inducement to overcome their ignorance of the language, or their indifference to the subject. Such persons, often female, could be seen to go from one cultural institute to another, swelling the statistics. In some quarters, they were nicknamed 'the knitters' because they liked to keep their hands occupied and were prominent in the front row; for the nervous lecturer they awoke memories of the *tricoteuses* who knitted at the tribunals in the French Revolution. The Germans were, later, to call the equivalent in their audiences 'ladies in hats'.

These open-house activities were not a particularly effective way of purveying information but they had a useful human function in encouraging access to, and familiarity with the ways of, the exponents of democracy. Newspapers, such as those run by the occupying powers in Germany and Austria, and radio broadcasts, cut more ice. On the other hand, institute-style activities were relatively cheap and they established some of the first contacts with potential target groups; also included in the audiences and the library membership were people who had an influence on larger numbers, for instance teachers. Such people became known as multipliers, and in time it came to be realized that multipliers can best be reached by making them a deliberate target. These postwar attempts to provide information seem undirected in comparison with the more developed techniques that characterize cultural relations at their best today. But it is worth reminding ourselves of the desperate hunger there was for information by considering the example of Germany.

George Murray (1978, p. 89) writes of the way British newspapers and periodicals used to vanish from army messes, 'as often as not ending their career on the local black market cut up into single pages and sold for cigarettes, the number varying in direct proportion to the topicality of the articles and in inverse proportion to the amount of advertisement on the reverse side'.

The British in Germany established *die Brücken* (Bridges), which were information and cultural centres named originally after a magazine of the information services called *Die Brücke*. The Americans had *Amerikahäuser* (American Houses) and youth centres. As the German Social Democrat leader, Kurt Schuhmacher, said, 'Total victory means total responsibility'. Most Germans today who remember this period immediately after the war would agree that this responsibility was well exercised so far as the provision of information was concerned.

But it was the French who first broke through the psychological barrier by bringing young French people to meet their German counterparts. The numbers grew from a few dozen in 1945 to 5,000 in 1959, in which year the frontier was opened to the Germans to go in the opposite direction (Grosser, 1974, p. 81). Obviously, the French had the advantage of proximity, but they seized the vital point that bringing young Germans together with young French people, on equal terms, was likely to establish better relations for the future than any amount of telling. Incidentally, a precedent was set up for the Franco-German youth exchange programme, which was to be one of the principal measures in the reconciliation between the two countries brought about by the Adenauer–de Gaulle agreement of 1963. The Franco-German Youth Office made possible exchanges of 1.8 million young people in its first five years of operation. The effects of this imaginative scheme will be considered in Chapter 15. It was founded on the realization that the best and most enduring way to inform populations of the truth about one another is to send the young to see for themselves.

The Federal Republic of Germany was also predominantly concerned with information as the main thrust of its cultural relations work in the year after 1949, when it assumed sovereignty in accordance with the Basic Law (*Grundgesetz*) of that year. The Federal Republic had to observe two main factors which conditioned its foreign policy: the Nazi past and the division of Germany. The living-down of the Nazi past will probably not be accomplished until there are no survivors from that period and it becomes part of history; even today, German cultural representatives abroad find themselves put under subtle or less subtle pressure on account of this legacy. Living with a skeleton in the cupboard can lead to constrained behaviour. The Federal Republic tended to concentrate on the arts, particularly music, in its cultural policy of the 1950s and early 1960s; these had the advantage of at once reviving the achievements of earlier history and emphasizing the common German tradition. The Goethe Institute, founded in 1932 and recreated in 1952, built up its activities and representation in pace with the growth of Germany's external cultural budget (from DM 4.5 million in 1952 to DM 324 million in 1970). The motive of national rehabilitation remained strong and information, or national self-projection, was the basic mode.

By the end of the 1960s, however, the Federal Republic had thought its way on to more forward-looking policies. By adopting the idea of an enlarged cultural concept (*erweiteter Kulturbegriff*) and co-operation in partnership (*partnerschaftliche Zusammenarbeit*) Germany was able to establish a position as the prime thinker among the nations practising cultural relations. These policies will be considered more closely later, but, by way of initial explanation, the first implies that culture should be treated in the broader sense to include various aspects of social activity, the second that cultural policies should not be aimed at national self-projection but at co-operation and exchange in matters of mutual interest. These are the two most important among fifteen theses that were presented to the cabinet by the foreign minister in 1970. They are not revolutionary or indeed individually new. The significance is rather in their being formulated as a strategy for enriching Germany's cultural relations with other countries. That, particularly at this high political level, was new. No better paradigm could be found to illustrate the advance from an information-based style to one concerned with mutual benefit.

French external cultural policy remained constant to its long-established traditions until modifications were introduced by the Rigaud Report of 1979 and the foreign ministry's statement of 1984, *Le projet culturel extérieur de la France*, which are considered in Chapter 13. France, enfeebled by the war in its substance and status, possessed the advantages of a culture that had flourished in spite of the occupation and even acquired glamour as a symbol of peacetime. Intellectually, it emerged from the ordeal with panache. France had been through the experience of defeat, occupation and resistance: the presentation of this experience, by writers in particular, gave it an immediacy of appeal. For France too there was an information role in its cultural relations. Most European intellectuals in the postwar years were left-wing, partly out of anti-fascist impetus and admiration for the wartime achievements of the Soviet Union, and partly because the instability of the political establishment encouraged receptivity towards a new way of ordering international affairs. What France had to offer that was peculiar to her intellectual traditions and her recent ordeals was the philosophy of Existentialism. This was very much aligned with the thinking of the Left.

Existentialism is not of course French in origin; it is Danish and German. But the formulation it received from Jean-Paul Sartre gave it a French manifestation appropriate to a time of readjustment and insecurity: Sartre's contention that man is the focus of his own universe and that what matters is his existence rather than his essence (or, more crudely, practice rather than theory) seemed to bring a new liberation. It was not a joyful liberation but it stimulated action. Sartre (1969, p. 553) wrote, 'man being condemned to be free carries the weight of the whole world on his shoulders; he is responsible for the world and for himself as a way of being'. The novels of Sartre and of Albert Camus (whose *La Peste* was a brilliant allegory of the contemporary human condition) presented the Existentialist world-view by showing characters in extreme situations that called forth fundamental responses. The link between Existentialism and Marxism was also of powerful topicality.

It might have looked as though France was about to reassert its cultural hegemony. Apart from fiction, there were theatre and cinema (especially the films of Marcel Carné) to arrest the intellect. Yet by the early 1950s France was discovering that a come-back on a scale commensurate with its traditions was impossible in a world where the English language and American models had introduced a new cultural balance of power. In an article in *Le Monde* on 26 December 1953 a French senator, Léo Hamon, wrote of 'French culture in danger' and of the way France was neglecting the fact that its language and culture were now in second place. He ascribed some of this decline to the rise of technology over the arts of literature and debate, and made the commercial point (which we have seen earlier to be a focus of interest for politicians), 'Fewer people will come to France, they will buy fewer dresses and luxury articles when French civilization is less known and valued'.

There was no default in the central administration of France's external cultural operations. The *Service des oeuvres françaises a l'étranger* became a separate directorate of the foreign ministry in 1945, as the Directorate-General of Cultural Relations (*Direction générale des relations culturelles*). This was expanded in 1957 to take account of the developmental needs of dependencies, as the Directorate-General of Cultural and Technical Affairs, and then again in 1969 to become the Directorate-General of Cultural, Scientific and Technical Relations. The Ministry of Education surrendered its *Bureau d'action artistique*, which funded the diffusion of the arts, to the Directorate in 1946. Cultural attaché posts were created at all major embassies, the French institutes were expanded, and French schools overseas adapted their syllabuses to the requirements of the host country so that they could attract more local children seeking a French-style education. The *Alliance Française* reopened its school in Paris to a growing number of foreign students and by 1949 had operations in 650 towns abroad. The Secretary-General said in his report of that year, 'We are absent only

in places where it is neither permitted nor possible to be present'
(Bruézière, 1983, p. 142).

The question that arises is how it could be that such a centralized
and well-endowed system nevertheless witnessed a steady decline of
influence. Part of the answer lies in the close identification in the
French mind of culture with language. Much of the generous
allocation to the Directorate-General for Cultural, Scientific and
Technical Relations (which by 1970 was nearly two-thirds of the
total budget of the foreign ministry) went on schools, institutes and
subsidized teaching posts in foreign institutions. And yet, in most
countries, French was overtaken by English; for purposes of international communication the discrepancy was even more marked.
The French response was to intensify the linguistic rearguard action.
With the organized cultivation of *Francophonie* from 1970 onwards
(see p. 169), France had a means of limiting its losses, but it was not
until the Rigaud Report of 1979 (published 1980) that full
recognition was accorded to the fact that French ideas, as a cultural
good for the benefit of other peoples, can be communicated by other
means than through the French language. The emphasis on the
French language contained some elements of that *messianisme*
which has been mentioned above. Albert Salon (1981, p. 1638)
concluded that although French cultural activities abroad can make a
material contribution to France's political and economic interests,
'as we believe we have shown, and as many inspectors of finance have
deplored, what France and most of the private and public operators
seek in cultural programmes is intangible advantages – a grandeur, a
glory, a prestige, a responsibility that is "cultural power" in itself and
for itself'. This contrasts with the rationale normally advanced in
Britain that the furthering of material national interests, even if in a
manner which can seldom be substantiated, is the ultimate
justification of external cultural policy.

Italy follows a similar pattern to that of France in its external cultural
policy and its implementation. There is a Directorate-General of
Cultural Relations in the foreign ministry, which co-ordinates the
total effort and collaborates with the Ministry of Education in
recruiting teachers for Italian institutes and schools abroad. Italy had
to live down the memories of fascism, but although Mussolini was in
power almost twice as long as Hitler the heritage was less burden-
some. Fascism in Italy was comparatively restrained in its
depredations and had less opportunity to subjugate other countries.
Indeed, the cultural image left by Mussolini has its favourable
aspects, because he understood how to turn the grandeur of the past to
popular effect.

After the war Italy expanded the number of institutes abroad on which much of its cultural activity was based. According to Umberto Gori, writing in 1970 about Italy's policy towards UNESCO:

> Italian policy has evolved from a Euro-centric and elitist view of the organisation's mission towards an attitude of mass-enlightenment and scientifically oriented technical cooperation; an attempt has been made to prevent the Italian speciality of 'tactile' culture from being overlooked; the tendency of communist countries to exploit the organisation's possibilities of political propaganda has been resisted in favour of a constructive approach towards understanding between different civilisations; and Italian experience has been drawn upon to help combat illiteracy in the developing world, to develop the use of audio-visual aids in education, and to encourage research into the social sciences. (Haigh, 1974, p. 95)

The Dante Alighieri Society, constituted similarly to the Alliance Française, soon had its world-wide network functioning again after the war. The millions of expatriate Italians and people of Italian stock retained a cultural connection even when they were integrated linguistically and culturally in their country of residence. They went back to Italy as tourists. Tourism was Italy's largest growth industry after the war. It has provided a profitable short-term answer to the question how Italy, with its incomparable cultural riches from successive civilizations, can assert its due cultural position at a time when, like France, it has been left on a linguistic side-line by the Anglo-American express.

For Britain the end of the war brought opportunities in its projection abroad that were not fully realized. Again, the government reduced expenditure rather in the same way, though less drastically, as the money was cut which had been spent by the Ministry of Information at the end of the First World War. In the period 1947/47 to 1953/54 the British Council's grant-in-aid from the Foreign Office was reduced year by year from £2,700,000 to £1,625,000. Britain enjoyed an upsurge of international prestige at this time. The English language was already establishing itself as the foremost lingua franca; literature and the arts were going through a reflorescence, which became manifest from the time of the Festival of Britain in 1951. It would have been a great time to reinforce success. If it had been consistent with the thinking of that period, it would have been an imaginative act to assert the political leadership that so many Europeans then expected from Britain and to support it with a vigorous external cultural policy. But the thoughts of politicians tended in very different directions. No one, not even Churchill, in spite of his Zürich speech of September 1946 when he spoke of a United States of Europe, saw the opportunity that existed. Its terms were unfamiliar to British foreign policy.

The British Council's information work, which had been part of its response to wartime requirements, continued to be important after the war, especially in those countries that had been cut off from knowledge of developments in Britain. However, the government was by no means unanimous in believing that the Council should continue to exist as a non-governmental organization. There was talk in 1946 of subsuming its work into the Publicity Division of the Foreign Office. Ernest Bevin, the Foreign Secretary, wrote a circular letter to heads of mission on 3 December 1946, *Definition of the Work of the British Council* (Foreign Office, 1946), enjoining more supervision of the Council and enclosing a paper, which has since come to be called the Definition Document. One of the provisions of this was that films and publications for the Council's use should in future be procured through the Central Office of Information. This measure reduced the specifically information work of the Council and led to greater concentration on cultural and educational activities.

It remains to mention one important development, which was a by-product of the war and which resulted from what was largely an information activity. The war brought to Britain large numbers of Allied merchant seamen, service men and women, and refugee civilians, who had very little rapport with the country. A meeting of government departments in 1940 decided that the British Council should assume responsibility for the educational and cultural welfare of such people. An Advisory Committee on Foreigners in Great Britain was assembled and the work was organized on a regional basis, consisting of English teaching, provision of books, film shows, lectures and concerts, etc. The significance of this development is that it left the British Council at the end of the war with a fully staffed network, which could be used for other human traffic. It was to prove invaluable when the number of visitors and students coming to Britain increased by leaps and bounds. The government considered this network especially important for looking after the students from colonies who came to study in large numbers as their independence drew near. As a result, the British Council acquired a unique triune structure, with representatives abroad, its headquarters in London, and its regional offices in major university cities of England, Scotland, Wales and Northern Ireland.

The transition outlined in this chapter from the postwar emphasis on information to the broader concept of cultural relations is typical of the countries that have been mentioned. As major belligerents they had to address themselves to the consequences of a war that had brought turmoil and change. Accordingly, they projected an image of themselves appropriate to their national policies; defeated enemies were infiltrated with concepts and precepts designed to preclude any recurrence of misrule. The conditions that made this necessary now belong to history. But in some countries today there is still, at least in practice, some identification of cultural diplomacy with information work. This is evidenced in the fact that both kinds of responsibility are frequently borne by the same attaché in embassies. The Press and Cultural Attaché is a convenient and economical amalgam. It is understandable that if a country conducts little cultural work this may well seem to serve as no more than a support for national projection. Nevertheless, the hybrid product must be classified as cultural diplomacy rather than as cultural relations as they are more specifically conceived. The realization of the full potential of cultural relations would call for a separation of competences.

8

The Organization

France having established the pattern of attaching responsibility for cultural relations work to the foreign ministry, Italy and Germany adopted the same pattern for similar reasons. They saw the need to maintain the loyalty of their communities abroad by the provision of schools, to extend their influence through and beyond those communities by enrolling local children and by promoting other educational and cultural activities. The pattern was logical because external cultural policy was seen to be an intrinsic aspect of foreign policy; this in many countries remains the view of government and the informed public. The British Council was set up as an autonomous body, but at the behest of the Foreign Office, in order to meet needs that were originally conceived in terms of foreign policy. When the Japan Foundation was set up in 1972, it was based on the example of the British Council's autonomy but under closer supervision by the foreign ministry. The USIA took over cultural relations work from the State Department but remained closely aligned with American foreign policy.

There are advantages and disadvantages in this primacy of foreign policy. On the positive side, there is a ready-made rationale in favour of cultural relations in this arrangement. Most politicians and taxpayers accept the necessity of observing their country's interests in the world through a foreign policy; they accept diplomacy as an instrument of foreign policy and, if they can be persuaded that cultural work plays an intrinsic part in this diplomacy, they will accept that too. This means that cultural relations budgets, vulnerable as they are, are more likely to be sustained if they are voted through the foreign ministry than if they were channelled through a domestic ministry, such as that of culture or education. Another advantage is that diplomatic missions provide a base to which attachés for cultural work can be posted, and to which other agencies or individuals operating abroad can refer. There is much convenience in having a recognized international network, which can be invoked for cultural purposes as for others (defence, labour, finance) that lie outside conventional diplomacy. Also diplomacy is enriched by the cultural element, which gives a longer-term, intellectual dimension to political and economic work; what intellectuals are saying and students are believing today will affect the political configuration of tomorrow. Friends in high places are perhaps yesterday's seekers of friendship and knowledge.

The principal disadvantage of this primacy of foreign policy considerations, however, is that it reinforces the one-way, outward concept. Also there is the danger of thinking and planning in the short term rather than in the longer term required by cultural relations. The justification for government expenditure tends to be sought predominantly or even exclusively in the direct benefit to the country providing the money. Evaluation of success is based on the same premise. The emphasis is on acquiring prestige and influence. While this primacy is appropriate, therefore, for cultural propaganda and for cultural diplomacy, it is less appropriate for cultural relations as a two-way process.

One reason for this is that a foreign ministry is not well placed to supply the co-operation with home institutions that is a prerequisite of reciprocity. There are ways round the difficulty, but structurally the problem remains and is likely to impede the more sensitive kinds of exchange. One solution is for the foreign ministry to remit cultural relations to autonomous agencies (such as the Japan Foundation and the British Council) and thus to modulate official involvement. Another is to rely on advisory committees and the domestic institutions they represent to secure a broad base of participation. The word 'constituency' is sometimes used to cover the institutions that make up the cultural and educational life of a country. For cultural agencies the constituency consists of institutions and elites which can relate, in cultural or educational matters, to their counterparts in other countries. On the whole, the constituency co-operates more readily with non-governmental than with governmental agencies. Academics, in particular, have expressed their preference for foreign mediation through autonomous bodies such as the German Academic Exchange Service (DAAD) and the British Council (also earlier the Inter-University Council, which was merged with the British Council in 1980) rather than through ministries and embassies. Some academics have even said that they would not give their time and services free if they were called upon to serve governmental purposes. There is for many writers, artists and specialists an essential difference between an organization that facilitates contacts with members of professional constituencies in other countries, for mutual benefit, and an official body that invokes participation in governmental programmes. This difference is another illustration of the distinction between cultural relations and cultural diplomacy, and of the greater economy in the manner in which the former uses and furthers the voluntary principle.

If the purpose of cultural relations is to achieve mutual exchanges rather than to promote national prestige, how does one pursue the argument that they justify their budgets by serving foreign policy? The answer is that they best serve foreign policy by developing international relationships. Each country engaging in cultural relations benefits not only by making itself better understood in other countries, but also by improving understanding of them among its own people. But here again we come up against the structural problem represented by the predominantly outward focus of foreign ministries.

On the whole, the 'culture-exporting countries' finance and direct their cultural relations through their foreign ministries. In some countries, however, it is another ministry (e.g. culture, information, education) that has the responsibility. Included among these are the 'culture-importing countries', which because of their stage of development or linguistic situation receive more than they give in the way of study awards, educational assistance and cultural events. In this category we can count, for instance, Indonesia, Korea, Malaysia and Pakistan, in all of which the ministry of culture bears the responsibility for co-ordination. Similarly, India bestows this responsibility on its ministry of culture centrally and on the Department of Arts in the individual states. One of the major agencies is the Indian Council for Cultural Relations, which is concerned with both foreign cultural activities in India and the Indian arts abroad. It does not follow, of course, that those countries which are net importers do not possess rich cultures. Even Japan has only in recent years gone through the transformation of becoming an exporter in cultural traffic to a degree that matches its century of imports since the Meiji restoration.

Another group of countries that tends to consign responsibility to the ministry of culture rather than to the foreign ministry (though not invariably) is in Eastern Europe. In Poland both ministries share the responsibility. In communist countries there is a high level of state subsidy for culture and also a policy of encouraging exhibitions and performances of artists abroad, often within the provisions of bilateral exchange programmes negotiated every two years with foreign governments; the central position of ministries of culture enables them to ensure that their own country's heritage and achievements are understood in other countries and that appropriate imports from abroad are encouraged.

One salient fact that emerges from these comparisons is that there is little in the way of an internationally accepted norm. This makes it

extremely difficult to relate different countries' categories of activity
and budgets to one another. (A limited attempt at this is made in
Appendix D.) Cultural relations funds may be channelled through
the foreign ministry, the ministry of culture, the ministry of
education, the ministry of development or a variety of other
ministries (e.g. the Federal Ministry of Information, Social
Development, Youth, Sports and Culture in Nigeria; the Ministry of
Information in Qatar; the Ministry of Guidance and National
Information in Sudan). And then there is the involvement of local
government, educational and research institutions, academies,
foundations and voluntary organizations. No one would want to see
cultural variety diminished. But it could be rendered more amenable
to international exchanges if there were a common denominator for
their encouragement and finance. The most obvious candidate is the
ministry of culture. This already has close contacts with the domestic
constituency. If it were more generally the channel for official funds
for external cultural policy the structural problem would be solved.
Just as nations interrelate politically through their foreign ministries
so they could interrelate culturally through corresponding ministries.

There are three models for the actual conduct of cultural relations:

Government control   The government, through a ministry or an
official agency, such as USIA, exercises direct control. Examples are
France, Italy, the United States; the communist countries; the
developing world in greater or lesser degree; smaller countries for
which it would be uneconomic to practise any other system.

Non-governmental, autonomous agencies   The government provides money through a ministry, normally the foreign ministry, but
delegates policy control and execution to an independent agency
such as the British Council or the Japan Foundation. The concept is
familiar in Britain: it embodies 'the arm's length principle' whereby
the state renounces control, as also with the BBC and the Arts
Council. Australia, New Zealand and Canada observe this model.

Mixed system   The government retains overall control but funds
and contracts non-official agencies to operate independently within
their competences. The Federal Republic of Germany is the prime
example. The foreign ministry maintains a large and important
Cultural Relations Department (*Kulturabteilung*), which is
responsible for formal arrangements such as cultural conventions
and relations with international organizations, services cultural
attaché posts in major embassies (which are normally filled by

members of the diplomatic service), subsidizes schools abroad, and handles major artistic events. The agencies are numerous. Those with representations abroad are the Goethe Institute and, on a smaller scale, the DAAD (German Academic Exchange Service).

In theory, one could also postulate a fourth, purely *voluntary system*, whereby institutions conduct their own cultural relations with opposite numbers in other countries without any government control or finance, though possibly with the encouragement of tax remission or some other indirect subsidy. This does not exist as an organized system; it is the way cultural exchanges used to operate (e.g. through academies and archaeological schools) before governments became involved. There are some countries in which private finance and initiative play a major part (for instance, the United States). The non-governmental element remains strong in academies, even when much of their international exchange work is paid for by government. Also some schools (for instance, British-type schools abroad) are maintained, without any official subsidy, by parental fees and local patronage.

In work abroad the degree and style of government control affect the status of the cultural representatives. In accordance with the first category above, the French and Italian representatives are attached to embassies and senior members have diplomatic status as cultural counsellors or cultural attachés. The French are career diplomats who are transferred as in any other branch of their service; the Italians are recruited from outside, especially from universities. The cultural sections of their embassies are responsible for the administration of institutes and schools and for co-ordination with, respectively, the Alliance Française and the Dante Alighieri Society. USIA staff also have diplomatic status; so do those of East European embassies, who are career officials and usually career diplomats serving in embassies as cultural attachés. Countries with a rich cultural heritage often have considerable obligations under cultural agreements. Austria, for instance, appoints the heads of its institutes from within the public service: this system makes available the requisite specialization for each post while at the same time ensuring the right degree of administrative experience. Until 1974 the ministry of education was charged with the administration of Austria's nine cultural institutes and with appointing cultural attachés to posts where no institute exists; then responsibility was shifted by legislation to the foreign ministry. The directors of institutes both run their programmes of cultural events (which do not usually include language-teaching: they leave that to the Goethe Institute) and occupy the position of cultural counsellor at the embassy. This arrangement is found to give them both the recognizable status and the disposition of resources that they need. The Netherlands uses serving diplomats, while Sweden brings in specialists in some branch of cultural administration (as may be appropriate for the conditions of each post) on contract for a few years.

Developing countries follow the system of government control. Their culture (or cultures) occupies a sensitive position in their national identity. Few have highly developed cultural representations, although many embassies administer their students on foreign study. India, which has increased its cultural exports in recent years (notably through the Festivals of India), seconds officials from its ministries of culture and education on assignments to its embassies.

The question whether having cultural representatives attached to an embassy has an off-putting effect on local contacts is one that has been much debated. It is true that to some intellectuals and artists officialdom may appear suspect; also that, in the eyes of the more radical, the diplomatic corps represents the essence of the establishment (of whatever persuasion) and in some countries may have sinister implications for individual security. But, in closed societies, governments do not in any case permit cultural relations to be conducted except by accredited diplomats and, in the case of most communist states, within the provisions of exchange programmes.

The experience of cultural attachés of various countries suggests that diplomatic status is no disadvantage to their work. On the contrary, they believe it announces to all and sundry what they are about and obviates the need often encountered by representatives of non-governmental organizations to explain their credentials. In operating official exchange programmes the merits and demerits of diplomatic status probably cancel one another out. But in work beyond those programmes there are advantages in not appearing too official. This applies particularly to the various forms of intellectual encounter that involve dissidents or innovators, who are inclined to shrink from officialdom.

Quite apart from possible local sensitivity to the 'taint of diplomacy', there are professional objections that have been raised over the competence of cultural attachés. The most articulate of these have come from Germany, whose mixed system affords comparison between cultural attachés at embassies and staff of the autonomous Goethe Institute. One of Germany's most revered ambassadors, Hans von Herwarth, who subsequently became President of the Goethe Institute, chaired a commission that studied possible reforms in the diplomatic service of the Federal Republic. The commission concluded that the appointment of outside specialists as cultural attachés was unrealistic, because the range of responsibilities was so wide, and that only an all-rounder with experience in political work and administration could manage. But it emphasized how important it was for the foreign ministry to ascertain that the right people were sent to these posts: 'It should be ensured by a long-term personnel policy that cultural attaché posts can be filled with qualified persons' (Herwarth, 1971, p. 52). The commission saw no objection, however, to the occasional appointment of well-qualified outsiders, normally for a limited period. A more severe view, directed at the central organization, comes from another German critic, Helmut Becker: he sees importance in the integration of cultural policy as an informing influence in overall foreign policy and argues against the suggestion of having a special authority in charge of cultural relations. But Becker (1966, p. 100) also presses for careful selection: 'Service in the Cultural Department of the Foreign Ministry should not be regarded, as it still sometimes is, as a kind of penal posting for diplomats who look upon culture as something subsidiary'. A similar point is made by Ulf Andenaes (1984, p. 13) in his report on the presentation of Norway overseas. He sees the arrangement whereby career diplomats are posted to the foreign ministry to look after cultural affairs as possibly leading to a lack of professionalism and continuity. There has indeed been a campaign in Norway to transfer responsibility for cultural relations from the foreign ministry to the ministry of culture, with a view to both raising Norway's profile abroad (which it believes to be obscured by Swedish dominance in the Nordic Council) and enriching the domestic cultural scene by more foreign contact. This reinforces the idea adumbrated above that ministries of culture would in theory be the most suitable counterparts for cultural exchanges if any serious attempt at standardization were ever contemplated.

The British Council is often cited as the prime example of an independent body that is largely funded but not controlled by government. The Council's policy is determined by its own Board; the Foreign and Commonwealth Office and the Overseas Development Administration, as the funding departments, are represented on this but do not dictate policy. The Council is, under its Royal Charter, quite outside the Civil Service. And yet about one half of the Council's eighty-one posts overseas are diplomatic, in the sense that at least the senior representative enjoys diplomatic status as cultural attaché. Even when Council staff are operating abroad under these official colours they retain their independence as representatives of an autonomous organization. The ground rules are the same whether staff have diplomatic status or not. In each country where the Council works, the ambassador is asked to agree the Council's statement of its policy, in recognition of his responsibility for the conduct of British policy as a whole. But the individual representative answers to the

Figure 8.1   Organization of an Independent Agency

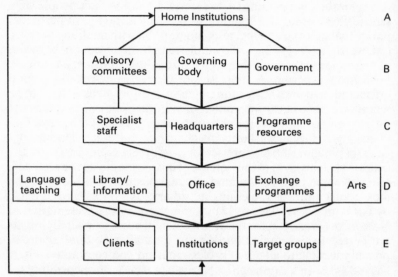

The diagram shows the strong line linking the institutions in the two countries and running through the agency's organization. The other lines show the application of institutional and operational resources. The direct connection between A and E indicates the desirability of forming and fostering relationships.

A   Home institutions: universities, research stations, arts bodies, professional elites, etc.

B   Control and advice: governing body which determines policy; responsible ministry and other parts of government; advisory committees.

C   Management: headquarters staff; resources as inputs into programmes and activities; specialist staff for advisory and support visits.

D   Representation: office and breakdown of principal functions (here in a major country with more than basic activities).

E   Contacts: institutions (including government and administration); target groups; clients for particular activities such as language-teaching and library/information work.

Note   The embassy has been omitted from this diagram.

British Council in London for the use of his resources and the execution of his business. This sounds more schizophrenic than it is in practice. Britain operates no separate network of cultural attachés. With the single exception of Moscow, all cultural attaché posts are occupied by staff of the British Council; whether they are in a diplomatic post or not, Council staff exercise responsibility for all aspects of cultural representation, from high-cost arts tours and exhibitions to English language teaching, educational enquiries and examinations. No other cultural agency has such broad responsibilities. The Council's non-official status enables it to act not only on behalf of government departments (for instance, it is the British government's principal agent in the execution of cultural conventions and exchange agreements), but also for educational institutions and private organizations. In financial terms, the bulk of the British Council's work is on behalf of the Overseas Development Administration, in administering technical co-operation under the British Aid Programme, especially in relation to education and training. The breadth of these responsibilities is possible partly by reason of scale: the Council had a total expenditure in 1983/84 of £200 million and its representation in eighty-one countries embraces most major countries of the world.

Other countries observing the 'arm's length principle' in some aspects of their cultural work (e.g. Canada, Australia and New Zealand) operate their cultural relations work through their embassies abroad, with cultural attaché posts, and might find it uneconomic to set up a separate service on the British Council model. Attaching a post or two to an embassy is a great deal cheaper than renting premises and meeting all the overheads of separate operation.

Figure 8.1 shows the idealized structure of an independent cultural agency and its relationship to institutions at home and abroad.

Germany's mixed system combines cultural attaché posts in embassies (which are answerable to the Cultural Department of the foreign ministry and to the ambassador) and the Goethe Institute (which works to its headquarters in Munich). The Goethe Institute abroad informs but need not consult the cultural attaché about its activities. In theory, the ambassador can apply a veto to an activity which he considers contrary to his country's interest, but this has rarely happened and, when it has been attempted, has sometimes redounded to the embarrassment of the ambassador concerned. Ambassadors, however, have recently been enjoined to ensure that co-operation between the embassy and the Goethe Institute is as close as it should be. This reminder followed the celebrated incident when Federal Chancellor, Helmut Kohl, opened the new premises of the Goethe Institute in Kyoto on 3 November 1983, while he was on an official visit to Japan. Herr Kohl made a speech that contained several significant points in the matter of cultural relations. One key passage ran (German Government, 1983, p. 1118):

This building will show our German Federal Republic to every Japanese for what it is – a liberal democracy whose existence and culture are based on statement and counter-statement and on free intellectual exchange at home and abroad. You will hear not only about the German past ... you will also hear about our present.

And you will certainly not hear only what the government thinks and wishes . . . you will also hear what the Opposition has to say on the policy of our country, for that corresponds to our conception of the political culture of our country.

At the end of his visit it was brought to Herr Kohl's attention that among the video collection in the institute were recordings representing political views contrary to his government's, especially some of an environmental nature. He conveyed his annoyance to the accompanying journalists and in no time the affair had assumed the proportions of a major scandal. In the event, most of the German media supported the Goethe Institute, and its President, Herr von Bismarck, came out strongly in defence of its policies. The *Bonner Generalanzeiger* of 30 November 1983 reported him as saying 'there are attempts from "certain quarters" to change the function of the Institute and to press it into the role of an organization pursuing the policies of the Bonn government'.

But this incident was not the only one of its kind to call into question the Goethe Institute's freedom of action. There was the notorious exhibition of posters by Klaus Staeck which were shown as part of the German Month in London in 1974. They aroused the anger of some CSU politicians because Franz-Joseph Strauss was represented as a butcher. Today, there is a vocal lobby in Germany which would like to see the Goethe Institute more in tune with the present CDU/FDP coalition and less 'Leftist'.

The airing of these differences is instructive for the student of external cultural policy. The agreement of 1976 between the Goethe Institute and the foreign ministry gives the Institute a great deal of independence. Certainly, the Goethe Institutes in Portugal at the time of Salazar, and in Greece under the colonels, allowed themselves a degree of independence in co-operating with dissidents which any member of an embassy would emulate at his peril. In matters such as this the Goethe Institute's relationship with its foreign ministry may give it more practical freedom of manoeuvre than is enjoyed by the independents themselves. This is illustrated by the operations of the Goethe Institute in Lisbon, 1969–76. *Die Zeit* of 20 August 1976 devoted a two-page article to the achievements of the director, Curt Meyer-Clason, on his retirement. He had brought Portuguese writers and intellectuals together and put them in contact with their German counterparts. He concentrated on those opposed to the Salazar regime, who would otherwise have lacked these contacts. He said that he had not endeared himself to diplomats; one can guess that his Munich headquarters had some anxiety about his activities. Meyer-Clason was appointed from outside. He had been a translator from Portuguese and Spanish, and considered his intimate knowledge of the language and culture of Portugal indispensable for his mission and the way he fulfilled it. He considered the cultural institutes of other countries stuffy and backward-looking and had a distaste for bureaucracy. He retired to the sound of panegyric and lament.

The German mixed system produces some explicit friction because of the diverse, and to some extent conflicting, elements within it. The several component parts (of which only the Goethe Institute and DAAD have been mentioned on the non-governmental side) have their interlocking functions. The German press is well-informed and carries many on the whole favourable articles about external cultural policy. For some years it was debated whether the Federal Republic should establish a 'German Council', on the model of the British Council, so as to unify the various agencies under one independent management. But the question was dropped. The greatest stumbling-block was the dispensation in the 1949 Constitution, which deliberately avoided centralization of culture and education by consigning the responsibility for them to the regional governments of the *Länder*.

9

Aims and Means

Economic straits since the oil crisis of 1973 have underlined the modern recognition that institutions, especially in the public sector, tend to ramify beyond their justified purpose and to degenerate into expensive bureaucracies serving their own interests. One way to avoid this slippery slope is to have a clearly expressed aim. This can serve as a yardstick by which to gauge the appropriateness of activities and to assess achievement. Cultural agencies need an aim no less than other institutions. Indeed, their need may be particularly great, because they have to steer clear of duplication with other organizations and to watch out for adverse criticism and the charge of superfluity.

External cultural policy is both a product and a component part of foreign policy. Foreign policy is made out of the observance of national interest; as this interest changes (always, of course, against a background of constant elements), so the policy changes. Now, it would be possible to express the business of foreign ministries as an aim, but to many of them the formulation would seem self-evident or supererogatory. The more cultural relations work is tied to foreign policy, the more it confines itself strictly to cultural diplomacy, the harder it is to achieve the statement of an aim possessing intrinsic long-term validity. In the mode of government control that we considered in Chapter 8, it might be stated that a country's external cultural policy has as its aim the support and enrichment of its foreign policy. That would be accurate perhaps, but not really helpful. A contingent definition such as this would make cultural diplomacy no more than a handmaiden to the day-to-day requirements of politics and reaction to the politics of other states. We have seen that cultural relations are too important to be relegated to such a subordinate role. Helmut Becker (1966, p. 90) goes so far as to say that the primacy of foreign policy itself is outdated in international affairs: 'The era of the primacy of foreign policy must be succeeded by a period of primacy for cultural policy (*Kulturpolitik*)'.

It is easier for autonomous agencies to state their aims; because they are not subject to political criteria – are beyond diplomacy, in fact – they can conceive their work in a specific long-term view. The British Council, for instance, stated its aim in 1982 as, 'to promote an enduring understanding and appreciation of Britain in other countries through cultural, educational and technical cooperation'. This is broadly conceived in its latter part in accordance with the extensive range of British Council activities, and it has stood the test of use and scrutiny. In the first part, however, it is one-way and makes no explicit allowance for the mediating role of helping to make other countries understood and appreciated in Britain, though this in practice happens as a side-effect of the Council's being represented in most major countries of the world and operating programmes that are intrinsically two-way, such as the exchange of persons. But the question remains how far the concept of mutuality should be built into an agency's aim.

The Japan Foundation's aim was formulated at the Foundation's inception in Article 1 of the Japan Foundation Law:

> In supporting cultural exchange, the Foundation's ultimate objectives are to contribute to the advancement of world culture and human welfare, to deepen understanding of Japan abroad and promote mutual understanding among nations, and to encourage friendship and goodwill between the peoples of the world.

This is idealistically worded. If these are the 'ultimate' objectives, what are the immediate ones to which members of staff should address themselves? However, the importance of mutuality is certainly more pronounced. The progression from deepening understanding of Japan, through promoting mutual understanding among nations, to encouraging friendship and goodwill between peoples, is logical and philanthropic. Indeed, the notion of 'goodwill between the peoples of the world' carries mutuality to greater lengths than would be countenanced in the external cultural policy of most countries. In some countries it would be fatal for a body dependent on the public exchequer to present itself in the guise of a 'goodwill organization'. It is encouraging that the Japan Foundation is able to assert the encouragement of goodwill as part of its aim. In an annual report seven categories of activities are listed. The first six are Nipponcentric and consistent with the practices of most other countries. The seventh, however, has a broader remit and clearly goes beyond the considerations of national interest; it carries mutuality beyond the bilateral or even the multilateral context to the world at large. The seventh category reads as follows:

> . . . other activities that bear upon the ultimate objectives of the Foundation. For example, where the Minister of Foreign Affairs

deems necessary, the Foundation may assist those educational and cultural programs of other organizations that are designed to promote mutual understanding and international goodwill and may lease and/or donate works of art, handicraft, animals and plants to such programs. (Japan Foundation, 1983, p. 9)

There are indeed examples of Japanese generosity in making grants to facilitate cultural activities between other countries. For instance, there is the grant of 5 billion yen (25 million US dollars) in 1978 to the ASEAN Cultural Fund.

It is difficult to frame a cultural organization's aims briefly in clear, unambiguous language. But this is what is required if its staff and collaborating institutions are to be able to judge the relevance to the organization of its existing activities and new enterprises. Also, of course, and this is a matter of vital expediency, the aims must be presented in such a way that politicians and others whose job it is to allocate public funds are firmly persuaded of the benefit of the organization's operations to their country's interests. These two criteria are not invariably easy to keep consistent with one another: some semantic balancing is necessary.

One basic consideration in the formulation of aims is whether the preference is for one-way or two-way policies, whether one is simply projecting the values and achievements of one's own country or also facilitating the import of cultural activities from other countries. It may be argued, of course, that import is the business of the other countries: that if each cultural agency were to address itself to national self-projection a lively and rational import–export business would result. But there are reasons why this could not work. For one thing, some countries – notably in the developing world – are not in a position to project their cultures; for another, the result would be a competition for cultural markets, a contest between national images, a recrudescence of nineteenth-century cultural nationalism, which would not conduce to understanding and co-operation. The style and methodology of cultural relations have to be two-way because they are to the benefit of the two peoples in any bilateral relationship. To some degree, therefore, the concept of mutuality needs to find expression in the aim, either overtly in the wording or by implication in the definition of the means (for example, in the British Council's aim, through the use of the word 'co-operation'; see p. 79). It will be helpful to represent the different styles of cultural relations diagrammatically in what may best be called a Mutuality Table. Before examining this, it will be timely to rehearse some of the key terms that have occurred so far.

Definition of Terms

Cultural agreements	Inter-governmental treaties outlining permitted cultural and educational activities and exchanges, which each country will facilitate. Also cultural conventions.
Cultural diplomacy	The involvement of culture in international agreements; the application of culture to the direct support of a country's political and economic diplomacy.
Cultural propaganda	The use of a nation's cultural attributes for the purpose of propaganda.
Cultural relations	The fostering of co-operative relationships between cultural and educational institutions and individuals so that nations can interrelate intellectually, artistically and socially.
Exchange programmes	Inter-governmental agreements, periodically renegotiated, defining those activities which are authorized, in terms of strict reciprocity with communist countries. Also, more generally, schedules of exchanges agreed between institutions.
Information	Telling others about one's own country's achievements. A more neutral term than propaganda.
Mutuality	The two-way concept in cultural relations that both sides benefit in a bilateral association and all sides in a multilateral one.
Projection	The deliberate display of a country's achievements and values in order to attract respect and prestige. Also self-projection, or national self-projection.
Propaganda	The diffusion of information and ideas, which may be true or false, in order to gain an advantage in a contest.
Reciprocity	Exchange based on comparability of activity. Reciprocity means, for instance, a choir for a choir; so many man-hours of training in each direction. Reciprocity is built into exchange programmes with communist countries.

Sending country   The side which provides the initiative and resources for an activity in the *host* country.

Mutuality Table

Table 9.1 shows on the horizontal axis how External Cultural Policy (ECP) projects its own culture, and on the vertical axis how ECP reacts to the culture of other countries. Horizontally, from left to right there is a progression through a scale of projection from the modest desire to achieve recognition to the more assertive desire to indoctrinate. Vertically, the progression is from top to bottom down a scale showing the reaction to the cultural scene in the host country, from indifference to a self-seeking interest. The fields in the table indicate the resultant styles of operation.

The definitions above can be applied to these fields. For instance, cultural propaganda (which is an elastic concept) might fit into A3, B3 or C3, but belongs characteristically in A3. Cultural diplomacy might be practised passively (under column 1) or actively (under column 3); A1 or B3 would be typical. Cultural relations belong ideally in B2 (which is the bull's-eye) but not exclusively there; some of their activities and approaches may fit better into A2 or even C2. There is no reason why all the activities of any one cultural agency should be placeable in the same field. Whatever the agency's aim, the execution will depend on conditions and receptivity in a variety of very different countries. Even if the aim of an organization were totally in line with B2, it might well happen that, in a developing country, the demands made by the authorities put it in position B3, or that, in a closed-society country, problems of access to collaborators forced it into position B1, or even C1 (but in this case without the finance!). However carefully aims are formulated and observed, they cannot be an exercise in isolation. As any cultural agency learns, sensitive response to the requirements of each individual country is essential. Flexibility is one of the cardinal virtues in cultural relations.

ECP and ICP

The logical connection between External Cultural Policy (ECP) and Internal Cultural Policy (ICP) is obvious enough but commonly obscured by that division of powers which tends to bestow the competence for ECP on foreign ministries and for ICP on ministries

Table 9.1 Mutuality Table

External Cultural Policy	in projecting its own culture →		
	1	2	3
in reaction to the local culture →	seeks recognition of its achievements	aims at two-way operation	wishes to influence/indoctrinate
A is indifferent	A1 national self-projection	A2 conventional programmes, without innovation	A3 propaganda in a vacuum
B has understanding and insight	B1 information, with entry points well identified	B2 mutuality, based on co-operation and exchange	B3 exercise of (benevolent) influence
C has informed but self-seeking interest	C1 exploitation of local response (and finance)	C2 abuse of local goodwill or strict reciprocity in closed society	C3 (covert) imposition of values/ideology

with a purely domestic remit. And yet, of course, no ECP is conceivable without recourse to the products of ICP, without, that is, the artefacts, performers and institutions that make up a country's cultural profile, and, in the modern age, depend on public funds for their maintenance as well as for their diffusion. In operating abroad, it is one of the most important duties of cultural representatives to mediate between their own culture and that of the host country. They are called upon to supply a variety of information and advice, which facilitates access to their country's institutions. The quality of their response will depend on their understanding of the local scene as well as on their familiarity with the facilities at home. Sometimes they will wish to support the resulting activity. But often the product of their mediation will find its own costs and administration. Representatives are often catalysts in activities that could not have happened without them.

At home, on the domestic scene, the link between ECP and ICP is usually less effective. This is where the division of powers works to the detriment of collaboration. There is usually little constructive dialogue between the authorities responsible for ECP and those responsible for ICP. Their funding is different and conceptually their purposes are not seen to correlate.

In general, government policy-making admits with difficulty and reluctance of inter-departmental convergence. The Think Tank (Central Policy Review Staff), which was meant to supply this deficiency in Britain, in an advisory capacity, and to introduce the capability of more inter-sectoral planning in Whitehall, expired in 1984 after fourteen years' existence. It is probably mourned by those outside government more than by those inside, whose minds are focused on operating departmental policies and budgets. In theory, the cabinet is the forum for inter-departmental debate (and the Think Tank was located in the Cabinet Office), but the pressure of governmental business allows too little time for this. Moreover, departmental policies tend to be conditioned by their traditions and mentalities, and to be filtered through the strainer of precedent and accepted wisdom. There is little receptivity for the distraction suggested by *New Society* in an obituary article on the Think Tank, 'A Think Tank worth its salt should always be like the Roman functionary who, on ceremonial occasions, walked symbolically tossing dirt over his shoulder and intoning "*sic transit gloria mundi*" ' (Hennessy, 1985, p. 12).

In France the problem of inter-departmental co-operation in cultural relations has been addressed in Jacques Rigaud's report (1980, pp. 16–17). This recommended the creation of an inter-ministerial committee for external cultural relations, under the chairmanship of the foreign ministry, which should meet twice a year. The idea was endorsed in the ministry's publication of 1984 on ECP, *Le projet culturel extérieur de la France*, which bestows on the committee the acronym CIRCE and explains that it was set up in 1980, met about ten times without achieving the hoped-for results and became dormant in 1981: 'A heavy apparatus, combining the representatives of some ten ministries, devoid of political directives, it served more to neutralize potential collisions between its members than to propose programmes of action' (Ministère des relations extérieures, 1984, pp. 140–1). CIRCE fell into desuetude after the coming to power of the socialist government, but there is now talk of resuscitation since several of the participating ministries see value in it. CIRCE, to give its less bewitching full title, stands for *Comité interministériel des relations culturelles extérieures*.

In Canada, the Report of the Federal Cultural Policy Review Committee recommended in 1982 that a new agency should be created, called perhaps the Canadian Cultural Relations Agency, 'under the ministerial direction of the Secretary of State for External Affairs' which must 'be able to respond to the needs of Canadian artists and scholars to present their work before international audiences ... This new agency should have a clearly defined mandate, but a mandate alone is not enough. We consider it essential to retain the confidence of the cultural community in Canada. We therefore propose an advisory board, representative of those cultural and academic interests to be served by this agency, be appointed to guide it' (Applebaum and Hébert, 1982, p. 337).

A structure of advisory committees is an effective way of achieving a degree of integration between external and internal cultural policies. Such committees have the function of helping to integrate demand and supply in the provision of cultural exports. In the arts, for instance, they have the merit of bringing together a selection of experts representing both the arts themselves and arts administration; the members relate to the situation in other countries both through their own professional contacts and on the strength of information supplied by the headquarters of the cultural agency itself, which is, of course, kept up to date by its representatives in the field. The British Council, for instance, runs fourteen committees on subjects covering most of its work, four of which are for the arts (Drama and Dance Advisory Committee; Films, Television and Video Advisory Committee; Fine Arts Advisory Committee; Music Advisory Committee).

Nevertheless, Britain illustrates the typical outward and inward dichotomy in the respective competences of the British Council and the Arts Council. The British Council is responsible for cultural exports, and the Arts Council for supporting the arts in Britain. Each organization has its own advisory committees and the liaison between them is ensured by cross-representation by officials. But the said dichotomy makes it difficult to correlate internal commitment and international demand. There is no connection between the allocation of grants to theatres, orchestras and ballet companies, for instance, and their being available to meet requests to tour abroad. The Arts Council grants are solely in respect of performances in Britain. This typifies the competence conundrum. Culture can hardly be packaged according to national frontiers. As will become evident in Chapter 17, it is particularly true of English drama today that 'All the world's a stage . . .'

The Canadian report referred to a general advisory committee or board. This is an important concept, calling for some comment. Cultural agencies with a degree of independence have a body of this kind to direct their policy and mediate with government and the home constituency. It is important for a board to have good relations with both, indeed to represent the interests of both. One of the board's functions is to protect the agency's interests, to be its foremost lobby; and this demands good connections. The United States maintains an Advisory Commission on Public Diplomacy, 'a bipartisan group of citizens, drawn from a broad cross section of professional backgrounds', which was established in 1978 to oversee the work of the USIA. As well as its more conventional responsibilities as a governing body, the Advisory Commission members (who are appointed by the President and confirmed by the Senate) confer with senior officials of government and with congressional committees, visit overseas posts, report to Congress, give public addresses and media interviews at home and abroad (US Advisory Commission on Public Diplomacy, 1983, pp. 10–11). The concept of 'public diplomacy' in American usage covers more than 'cultural diplomacy': it also has a major information ingredient, as the USIA itself also has.

There are less obvious ways in which ECP and ICP should interrelate. Tourism is another connecting point. Each country that cultivates tourism uses its representation abroad, including its cultural representation, for promotional purposes. One of the attractions is the cultural scene, not just the heritage but the living arts. For instance, 46 per cent of foreign tourists questioned in London said they intended to visit a theatre. Albert Salon (1983, p. 58) remarks that France's touristic riches constitute an *exportation sur place*. But except for reasons of promotion there is little co-ordination between the cultural attractions at home and cultural relations work abroad, and rarely at the level of government policy. And yet, according to the Economic and Social Committee of the European Communities, tourism provides over 4 million jobs and will be among the world's largest industries by the year 2000. More co-ordination might encourage the realization that national frontiers are not cultural frontiers – and take some of the force out of the campaign for the return of cultural property to its country of origin.

The hiatus between external and internal cultural policies is reduced, if not eliminated, in countries where both are in the hands of the same ministry, usually the ministry of culture. Not a few countries have this arrangement. Among the others, there are some that would have political difficulties over the creation of a national ministry of culture (in the Federal Republic of Germany constitutional changes would be necessary) and some that would encounter a great deal of public opposition to what might seem like interference by government in cultural activity. Several countries, such as France, which have a ministry of culture but consign their external cultural policy to the foreign ministry, would need to reconsider the question of ministerial competence.

One country where opposition to the introduction of a ministry of culture would be particularly strong is Britain. It would be perfectly possible, in fact, to preserve Britain's characteristic 'arm's length principle', whereby the state makes grants of money without seeking control, but the principle might appear under potential threat. The only significant lobby in favour of a ministry of culture in Britain is the Liberal Party. The Liberal Manifesto for the Arts (Liberal Party, 1984, p. 7) argues for a ministry of culture with cabinet status, as a means of improving the status and financing of the arts and over-coming the fragmentation of responsibilities among different ministries at present (the Board of Trade for films, the Home Office for broadcasting, the Department of the Environment for historic buildings and some national collections, and the office for the Arts and Libraries for grants). The Manifesto makes no mention of the international dimension.

Another way of achieving co-ordination would be to rely on inter-departmental co-ordinating committees, but like CIRCE these might turn out to be 'heavy apparatus'.

10

The Cultural Dimension in Development

The preferred mode of cultural relations is one that induces mutuality through exchange and co-operation. Whatever the relative political significance of any two countries, they will best succeed in their cultural relations if they operate according to this mode, if neither country assumes a position of superiority towards the other, and if they consider long-term understanding between them to be more important than short-term advantage. Every national culture is of value; each makes its contribution to world culture, to the common heritage of mankind. Part of the rationale of cultural relations is to render people conscious of this shared resource and to make it more accessible. The question we must next ask is how this postulate applies to the aid relationship. Is this not by its very nature one-way rather than two-way? Can one genuinely talk of mutuality in the process whereby the North transfers its values together with its capital and technology to the South?

The issue is different from that of 'global responsibility for economic and social development', which is central to the Brandt Report (1980, p. 8). The Brandt responsibility could be honoured simply in the spirit of obligation and self-interest, without thought for the cultural effects in the receiving countries. Indeed, the Brandt Report does not go into the question of receptivity. Aid lobbies in the North tend to assume that more development aid is good and necessary, regardless of the social effects on the recipients. This approach presupposes that the norms of the Western world are implicit in the transfer process. However philanthropic, it rests upon assumptions that have become unaccept-able to the Third World. To the recipient, it can indeed appear that the whole aid enterprise is a conspiracy to hold the developing world in cultural as well as economic bondage. No wonder, then, that the term 'cultural imperialism' gains currency. It calls for a cultural response.

One reaction in the Third World is the assertion of cultural identity. The force of this concept, which inevitably has strong emotive elements, is revealed in the Final Report of the UNESCO Conference on Cultural Policies, which was held in Mexico City in July–August 1982 and attended by 126 member states and 960 participants. The conference was arranged 'to review the experience acquired with respect to cultural policies and practices since the Intergovernmental Conference on Institutional, Administrative and Financial Aspects of Cultural Policies (convened by UNESCO in Venice in 1970), to give rise to searching consideration of the fundamental problems of culture in the contemporary world, and to formulate new guidelines for accentuating the cultural dimension in general development and facilitating international cultural cooperation' (UNESCO, 1982, p. 5).

Under the heading 'Culture and cultural identity', these four excerpts from the summing-up show the drift of the deliberations:

> The concepts of culture, the right to culture, cultural democracy and cultural development as an essential dimension of development, the relationship between culture and the other areas of life of society: culture and education, culture and cultural communications and industries, culture and science and technology, international cultural cooperation, and culture and peace, were considered at the conference...
>
> The conference was unanimous in recognizing and reaffirming with conviction and force the equal dignity of all cultures, rejecting any hierarchy in that area, since nothing could justify discrimination as between 'superior cultures and inferior cultures...'
>
> Cultural identity was the defence of traditions, of history and of the moral, spiritual and ethical values handed down by past generations...
>
> It was strongly emphasised that the legitimate insistence on identity in no way signified a turning inward, but rather placed relations within the context of mutual enrichment through dialogue among cultures in a framework of cooperation among free and equal partners. (UNESCO, 1982, pp. 8–9)

And in his closing address, Mr M'Bow, the Director-General of UNESCO, said: 'Among the many topics discussed, that which, to my mind, ultimately carried by far the greatest weight was the notion of cultural identity' (UNESCO, 1982, p. 189).

The fact is that in the acquisition of national independence the most difficult attainment is that of cultural identity. For this requires the consolidation of tradition and the establishment of a basis of popular support. It can take a long time. Furthermore, cultural identity is far from being conterminous with statehood. In many developing countries the cultural roots are more realistically defined according to tribal or racial boundaries rather than according to frontiers bequeathed by the colonial past. Political independence comes with the raising of a flag, economic independence can follow with prudent husbandry and development aid, but cultural independence often trails far behind. The demand for cultural identity is a recognition of this. The difficulty is exacerbated by the preference of dominant classes in newly independent countries for cultural values from outside, as a means of reinforcing their political or economic power, or simply as a way of rendering life more congenial for them and more consonant with their personal background. Their background may, however, be that of a deracinated, urbanized minority, and bear little relation to the ultimate interests of the population at large. This minority may in some countries favour Western values and ways, and it may in others take the communist model as a rationale for the seizure and maintenance of power. Either form of minority is likely to be cultivated and supported with the injection of aid by states who see their interests as being thus best served. Cultural identity, therefore, if it means an affirmation of a sound basis of nationhood, should operate as a defence against distortion by minorities. The thesis begs many questions, but is manifestly important for the evolution of the Third World. It is important also for foreign cultural agencies.

The cultural dimension for aid-giving countries consists in mediating between their own culture and values and those of developing countries. Inevitably, there will be a flow of influence from a dominant to a receptive society; this has happened in all periods of human history. The task of cultural agencies is to make this process beneficent and to modulate its effects. We might call this exercise of influence – in the anthropologist's term, acculturation. There are enough examples of unguided acculturation in history (the Australian and the North American aboriginals to mention only two) to illustrate the dangers of alienation that can result.

It is a prerequisite of cultural relations work that it should be founded on an understanding of the social configuration of the host country. It is only too easy, in terms of the Mutuality Table (see Table 9.1, p. 83), to show up badly on the vertical axis, which measures sensitivity to the local culture; easy, because operating in an expatriate environment can encourage superior, dismissive attitudes, and because ready-made contacts with the local people are likely to be among minority groups that tacitly echo these attitudes. This applies especially to developing countries.

The need for staff training will be considered in the next chapter. It is no less essential for work in developing than in developed countries. Primed with an advance knowledge of the country and some degree of linguistic skill, the cultural representative should be able to acquire on the spot that degree of understanding which is a precondition of mediating between cultures. Anyone with experience of the Third World would agree that Frau Hamm-Brücher, who was State Minister in the German foreign ministry responsible for cultural policy 1976–82, does not stand alone when she says:

> Above all, we must change our own attitude to developing countries in cultural co-operation. I have constantly found myself having difficulty in penetrating the culture and thought categories of so-called developing countries and also found myself unconsciously transferring my own thought and behaviour patterns on to other cultural conceptions. That is probably the way with most of us. (Hamm-Brücher, 1980, p. 207)

Serving in a developing country is a challenge not only in the humanitarian sense but also in the intellectual sense. The cultural representative can by the exercise of intellectual sympathy and the facilities at his disposal help make the developing country's acculturation a more positive experience.

One fruitful field of activity for this purpose is the exchange of persons. This tends to be directed mainly at the provision of training in the institutions of the donor country. Careful preparation and induction before departure and on arrival in the country of study, together with the necessary care during residence and follow-up on return, are essential. They may be seen as commonsense measures to achieve maximum returns on an investment, and that is entirely reasonable. It is important that they should be carried out in full understanding of the socio-cultural problems experienced by the student. The longest favourable memories students take back home are often of those people (for instance, landladies) who were sympathetic to them as individuals. Daniel (1975, p. 12) quotes the contrary impressions of a foreign student:

> Most of those exaggeratedly friendly people, whether they are aware of it or not, believe that the African is a destitute, who will rejoice to see a white man friendly to him, however impolite the method of contact. Their approaches are therefore often very impudent despite their good intentions.

In terms of the transfer of experience the exchange of persons is the programme with the deepest and most abiding effects because it is one that most directly contributes to human development. At its best, it is not a one-off exercise in manpower training but a way of establishing relationships with individuals selected because they are, or are likely to become, members of influential elites. Because of the value of these personal relationships for the two countries, it is a sensible arrangement if the exchange of persons, including those financed under the aid programme, is administered by cultural agencies that have the 'people' rather than the bureaucratic approach. This enables cultural agencies to use their other facilities (such as libraries, language classes, film shows, etc.) as a means of sustaining the relationship. Enduring relationships with the institutions where people have trained are another benefit. These will not of course be universal: they will not be so relevant to vehicle inspectors and police dog handlers as to scientists and technologists. Relationships between academic institutions in the two countries can, with some assistance, flower into faculty links and joint research projects.

Once the talk is of relationships and common benefit the relevance of mutuality in the aid context becomes more evident. Benefit for aid-givers may take several forms. There are, self-evidently, unique conditions in developing countries for research in tropical medicine and agriculture, anthropology and art. But what is less apparent is that those receiving higher education are an inestimable resource, not only the best brains but often the first to be exposed to the accumulated knowledge of the industrialized world. The phrase 'a new Einstein in Chad' has been coined out of the optimism that this prospect induces.

What has been said is a partial response to the charge of cultural imperialism. The expression is admittedly sometimes a catch-phrase, especially in the mouths of Marxists, whose selective application of the word 'imperialism' appears to exonerate them from any implication. Kemp (1972, pp. 17–18) says of the Marxist theory of imperialism that it:

> uses the term 'imperialism' in a technical sense which has to be carefully distinguished from the variable meaning attached to it by historians and others. For the latter it generally means principally or exclusively the relationship between the advanced, imperial country and the colonial or semicolonial areas falling within its formal or informal empire. The Marxist theory does more than this. It uses the term to describe a special stage of capitalist development...

Similarly, it is a belief propagated by Marxists that cultural imperialism is an outreach of capitalism. Yet it appears that communist countries practise what one might, in objective parlance, call a policy of cultural imperialism in that they start from seemingly immutable assumptions about the superiority and ultimate rightness of their own system. Danckwortt (1973) relates this to the self-projection which, as we have seen in Chapter 7, was the mode mainly followed in external cultural policy after the Second World War:

> In the case of partner countries which are only just discovering their own cultural identity, a massive import of alien value concepts of this kind can have a depressive effect. It alienates the upper class from the mass of the people, awakes demands that cannot be satisfied, distracts from their own problems and paralyses their own creativity. The will to self-help, the motive force of every kind of development, is slowly but surely killed . . . In its naïve phase after the war German external cultural policy simply did not consider these consequences of its programme . . . It should be noted in passing, that the Eastern Bloc states pursue in this sense an unconscious and naïve cultural imperialism. Especially the GDR makes a point of selling the value concepts of its social system as a panacea and of decrying as a capitalist trick the new critical idea of an external cultural policy which wants to let the developing countries go their own way. (Danckwortt, 1973, pp. 39–40)

The extension of Marxist theory to development economics is an argument in favour of revolution in Third World countries to which some intellectuals are prone. The situation outlined above of an entrenched minority, reinforced by foreign capital and dominating a society with alien models, creates receptive conditions for revolutionary impulses whether populist, religious or Marxist. Marx's insistence on social struggle as class struggle provides a paradigm waiting to be invoked. And Marxism as a rationale for the seizure and maintenance of political power by an equally, perhaps even more, unrepresentative minority is attractive to those who seek the fruits of membership of it. As Taylor (1967, p. 46) says, 'Revolutions in short are made in the name of the proletariat, not by it, and usually in countries where the proletariat hardly exists'.

In so far, therefore, as the Western cultural presence and aid programmes are intended partly at least to erect a bulwark against communism, it is important to take the Marxist ideological ambitions seriously. Efforts in this direction will lack finesse unless they are based on an appreciation of the need to reach the semi-westernized intellectuals (e.g. schoolteachers, middle-rank officials and media personnel), who should constitute one of the most important target groups, standing as they do between the westernized elite and the diffused mass of the population. This task calls for greater resources than are available to cultural agencies alone. But these should play their part by appealing to the interest and sympathy of their own target groups among intellectuals. Frankel (1966) writes about the equivocal feelings of such intellectuals:

> This is one reason for the appeal of Marxism, a philosophy which, at one and the same time, offers both a convenient synthesis of Western tradition, and a radical critique of that tradition. Marxism allows the intellectual of non-Western societies to feel that he is taking advantage of Western thought without being taken in by it. In contrast, any United States program of educational or cultural exchange with a developing country, much as it may be to the interest of both sides, almost inevitably raises the spectre of 'cultural imperialism'. (Frankel, 1966, p. 60)

For all the emotionalism with which the term 'cultural imperialism' is employed, the concept behind it should exercise serious minds. The point can be illustrated by the juxtaposition of two more quotations from the World Conference on Cultural Policies, the first showing the primacy accorded to culture in development and the second the fear of alien domination:

> The conference was unanimous in placing special emphasis on the dialectical relationship between culture and development, recognising that the notion of cultural identity was central to the whole question of development (UNESCO, 1982, p. 10).

> Several delegates from the 'South' – but also some from the 'North' – expressed their alarm at the threats to other cultures represented by the present-day trend towards standardization and the world-wide distribution of certain patterns of cultural life which would thus eventually come to dominate. They censured and denounced the way the world had been taken over by the mass media and cultural industries in the hands of transnational corporations. Their impact was such that the patterns of life they carried with them in fact exercised cultural imperialism, albeit insidiously, violating and directly manipulating people's conscious minds and restructuring their subconscious minds and thereby impairing and distorting the cultural identity of others. (UNESCO, 1982, p. 11)

The second passage echoes the proposal for a New World Information and Communication Order already put forward by UNESCO's MacBride Commission. The fact that most of the world's information is carried by five press agencies (Reuters, AP, UPI, Agence France Presse and Tass) and the domination of Third World television programmes by imported material, which is not only alien in content but also often unsuitable, are matters that go beyond our concern in this chapter. They are nevertheless part of the cultural identity issue. There are, however, many people in the developing world as well as elsewhere who see the alternative of state control of information as a greater menace.

The answer to the question with which this chapter opened is that mutuality in the practice of cultural relations between North and South is desirable and possible. There is an important cultural dimension of development aid, which can be made two-way by the cultivation of relationships. Such relationships are encouraged and enhanced by the mediation of well-informed and sympathetic individuals working in aid and cultural agencies, who can assist the process of acculturation by demonstrating human as well as administrative qualities.

Political confrontation is not the business of cultural agencies; but it is a fact that in the Third World the East–West divide and the North–South dichotomy intersect. Politics is a manifest part of the background to urban life, where the structures of new societies are being fashioned in the mingled shadow of luxury apartment blocks and shanty-land. Revolutionary doctrines, such as Marxism, may appeal to Third World intellectuals as a way of making sense of the political and economic challenge facing them. Those who are ambitious for power may see in Marxism a quick way of justifying the seizure of it. Aid programmes and Western sophistication are not in themselves an antidote. Nor is the fine but in some situations remote theory of democracy. Old-fashioned human agency, equipped with local knowledge and professional skills, is one effective answer; it can best be brought to bear through cultural dialogue and exchanges founded on the recognition of cultural identity. In the long run, everyone can distinguish between those who genuinely offer help and respect and those who seek to exploit by presenting false credentials.

11

A Personnel of Paragons

It will be obvious from the argument so far that cultural relations work is not the easiest profession to pursue. A combination of qualities is required of those who act as mediators between cultures and societies; it is one that is rarely found in its ideal completeness. Such persons go under a variety of titles in different languages. Reducing them to a common denominator defies the translator's art, for the appellations reflect the diversity of the systems to which they belong. The term 'cultural representative' will continue to be used in this book; when there is no risk of ambiguity, 'representative' alone. It applies to persons of any seniority who represent their country's cultural services abroad, whether in a diplomatic or non-diplomatic capacity.

What renders cultural relations work particularly demanding is not just its intrinsic difficulty but the high degree of personal engagement it calls for. Cultural relations cannot be conducted from a desk – although there is enough desk work that goes with it – but require constant contact with people. The success of such representatives will depend on their ability to keep the paper moving while they go out and about. They must know how to be friendly and yet purposeful in dealing with a wide range of people, how to manage their resources, including themselves, and above all how to communicate. Communication involves more than talking their own language to the circle of converted *habitués* who tend to close in on a newly arrived monoglot like bodyguards; it means having a sufficient mastery of the local language so that they can use it for official purposes and above all for the quintessential task of intellectual encounter. It would be unrealistic to insist that everyone in a cultural representation should possess an advanced linguistic proficiency; there are staff in administrative posts, for instance, who can manage with less, and they will have indigenous colleagues to help them. But anyone who is fully engaged in cultural relations must be able to communicate with members of the academic, scientific, artistic, educational and intellectual target groups who are the counterparts of similar elites at home. This is the stuff of mutuality. Old-fashioned cultural propaganda could get away with monolingualism because it relied upon projection and information; officials administering a programme of documentary film loans, standardized book presentations or informational handouts, and corresponding with their headquarters to indent for further supplies, could manage their contacts with the help of an intelligent local secretary to translate what was necessary for them. As their work was one-way this did not need to be much. Their social life was among expatriates, with a light sprinking of *habitués* for local flavour. In the front line of sophisticated cultural relations as we understand them today, such persons would be anachronisms, not only incompetent but illiterate.

In some countries, indigenous people in key positions speak English or French, for instance, so well that they can, and may prefer to, communicate in the adopted language. It has become for them an extension of their personality into the international sphere, and they will expect to use it in dealing with members of appropriate cultural agencies. This will clearly reduce the need for language proficiency, but it does not remove it. It is easy for cultural representatives to limit themselves to a particular set of contacts, to the exclusion of others, because their language is spoken by this set.

McMurry and Lee in *The Cultural Approach*, writing immediately after the war, quote the far-sighted view of the General Advisory Committee of the US State Department on the qualifications required for what were then called Cultural Relations Officers:

> they should have a suitable personality that would assure their ability to work effectively with the people of the country in which they may be located; they should have broad intellectual and cultural interests, which should be capable of understanding and appreciating matters of which they may not have specialized knowledge; they should have constructive imagination and enthusiasm; their point of view should be that of a mature, educated person, and they should have good judgement and common sense. It may be assumed that they have a fluent command of the language of the country to which they are sent, but they should be willing to endeavour to learn to use the language with distinction, as well as with readiness. (McMurry and Lee, 1947, p. 215)

Another American observation by Frankel (1966) is perhaps closer to experience (the author had been Assistant Secretary of State for Educational and Cultural Affairs) and does not shun the irony implicit in the description of a rarely attainable excellence:

> It is, indeed, an assignment that calls for an unusual combination of qualities. As the description of two days in the life of a normally

competent, normally harassed Cultural Affairs Officer may suggest, the ideal or 'compleat' Cultural Affairs Officer would be a protean character. He would be an intellectual with gregarious instincts; a warm-hearted communicator between two cultures and yet a hard-headed negotiator; an administrator of a large staff and program who keeps his staff and program in hand while he spends most of his time out of the office; a faithful bureaucrat who nevertheless can deal with the temperamental idiosyncracies of professors, musicians, athletes, and VIPs. In short, he would be a man of parts with the tastes of an aristocrat, the patience of a saint, and the constitution of a shot-putter. If he can manage it, he should also be a man who has a beautiful and charming wife who loves his job as much as he does, speaks the language of the country as well as he, and has inherited a comfortable sum of money so that she can supply what his representation fund lacks. (Frankel, 1966, p. 20)

In the intervening decades since Frankel wrote this, it has become customary to acknowledge in linguistic usage that cultural representatives may be female. For this reason, the word 'spouse' is often preferred to 'wife'. However, it remains true that the contribution, positive or negative, of a wife is a considerable factor in the success of any married male representative. Some wives make their home a place of pilgrimage for the entertainment of those who matter for their husband's work; others do not have it in them to transcend domesticity or xenophobia. Official entertainment in addition to bringing up children and running a household, especially in countries where servants are unobtainable, can be a major task in itself. But there are wives who also make a contribution in their own right. *The New York Times* of 4 September 1956 reports the director of USIA, Theodore C. Streibert, telling Congress, after a tour abroad, that many Agency wives were doing such good work teaching English (or whatever) that the US government often got 'two first-class representatives for the price of one'. In 1956, USIA wives were more likely to feel flattered by this remark than they probably would today. The mood of a growing number of wives in different cultural services is that they should be getting a bigger cut of 'the price of two'. Several wives feel that their services should be recognized not only in their husbands' allowances but also by personal remuneration. A larger proportion of wives today have a professional qualification and wish to exercise it. Frankel's picture of the ideal wife, ready to supplement her husband's finances to the end of improving cultural relations, must appear rather more of a parody than a jest today. Nevertheless, and in spite of these social and generational trends, the traveller on a country's cultural network is repeatedly struck by the positive and sympathetic attitude of wives to the country where their husbands' job has landed them. Not for them the 'expatriate stress' mentioned in an article in *The Times* of 1 October 1984, called 'Life as an Englishman abroad', in spite of its being written by a woman and mainly concerned with female case histories. Frances Donaldson, whose preparation of her book on the fiftieth anniversary of the British Council took her to a selection of its offices abroad came to this conclusion about the wives, 'Unpaid but not unappreciated, in the old-fashioned role of housekeepers and hostesses they are an indispensable part of the scene' (Donaldson, 1984, p. 365).

The question how far cultural representatives collectively measure up to the criteria demanded of their profession is interesting but impossible to answer. There are no generally accepted standards which are susceptible of more than subjective application. Some observers praise the talented amateurs they have known in the less regulated past and recall with admiration the mark these made on whole nations. They see their epigoni of today as faceless in comparison, harassed by bureaucracy and bemused by administration. Certainly, it is true that the good communicator is often a person with something to communicate and that the demands of the work as it has developed are not always favourable to individualism. Yet it remains a profession that offers enormous opportunities for personal fulfilment, and it has gained immeasurably in general recognition, not least because of the professional discipline it has developed.

Staff and Posts

One question for each country engaging in cultural relations is how its service should be structured and organized in order to fulfil its aims and objectives. It will be helpful first to consider some typical staffing patterns.

Personnel are normally divided into these categories:

1   *Home-based staff* are recruited in the home country and serve in posts abroad as generalists or specialists. They may belong to a career service (the Goethe Institute, the USIA, British Council) or be seconded from an educational institution (France and Italy), or from a home ministry (Austria) or cultural institution (Sweden). They may be attached to their diplomatic mission or may be independent of it.

2   *Local staff* are appointed in the host country. Usually, but by no means always, they are local nationals. It is economical to employ one's own nationals on local contract because this saves expatriate

salaries and allowances. Nationals from third countries living abroad present the same advantage.

3 *Teachers* are not usually members of the career staff, but are recruited at home or in the host country to teach in the cultural representation's own classes or at local schools and colleges. Their subject is overwhelmingly their own language and literature. They may act as *surrogates* for cultural relations work, for instance in remoter areas that the cultural service finds it difficult to cover; they may also be surrogates in countries where the cultural agency is not represented.

4 *Agents* are institutions or persons who act on behalf of the cultural service in a country or region where it is not represented. They include embassies, consulates-general, and may also include individuals who devote only a small part of their time to this work. One form of agent is the local resident, who has valuable connections operates rather like an honorary consul, with minor allowances for his expenses.

Home-based staff are expensive. According to *The Times* article 'Life as an Englishman abroad', 'It may cost £100,000 a year to keep a senior executive abroad: a high salary; school fees; acommodation and travelling expenses for the family leave'. For cultural representatives, the cost will average about half this in most countries, but the basis of remuneration will be similar. Posts abroad represent high expenditure, and they have to be deployed economically. In a larger representation there will be both generalist and specialist posts. The generalists include the officer in charge and a deputy or assistant; the specialists those whose work involves skills in such areas as language, books, the arts, science, and accounts. In a career service, staff will be transferred from one post abroad to another, with postings at home in between for their greater experience and reintegration into the domestic scene. They will be motivated by their sense of vocation and by career prospects. The advantage of a career service is professionalism; the disadvantage is that staff cannot be expected to possess or acquire the necessary degree of local insight and linguistic proficiency required in a series of postings. As Max Beloff (1965, p. 485) says, 'It is not self-evident that years spent arranging for English-teaching in tropical Africa are a good preparation for acting as an official representative of British culture in an ancient European capital'. One might add – or vice versa.

Professionalism brings an inside knowledge of the discipline and resources of the organization. This is important for an integrated world-wide service particularly. All posts overseas can then work with continuity to their headquarters, with a common identification of targets and objectives. On the other hand, appointing outsiders on limited contract makes it possible to bring in people who possess the deeper expertise necessary for the more sensitive and demanding requirements of exchange and co-operation. Also, on a practical note, outside appointments introduce flexibility in establishment structure and personnel management. There is always the danger that career staff build up an organizational mystique, that professionalism can become inbred and perpetuate exclusive, complacent attitudes that are inimical to new ideas.

Local staff are not simply the executors of subordinate functions. They also secure an important continuity in the standing and contacts of the representation because they stay longer, often much longer, than their home-based colleagues. They know the language and they have protracted experience of the conditions affecting the work in their country. What they do not possess to the same extent is the organizational professionalism and the ability to perform representational duties. But this depends on the kind of staff employed and the salaries and responsibilities offered to them.

The British Council has local staff in charge of some of its smaller offices abroad; also it has local staff in some posts which in other representations are occupied by the home-based. In 1983/84, of the 2,500 staff the Council employed overseas, 300 were home-based and the rest local. The terminology that the British Council itself uses for those two types is 'London-appointed' and 'locally engaged'. In view of the lower prospects of the latter, this typology has been corrupted to 'London-anointed' and 'locally enraged'! French employees, responding to a questionnaire (Grémion and Chenal, 1980, p. 15) about their work, saw themselves in Dantesque terms either in limbo (local staff who do contract-teaching and other supportive tasks), or in purgatory (staff seconded from the ministry of education as teachers) or in heaven (cultural representatives, who do not teach – directors of institutes and cultural attachés). The fact that they never actually see themselves in inferno may be due to the *messianisme français*, which was mentioned in Chapter 5 (p. 35).

Teachers are not always in happy relationship with the cultural representatives to whom they work; they feel disadvantaged when they compare their salary and conditions. But the teachers can choose where they serve, whereas the cultural representatives who are members of a career service must go where they are sent. The itinerant language-teacher has become a noteworthy feature of expatriate life and figures in a good deal of modern fiction. Also, many writers, especially in English, have taught abroad and acquired material for their books. The line stretches from James Joyce and Christopher Isherwood to include many more in the postwar period, for instance, D. J. Enright, Anthony Burgess and Francis King. The language teacher is an interpreter between cultures; so is the writer concerned with foreign societies and expatriates resident in them.

Italy, like France, recruits teachers through the ministry of education for deployment by the foreign ministry, which has the funds in its allocations to pay them. It offers them the inducement that two years abroad count as three years service at home. They can teach for as long as fourteen years and can return to their old post if they spend a minimum of three years abroad. Recently, the Italian teachers' unions have put restrictions on the employment of locally engaged teachers (that is, those in limbo in the French quotation).

The idea of using teachers as surrogate cultural representatives tends to meet with opposition from trade unions, as does the notion of using agents. Both possibilities present the opportunity of keeping down staff costs. A partial presence on behalf of a cultural organization in a remote but significant town is better than no presence at all.

The German Commission of Enquiry on Foreign Cultural Policy made an original point in this connection:

> The Commission declares itself in favour of giving more consideration than heretofore to persons from cultural life in the appointment of honorary consuls. This is all the more appropriate since for the consulates cultural work has gained much significance in comparison with the traditional activities in the economic sphere. (Bundestag, 1975, p. 36)

Training

It is difficult to exaggerate the need for training. Cultural representatives in a career service need it for learning the languages and conditions of their countries of posting; they need it for the performance of their professional duties when they take on new responsibilities; they need it for refreshing their familiarity with what is going on in their own country. Non-career representatives, or diplomats doing a stint in a cultural post, need it for these reasons but also in order to learn how the cultural service works and how it draws upon the institutions in the home country.

One form of training, which is little given but which is indispensable for all but those who are already really expert in the country of posting, is in the workings of its society. Being able to mediate between cultures and societies calls for a profound knowledge of the social structure; this is too fundamental a need to be left to be satisfied by chance reading, second-hand opinions or uninformed observation. To revert to the Mutuality Table in Chapter 9 (p. 83), the target field B2 is the one where the most significant action is. This is the scene of intellectual encounter, where original thought and experience is turned to account for mutual advantage by the elites of both sides. To operate there calls for the understanding and insight postulated for the B axis.

Training is admittedly expensive, both in the actual costs and in maintaining enough spare capacity to release staff for the purpose. The former costs could be reduced, however, by more sharing between friendly, like-minded countries. Another kind of cost-sharing that might be practised is in the production of a *vade mecum* on the culture and society of individual countries. At present there is little pooling of such guidance information. National representations often produce their own post reports, including perhaps information from the local embassy, which can be useful even if they do not go much beyond a list of do's and don'ts. What is required for guidance in the cultural relations work, however, is something of greater profundity specifically prepared for this purpose, which treats the society in the context of history, politics, national culture and social forces. Since most democratic countries now have a similar approach to cultural relations, the production of briefing and reference material of this sort might well be a joint activity between them. This might happen, for instance, in the framework of co-operation between member states of the European Community. It could facilitate closer co-operation between them, as discussed on pages 214–15.

Country-specific training is not easy to arrange with existing facilities. There are academic courses, but they are too diffuse and too long; there are individually tailored programmes of visits and consultations, but they are too superficial. An idea mentioned by two commentators on the British Council in the postwar years, T. R. Henn (1946, p. 239) and W. C. Atkinson (1946, p. 98) was that of a 'staff college'. Henn wrote in some reflections on the British Council, 'A staff college for the Council would add enormously to its efficiency, and it could run "refresher courses" for the gaps between tours in the field'. This idea of a staff college has become even more attractive with the expansion of cultural work. It might be uneconomical for any one country to maintain alone, but on a shared basis it would be more viable, and again this might be a task for European Community countries, if it could be done informally and unbureaucratically. It is surely time that an international training centre was set up. It could have an academic and research aspect, as recommended for France by *Le projet culturel extérieur de la France* (Ministère des relations extérieures, 1984, p. 142), but the greatest need would be for professional training in relation to regions and countries. After attending a course aimed specifically at their country of posting, cultural representatives would arrive equipped to penetrate that country's society and culture, without an initial period of disorientation.

The kind of cultural service any country runs and the way it is organized must obviously depend on the policy behind it. Existing cultural services have grown up by an accretion of functions. The rapid evolution of cultural relations in the twentieth century is an indication of their vitality. They have been transformed to meet a new international situation. The accretion of functions has produced services with a high degree of administrative responsibility, whether they are independent career services, such as the Goethe Institute and the British Council, or those, such as the French and Italian, that are closely interwoven with their diplomacy.

What may get lost in large organizations is precisely the intellectual mediation that is the prime opportunity of cultural relations in our time. The facilities we possess for communication and travel present us with an unprecedented opportunity to bring about understanding and co-operation, first between intellectual and cultural elites, then through them more widely between societies. Cultural services are there to seize this opportunity and it is important that they devote adequate resources to it. Yet what easily happens is that, with straitened budgets, they have little margin to do more than meet their existing obligations, which include a heavy burden of administration of official schemes.

The activity in question will typically comprise the organization of bilateral (and multilateral) seminars, lecture series in the universities and learned institutions of the host country, informed contact with the avant-garde in the arts and literature, identification of sensitive points on the frontiers of contemporary scholarship and research, and penetration of student opinion at first hand. Such undertakings may be seen together under the generic term 'intellectual encounter'. It already figures to some extent in existing cultural programmes; the point is that it needs to be extended and developed. It should contain a literary content, for, as Frankel (1966, p. 54) remarked, from an American point of view, 'the education and mental formation of most foreign intellectuals is literary in character, and their approach to social issues is marked by a high degree of reliance on broad and abstract theories and ideals'. This activity should go beyond what one might call the established culture; Walter Wassener (1971, p. 262) makes the undoubtedly valid point from a German and European view, which could be applied to a variety of other countries in both the developed and developing world, that culture-producing elites do not identify with established cultural patterns so much as with alternative values, and that the cultural representatives whose mission is to secure their co-operation should themselves give the impression of being open-minded and critical. This requirement has admittedly to be reconciled with the operation of more formal programmes and good relations with officialdom.

In so far as a cultural service cannot meet the exigencies of this more forward-looking work from its own staff, it has two solutions: either to recruit people from appropriate institutions as cultural representatives for specific postings, who possess the requisite qualities and expertise, or to recruit people as supernumeraries to the establishment of existing cultural representations, who would operate, for instance, from a local university teaching position. In either case, it would be important to ensure that they enjoyed a due measure of freedom from routine duties. The former method would be more suitable for smaller countries which maintain the cultural attaché system, and the latter for countries with autonomous cultural services. The secondment of well-qualified people from universities and cultural institutions (museums, galleries, research institutes), who already possess an intimate knowledge of the language and conditions of the host country, would not only be effective for this key task but would strengthen contacts between the two countries and enrich understanding in each. Such persons could be offered inducements to carry out the kind of long assignment (for example ascending remuneration and a lump sum) which is not normally possible, or even desirable, within a career service. Contract employment on this model may well become more widespread as the needs and opportunities of intellectual encounter grow more manifest.

Rigaud (1980) came to the conclusion that being a cultural representative was more a function than a career and that it should be for a limited term rather than for life-long service. He admits that several interlocutors during his enquiry expressed a contrary view, but abides by his conclusion that:

the functions concerned should be exercised by agents already possessing professional experience in other areas which has put them in contact with the realities of national life and French cultural activity;

interested people should be discouraged from devoting a complete professional life to this work, if only so as to give them the possibility to return to France and to resume contact, as diplomats do, with national reality. But exceptions can be made to this general rule. (Rigaud, 1980, p. 101)

The arguments are persuasive in favour of contract service for a few years by eminently suitable and ideally distinguished people, with a background of regional experience and advanced language proficiency, who would return to their own institutions and bring the benefit of their foreign associations with them.

In contradistinction to this is the question of outside appointments to the top positions in cultural services. This arises in respect of the independents particularly, since the diplomatic system, such as that of France and Italy, has senior foreign ministry officials in charge. In earlier years, cultural services did not possess staff with enough experience for the top echelons. But now they have come of age. It would be more in keeping with their professional maturity if such posts were normally (though not necessarily invariably: there should be scope for the outstandingly suitable appointment) filled by insiders. Also it would encourage the most able and ambitious people to work for such services.

The officers of USIA felt so strongly on this subject that they wrote a letter to the director, Charles Wick, in the *Foreign Service Journal*, which is published by the American Foreign Service Association. The *International Herald Tribune* of 3 August 1984 reported their allegation that there were four times as many political appointees in USIA as before and that many of them were underqualified. Wick, himself a Presidential appointment, is reported by the same paper of 4–5 August 1984 as having replied defending his appointees as people with 'unique talents'. He said that, under his direction, the USIA budget had climbed from $454 million in 1981 to a proposed $885 million for 1985.

It is salutary for any service to refresh itself with new blood. In cultural relations the desirability is in the very nature of the work, which at its most significant is concerned with originality and innovation. But the most eligible posts for outside appointment are those concerned with setting up exchange and co-operation abroad, especially in the area of intellectual encounter. The rationale for bringing in outsiders should be that they have qualifications to offer that are required for particular aspects of the work and that do not already exist inside.

12

Analysis and Evaluation

It is a besetting problem that cultural relations work does not lend itself to evaluation. Evaluation is practicable within limits and there exist various ways whereby it can be improved. But it will never carry cast-iron conviction. The same applies to most cultural activity, whether at home or abroad. The effect on minds, sensibilities and attitudes will be perceptible (although unlikely to be fully perceived) in years to come rather than immediately. The justification of investment in cultural activity must therefore include an element of faith. That faith is more likely to be forthcoming in societies where there is a traditional belief in the importance of culture and of devoting public resources to it; elsewhere, it has to be cultivated and propagated by people of conviction. So we find that, in the battle for government funds, lobbies and pressure groups have a critical role.

Competition exists by virtue of comparison. It is not obvious to politicians, or anyone else, how one can compare the benefit of spending a million pounds on cultural relations or on, say, public health. The answer is that you cannot. Both matter on different wavelengths and different timescales. Remembering the comment by Eliot (1948, p. 22), 'Culture may even be described simply as that which makes life worth living', one might say that the perfectly healthy would die of boredom if they had nothing to do but rejoice in their fitness. Try telling that to a sick man, may come the riposte; to which one can counter, Try telling the opposite to a sick world. It is a controversy that will never be resolved. Decisions about the allocation of resources are made in individual instances, according to the priorities a government sets itself in the light of what it believes to be the national interest and the public will.

It is prudent for cultural agencies to foster public support of their work. Their prime target for persuasion therefore, outside government and opinion-moulders, will be those elites that are both the immediate beneficiaries and the predestined carriers. The proximate target will be public opinion at large. It must be acknowledged to be an unhealthy state of affairs when even educated members of the public know little of the way their country presents itself abroad. Indeed, it might be argued that there is an obligation to inform them. Public relations on the home front are therefore important, just as they are important abroad for maximizing the effect of activities and raising the local profile of cultural agencies. Since the British Council set up a Public Relations Department in 1981 (later called Press and Information Department) there has been a remarkable increase in the number of recorded mentions in the British press: 486 in 1982; 763 in 1983; 1,422 in 1984 (*Source:* The British Council).

Admittedly, the doubling of mentions from 1983 to 1984 is largely due to the celebration of the Council's fiftieth anniversary in 1984, but the steady rise is impressive. Professional expertise in handling the PR side of any country's cultural relations is likely to pay off. We saw earlier (p. 40) how the term 'publicity' found favour compared with 'propaganda' in the inter-war years in Britain, when further-sighted interests were groping towards a more efficacious presentation of Britain and its culture abroad. The term no longer needs to be invoked as a euphemism. Publicity has its own place in cultural work, both at home and abroad. Its techniques are instructive for the way a country should present its image to others, and for those concerned with the profile cultural agencies convey of their nature and functions. Dr Alois Mertes, the State Minister in the German foreign ministry, in whose responsibilities external cultural policy is included, made a similar point when he said in an interview:

> No modern state can afford to pursue a foreign policy without a goodly measure of public relations work. A good German cultural policy is a form of public relations work, creating a liking for our people, for our democratic state. Artists and scientists, in their way, are indispensable ambassadors of the spiritual substance of our nation and our political order which embodies a measure of freedom hitherto unknown in German history. (Bildung und Wissenschaft, 1984, p. 72)

Perhaps the public relations approach is most necessary in countries such as the USA and Britain, where there is an anti-culture prejudice waiting to be exploited. As we have seen, the word 'culture' itself has dubious overtones in English, so it does not take a very talented publicist to stir up hostile prejudice. Lord Beaverbrook's campaign against the British Council has already been mentioned; the motive for this has never been made clear, but it is commonly supposed to have derived from his animosity towards Lord Lloyd, the Council's Chairman, 1937–41. It may also have been his feeling that, because he had been Minister of Information in the First World War, he should have been given more say in the Council's work himself. Whatever lay behind it, the method was to miss no opportunity of attacking the British Council by distortion and misrepresentation in his newspapers, the *Daily Express, Sunday Express,* and *Evening Standard.* The campaign, in retrospect, is not without its amusement. It played upon the philistinism of the less-educated members of the public, referring to Council staff in such phrases as 'long-haired lads and lasses' and making the Council's activities seem extravagant and wasteful. In 1954 the British Council Staff Association published a pamphlet drawing attention to the inaccuracy of Beaverbrook's reporting. It is worth considering one example the pamphlet quotes.

The *Daily Express* of 16 October 1952 carried a front-page headline, 'British Serenade the Germans', reporting that British madrigal singers (an ideal target) were giving a concert in Stuttgart, provided by the British Council 'as the highlight of the fun'. The *Express* ignored the information supplied by the Council that the concert was taking place entirely at German expense. It said in a leading article the next day, 'With a fa-la-la! Observe what the British people get for their money. "British Serenade the Germans" said a Page One headline yesterday, announcing that the Council's carollers are to woo the beefy, beer-drinking Bavarians with Elizabethan madrigals.' Madrigals and Morris dancers were two recurrent themes in such attacks. In this particular one, the misrepresentation continued in the *Evening Standard.* To the end, the Beaverbrook newspapers persisted in disregarding the facts, though a brief correction was published, and in placing Stuttgart in Bavaria. This was an example not only of philistinism but also of the crudest cliché being used to play on anti-German feeling, shortly after the war, and to make the British Council appear misguided and unpatriotic as well as extravagant.

It is a minor irony of history that Beaverbrook may have contributed to the British Council's survival in the first year of the war, when Duff Cooper, the Minister of Information, was anxious to control all forms of propaganda, including culture. There was internecine conflict between ministries. The account in Eastment (1982, p. 33) says:

> Churchill called on Beaverbrook to put an end to the ceaseless squabbles. In his report to the War Cabinet, Lord Beaverbrook outlined two choices in regard to the Council: absorption by the MOI [Ministry of Information] or the restriction of the Council 'to cultural activities, entertainments, scholarships and systems of education'. On the question of overseas publicity Beaverbrook

reaffirmed that the Foreign Office must be responsible for the strategy and the MOI for the execution . . .

The second course was the one followed. This meant that the Council had a further mandate as an independent body under the aegis of the Foreign Office.

It is on financial grounds that external cultural services can be most tellingly impugned. The absence of automatic returns to justify expenditure lends force to the attack. Moreover, it has become part of the mythology of our time that governments waste money by the million; people can easily be stimulated to believe that cultural organizations of all others are expensive and expendable. The American, Eugene Castle, chose for his book, in which he criticized the USIA in 1955, the title *Billions, Blunders and Baloney: the fantastic story of how Uncle Sam is squandering your money overseas.* In particular, he maintained that the films made by USIA were a waste of money. According to *The New York Times* of 25 April 1955, he was a New York investment banker and former president of a film company. The USIA budget was at that time the subject of repeated debate in Congress and the media. But, even when USIA was longer-established, its methods and expenditure were constantly being criticized. The *Daily Telegraph* of 8 July 1965 summed up the argument by saying that the Americans were masters of advertising techniques and yet had not discovered how to sell themselves abroad. What weakens the defence of cultural and information organizations is that they have not always been good at answering criticisms and justifying their expenditure. It behoves them, therefore, to employ evaluation of their work, both for the better functioning of their own services and in order to convince their critics.

We might expect that France and Italy would find it easier to sustain the importance of cultural relations because, in their systems, these are so closely wedded to diplomacy and national interest. Yet this is no longer self-evident. Perhaps because they have in the past been able to make generous assumptions about their cultural relations, France and Italy have had less practice in dealing with challenges to them. Admittedly, these challenges, when they come, are about the conduct of rather than the need for cultural relations, but some fundamental questions get asked about the cultural base itself. In their study of French cultural centres and institutes in Europe, Grémion and Chenal (1980, p. 1) consider that the erosion of French national cultural identity cannot be denied. They point to several indicators: 'the increasing vulnerability of the language within France itself, the weakening of the capacity of the school system for integration, the recrudescence of regionalisms, the value attached to access to centres of foreign dominance for the new ruling classes, and the "peripheralisation" of the centre [that is, Paris]'. And when it comes to cultural policy, the authors' conversations with cultural representatives produced discomfiting responses, such as:

A brutal fact: the answer to the question 'Do you perceive a policy for the country in which you are?' is unanimously negative. On this point there is a massive consensus, whatever the position in the organization and the degree of access to the Directorate-General [the division of the foreign ministry responsible for cultural relations] there is no country policy or indeed policy at all. (Grémion and Chenal, 1980, p. 40)

In Italy, too, far-reaching policy questions have been raised, particularly about the relationship between internal and external cultural policy. In an article in *Il Messagero* of 10 October 1984, Giuseppe Tamburrano, the spokesman of the Socialist Party for cultural affairs said, 'The vast world of cultural organizations and institutions is a chaos'. He repeated the plea (which had emerged from the conference on external cultural policy he organized in December 1983) for the creation of a ministry of culture to bring order into this chaos, and said it should tackle the 'cultural colonization of which Italy is the object, especially from the United States'. *Il Giorno* of 2 December 1983, reporting on that conference, singled out the mismatch between Italy's cultural riches ('our oil wells are to be seen in our churches, ancient palaces, monuments in the middle of squares, art galleries, theatres and film studios') and the actual benefit Italy derived from them. Professor Tamburrano is quoted as saying, 'The future of our exports is largely in the cultural market'. The newspaper referred to Italy's external cultural budget as 'loose change' and said, 'The fulcrum of Italian external cultural policy should be the cultural institutes: eighty altogether in the whole world, of which few are working.'

An Analytical Approach

Analysis and evaluation are necessary, therefore, not only to ensure success in the conduct of an organization's work (although this is the primary purpose), but also in order to supply a rationale towards the justification of cultural relations and, not least, to attract the requisite funds from government.

Salon (1981), writing from his experience as a French cultural representative, comes to the conclusion:

> In fact, one of the principal difficulties of evaluation in general comes from the almost complete absence of quantifiable data and their unreliability when they exist. Cultural work bears fruit only in the medium and long term, very rarely in the short term, and it operates essentially by people and through people, with all the fortuities and imponderables that this brings with it. Evaluation runs the risk of being reduced to a qualitative appreciation, vague and almost inevitably subjective. (Salon, 1981, p. 1501)

Although this point is certainly valid, it applies less to discrete activities. One technique of evaluation, therefore, is to conceive the work in terms of the component parts (language, libraries, arts, etc.) and to treat each individual activity as something that has a beginning and an end on a time-scale; each activity can then be subjected to evaluation after it is completed. The techniques of business studies, such as management by objectives, can usefully be invoked as a discipline. It is much more constructive, for instance, to have a formulated objective for each activity rather than to regard it as self-justifying because it has always been done, is expected by one's audience, or fits into one's resources. If it has always been done, the time will certainly be ripe to ask whether it has outlived its usefulness; if it is expected by one's audience, whether the audience is the right target; if it fits into one's resources, whether these would not be better employed on some other activity. It is a mark of positive management to handle each item of activity, so far as possible, as a project – to 'projectize' it – so that it has a definite conclusion and can be evaluated. Also, this heightens the individual representative's sense of achievement. The converse – to maintain the same activities year in, year out, without concern for objectives or evaluation or change – may produce staff frustration and even fundamental doubts about the value of the work. In a number of the *Zeitschrift für Kulturaustausch* devoted to evaluation, Schlaginweit (1975, p. 5) argues in favour of the prior formulation in writing of 'the objective and/or the expected effect, before the project is included in concrete budgets' for each intended activity. He points out the need to avoid sweeping statements, such as to 'secure peace, improve Germany's image' and to concentrate on limited goals. He states how difficult it is to determine in concrete terms:

> what one hopes to, and believes one can, achieve with a particular enterprise;
> whom one hopes to, and believes one can, address;
> what resources will be necessary;
> what side-effects are to be expected.

Schlaginweit also remarks, 'For the language of evaluation is numerical'. And it is the common experience that evaluation, if it is not to be subjective, requires quantification. This may be expressed, for instance, in size of audiences, number of students or library users, in dossiers of press mentions, box-office receipts or in terms of financial contributions from partner organizations. These have the advantage of being susceptible of comparative analysis, so that the measurable effects of activities can be assessed against one another. But, of course, quantity tells only part of the story. It does not follow that a capacity audience paying for expensive tickets to sit through the whole of Shaw's *Back to Methuselah* or Wagner's *Ring* is going to end up actually understanding or liking more than before the countries that produced them. We come back to the difficult area of judgement. To prevent this becoming subjective (which easily means a rationalization of the conclusions hoped for), it is helpful to conduct evaluations in conjunction with partner organizations of the host country. In cultural relations between democracies with open societies, when mutuality is practised, there is everything to be said for an open declaration of an activity's objectives and for the invitation of partner organizations to participate in evaluation.

Overall, evaluation has to be seen in the context of an organization's general aim and policies. These are conceived at its headquarters or in each individual representation, or ideally in both. Most cultural organizations find it necessary to co-ordinate policy by some institutionalized system, which includes inspections, consultations, policy seminars or whatever. Evaluation clearly cannot work except in consonance with agreed policy. And everyone working for a cultural agency needs to know very precisely what its policies are, both in general and in sectoral terms. This is a first step to evaluation and to the measurement of success.

The Mixed Commission also has an evaluative function. Its purpose is to secure closer cultural co-operation. This is expressed in the Cultural Convention between the United Kingdom and France (see Appendix A, p. 233) as being 'to promote in each country the fullest possible knowledge and understanding of the intellectual, artistic, scientific, technical and educational activities and of the history and ways of life of the other'. Mixed Commission meetings are a forum for consultation between the two sides. They review activities since the last meeting and consider those planned for the future. The Agreement with the Soviet Union (see Appendix B, p. 235) and the Exchange Programmes with East European countries are much more prescriptive and constitute the authority for agreed exchanges. There is no Mixed Commission. Both sides send their representatives to inter-governmental talks to agree the programme for the next two-year period. Although these talks are not conducted with the same openness as Mixed Commission meetings, there is an evaluative role here too. In both forms of bilateral consultation, the delegation of each country, consisting predominantly of officials, is able to assess the effect of its activities from the reactions of the other side.

Reports and Reviews

Any cultural organization would be well advised to have some up-to-date examples of evaluation available for briefing purposes or for scrutiny by politicians or others who ask searching questions. We have seen above (p. 57) that Ed Murrow said of USIA when he became director in 1961 that it had had five titles in the twenty years of its existence. In the fifty years of its existence, the British Council has had twenty reviews. Small wonder if its staff talk of its being like a plant that is continually uprooted to see if it is still alive. It is one of the ironies of such reviews that they leave some of the most fundamental questions unasked and unanswered. There are certain basic issues in the business of cultural relations, which have already emerged in this book. A comprehensive review of cultural policy or a cultural service would be expected to cover the following:

• the aim as part of national policy; the relevance of the objectives;
• ministerial responsibility; how far the requirements of mutuality are satisfied;
• budget required for execution of policy;
• representation world-wide or in selected countries only;
• areas of activity;
• cultural dimension of aid; how this links up with cultural agencies;
• diplomatic: non-diplomatic;
• the agencies and their co-ordination;
• relationship with external broadcasting;
• bilateral: multilateral.

Four major reports will be considered in Chapter 13. Of these, that of the German Bundestag of 1975 comes closest to dealing thoroughly with all these aspects. It is unfortunate that very few of the countries engaging in cultural relations with any real degree of seriousness possess the critical apparatus they would need for a running evaluation. Little attempt is made to see this work continuously in relation to national policy, geographical priorities, the resources and interests of the home constituency, and financial resources. The result is an undue element of the fortuitous. This may be to the advantage or disadvantage of individual cultural agencies: some agencies are spared the searching investigation that might otherwise be applied, others fail to receive the backing they deserve. For cultural relations as a growth area in international understanding, the effect is adverse. The justification for its work tends to be seen as incidental to conventional diplomacy and subject to undefined generalizations about the national interest. Budgets are straitened or reduced, not for any intrinsic reason, but because economies are sought wherever they can be found. Uncertainties arise, which complicate forward planning so that action in accordance with well-considered policies gives way to *ad hoc* expediency.

For want of the means of analysis and evaluation, public judgements tend to be tentative, sectoral or ill-informed. Few assessments of cultural relations or their agencies are based on sufficient information or an appreciation of their place in contemporary international affairs. Certainly, in default of a critical apparatus or statement of government policy, it is good tactics to encourage and welcome commendatory judgements. They create a conducive climate of opinion even if they sometimes start from false premises. It is better to justify expenditure on cultural relations in the wrong terms than to wait for the acceptance of terms that have not yet achieved currency. One should not be too far ahead of public opinion. But it will be a PR priority to create a greater appreciation of the purpose of cultural relations and to present them as being necessary and justified in their own rather than in contingent terms. They will be expected, of course, to contribute to the national good, political, economic, social – as well as cultural. It is important to collect evidence demonstrating that they do. Any cultural agency will be well advised to collate and evaluate examples so that these are available for the information of politicians, publicists or those who conduct periodical reviews. Examples from other countries will also carry weight. Cultural relations are well enough established by now for a considerable case-history and descriptive literature to have accrued. It is in the analysis of these that the authentic rationale is to be elaborated. Priming lobbies and supporters with their conclusions is one effective means of achieving a constructive appreciation. Because of the financial vulnerability, the strategy of cultural agencies is bound to be in part defensive.

13

Four Major Reports

It will be timely to pursue the theme of evaluation further by considering four important reports published in different countries since 1975. They are all typical of attitudes prevailing in the countries that produced them. All of them, except that of the Central Policy Review Staff (Think Tank), have had directly positive consequences, which have reinforced cultural relations in the public recognition. They will be considered in the following order, which is not chronological:

1 The Stanton Report of 1975, *International Information Education and Cultural Relations, Recommendations for the Future.*
2 The Rigaud Report of 1979 on external cultural relations, *Les relations culturelles extérieures.*
3 The Report by the Central Policy Review Staff of 1977, *Review of Overseas Representation.*
4 The Report on Foreign Cultural Policy of the Commission of Enquiry of the German Bundestag of 1975, *Bericht der Enquete-Kommission Auswärtige Kulturpolitik.*

The Stanton Report

Dr Stanton was the chairman of an Independent Panel on International Information, Education and Cultural Relations, which included all members of the two US Advisory Commissions on Information and on International Educational and Cultural Affairs (later to be combined into one Commission). There was general agreement that an investigation should be carried out, the panel was constituted, private funds were raised from foundations, and various informants were consulted, ranging from the Secretary of State, Henry Kissinger. It says in the preface (Stanton, 1975, p. v):

'American programs in information, education, and culture are a means of fulfilling our national identity, of practising the philosophy in which we believe. Public diplomacy is a central part of American foreign policy simply because the freedom to know is such an important part of America'. The fact that all the expenses of the exercise were met from private sources is significant.

When the USIA was founded in 1953, it was conceived as being concerned with information only. It took over the responsibilities of the International Information Administration from the Department of State. It was essentially a mouthpiece for American policies, a channel of information about America, and a defence against hostile propaganda. It ran the Voice of America radio broadcasts, US libraries, the foreign film service and various news facilities. But the cultural and educational work, including such exchanges as those under the Fulbright programme remained in the Department of State. From 1954, these were the responsibility of the Bureau of International Cultural Relations (CU), which was established in that year. USIA staff working overseas (where their organization is confusingly known as the United States Information *Service*) therefore had two masters and two sets of interests to serve: the USIA and the State Department. The need to combine the hard-nosed projection of America with the subtler requirements of cultural exchange set up operational tensions.

Stanton came up with three major recommendations:

- An autonomous new agency should combine these dual functions and be called the Information and Cultural Affairs Agency.
- A new Office of Policy Formation should be set up in the State Department to bring together all programmes that explain US foreign policy.
- The Voice of America should be set up as a federal agency under a board of governors.

The Report ends on a note of liberation: 'USIA and CU have done admirably in circumstances very different from those for which they were designed. These dedicated officials, however, have labored too long under needless structural burdens. It is time, in the Panel's view, to set them free' (Stanton, 1975, p. 41).

Leaving aside the second recommendation as outside our subject, we note that the two functions in the first were indeed combined. Nomenclature was satisfied by changing the name USIA to USICA, the United States International Communication Agency. The change took effect on 1 April 1978. The *International Herald Tribune* of 6–7 May 1978 reported that the new Director, John Reinhardt, ceremoniously removed from the USIA building a plaque that bore the inscription 'telling America's story abroad' because, as he explained, the new agency 'will listen as well as speak'. But the new title was not popular. Some people thought it sounded too much like the CIA, and 'communication' had become hackneyed from over-use. Other suggestions were made: Senator McGovern proposed USAICE (US Agency for Information and Cultural Exchange). Those who did not like the name USICA maintained that the word, or something sounding like it, meant horse-dung in Chinese.

The concept behind the new USICA was more Carter than Reagan, and under the latter's Presidency, in 1982, the name was changed back to USIA, and so it rests. The combination of functions remains. This has been structurally beneficial because it has obviated the schizophrenia that obtained before. But it has meant that cultural exchanges have been financially at risk. When President Reagan's administration introduced public expenditure cuts in the autumn of 1981 it looked as though most of the weight of a 12 per cent overall reduction in the USICA appropriations would fall on the exchanges side and that the Fulbright Scholarship Program might be decimated. Priority was to be given to preserving the strength of the information side of USIA, which President Reagan himself and the new Director, Charles Wick, believed to be of overriding importance. If economies had produced this disastrous effect, it would have been an ironical consequence of the Stanton Report. The *International Herald Tribune* of 29 October 1981 pointed out that cuts of this magnitude would leave the Soviet Union unrivalled champion of education and culture for the poorest nations of the world. But the situation was saved and USIA, as it then soon became, was able to maintain the exchange of persons programmes.

The Voice of America remained under USIA direction. VOA has been the subject of much controversy since it was founded in 1942, especially during the Cold War. There was much criticism of programme content and of effectiveness. The idea of a radio service designed for foreigners and, on the vernacular side, largely run by expatriates, was repugnant to those who believed that the best message the United States could deliver was its ungarnished self. Indeed, Walter Lippmann suggested in 1953 that the VOA should be abolished and the government should instead regularly transmit domestic news broadcasts to other countries; he questioned whether VOA had a real control over the content of broadcasts in the rarer languages, such as Albanian (*New York Herald Tribune*, 17 April 1985). But President Reagan and Mr Wick had no doubt about the necessity of putting across a specifically designed message. The Stanton recommendation that VOA should operate under a board of governors was inspired by similar measures taken in respect of Radio

Free Europe (broadcasting to Eastern Europe) and Radio Liberty (broadcasting in various languages to the USSR). We have seen above that these two radio stations were typical products of the Cold War. For years it appeared that they were financed by the same Crusade for Freedom, under the sponsorship of the National Committee for a Free Europe, which had been responsible for the balloon campaign mentioned in Chapter 6 (p. 55). After the truth was revealed that they were receiving money from the CIA, it was decided to channel federal funds through a less questionable organization, and they were both put under a Board for International Broadcasting. The Stanton Report acknowledges the difference in nature between Radio Free Europe and Radio Liberty, on the one hand, and the VOA, on the other, as the official mouthpiece of the US government. Subsequently, all three stations came under the International Broadcasting Committee.

The Rigaud Report

It is indicative of the honour accorded to cultural relations in French foreign policy that shortly after he became foreign minister, M. Jean François-Poncet should commission a study to consider their future. Jacques Rigaud, *Maître des requêtes in the Conseil d'État* (a post that might be translated 'Master of Petitions'), chaired a working group consisting of civil servants, a university rector and the Secretary-General of the French Commission to UNESCO. The report was prepared in two carefully planned stages. First, a draft was circulated after consultations with members of the Directorate-General of Cultural, Scientific and Technical Relations in the ministry; then this was modified in the light of comments on it submitted by 200 parliamentarians, diplomats, academics, scientists and cultural figures. The report was submitted to the foreign ministry in September 1979.

First, the report considers the position of France as the leader in the field of cultural relations ('French culture belongs to the whole world and we are simply its trustees', Rigaud, 1980, p. 13) in a changing world where 'the involvement of people in international affairs' (p. 12), is part of the 'multipolarity towards which the world is tending'. The report believes that France is in danger of losing its pre-eminence and that it is a necessary counter-measure to develop more inter-ministerial co-operation and to bring French external cultural policy into more of a relationship of mutuality with other countries, since national cultures are interdependent. In the controversy about the dominance of English in the modern world, the report recommends 'plurilingualism', a policy favouring the international use of other languages besides English, which it says tends to have political overtones.

In the execution of these policies, the report recommends that French institutes and cultural centres should not be 'bastions of French culture' but places of exchange, rooted in local life (p. 12). The world-wide teaching of French should be maintained by co-ordinating the available resources (schools, institutes, Alliance Française, local academic institutions) and concentrating on the training of teachers of French in other countries (p. 49). In developing countries, there should be a concerted strategy combining cultural and technical with economic and industrial co-operation (p. 54).

The report claims that France occupies a leading place in intellectual co-operation. In spite of the competing opportunities provided by the mass media (*'vulgarisation'*), and in spite of the discredit they have sometimes earned, lectures by distinguished French people travelling abroad should be cultivated as an economical way of winning prestige. The symposium and seminar should also be employed as lively forms of intellectual encounter. The central role of information and its particular importance for science and technology is emphasized (pp. 59–62).

In the arts, the report attaches continuing importance to performances and exhibitions abroad and to the attraction of artistic events from other countries; such visiting *manifestations* reinforce the place of Paris as a 'cultural crossroads'. (It is significant that the cultural prerogative of Paris is so automatically assumed.) But such cultural exchanges should not be seen as elitist events limited to a select public but as part of totality including industry as a sponsor and propagator (pp. 63–6).

The report expresses concern at the fact that less than 20 per cent of French book production is exported and that 80 per cent of that goes to Francophone countries. The French government's support for the book had been consigned in 1976 to the Ministry of Culture, which disposed of a fund of 13 million francs for the purpose of promoting exports and subsidizing the translation of French books into other languages. The report recommends a boost for the diffusion of French literature, in which the foreign ministry and French embassies should play a full part. So far as the film, television and other audio-visual means are concerned, much more planned promotion was considered necessary.

After considering these various sectors of French cultural activity, the report tackled the two crucial questions: how cultural relations should be aligned with foreign policy and how bilateral and multi-lateral demands should be reconciled. The answer given to the first of these issues is in keeping with the tradition of France as the first Western country to define an external cultural policy and consign its management to the foreign ministry: the government has an inalienable responsibility not only to assist but also to supervise the process and content of cultural programmes, especially towards 'socialist' and developing countries. This should not entail ideological intervention or treating culture as a 'storehouse of diplomatic accessories' (p. 76), but in the long run it has to be political criteria that prevail. Similarly, the national economic interest in cultural exports should be observed and commercial sponsorship encouraged (pp. 74–9).

On the multilateral issue, the report assesses the advantage to France of participation in international organizations, such as UNESCO (from the presence of which in Paris it has been elsewhere estimated that France derives twelve times the expenditure it contributes). The report contradicts the view that multilateral development aid is less politically rewarding for the donor than bilateral; it says that multilateral aid is more neutral and that French experts and procurements provided within its terms carry, nevertheless, a cultural message, which is all the more effective for being devoid of political overtones.

As for bilateral relations, the report makes one statement about the inter-governmental cultural agreement that clearly belongs in the 'influence/indoctrinate' column of the Mutuality Table: 'it enables France to persuade its partners to accept modalities of intervention about which they might be initially reluctant' (p. 81). But the report also cautions that such agreements may encourage a certain fixation on existing programmes rather than on their evaluation (pp. 79–84). Finally, in this section, the report relates cultural relations to national cultural life. It is paradoxical that, although the foreign ministry bears responsibility for external cultural policy, this responsibility does not extend to the resources themselves. While accepting and even applauding this separation of powers, the report would not wish to see the foreign ministry reduced to running 'a tourist agency or an import–export business for the things of the spirit' (p. 85). It recommends, therefore, that the ministry should maintain a dialogue with relevant French institutions. The report recommends also that an Institute for External Cultural Relations Studies should be set up, presumably in a French university (p. 86).

The searching and positive nature of this report is impressive. It leaves the reader in no doubt about the crucial position occupied by cultural relations in French thinking. It asserts French national interest and, at the same time, displays sensitivity towards the cultural requirements of other countries at different levels of development. Its recommendations were subsumed into the policy document published by the French government (Ministère des relations extérieures, 1984) *Le projet culturel extérieur de la France* and therefore provided the basis for this detailed sectoral and geographical policy document.

The Report of the Central Policy Review Staff (CPRS)

This publication differs from the others in two important respects. First, as its official title, *Review of Overseas Representation*, implies, its scope was much wider: its terms of reference, prescribed by the then Foreign and Commonwealth Secretary, embraced all aspects of the United Kingdom's overseas representation, 'including political, economic, commercial, consular and immigration work, defence matters, overseas aid and cultural and information activities, whether these tasks are performed by members of Her Majesty's Diplomatic Service, by members of the Home Civil Service, by members of the Armed Forces, or by other agencies financially supported by Her Majesty's Government' (Central Policy Review Staff, 1977, p. v). One chapter is devoted to 'Educational and Cultural Work' (Chapter 12) and two others, 'The Administration of Overseas Aid' (Chapter 11) and 'External Broadcasting' (Chapter 13) have a relevance to this book. The second difference is that its purpose was 'to judge whether what is being done is relevant to the UK's objectives overseas and whether the resources devoted to it are proportionate to its present and future importance' (p. xvi) and not to produce a functional analysis.

The review was carried out by members of the CPRS. The CPRS was set up in 1970, shortly after Edward Heath became Prime Minister, in order to consider and question policy across the divisions of individual government departments. Its major preoccupations were domestic, and it produced a series of reviews for the guidance of politicians and officials. One of the criticisms levelled at this particular report was that the CPRS did not possess the expertise to review aspects of foreign policy.

The report was deliberately radical. It was a pity that what *The Times* branded its 'modish iconoclasm' was so markedly conditioned by the pessimism about Britain's future that was widespread in the late 1970s, when Britain's economy registered low growth and relative decline among OECD countries, and North Sea oil was not yet in full flow. The report was conditioned also by a smallness of vision – some would say meanness of vision – in geopolitical appreciation. The general thesis of the report was that Britain was cutting a grander figure in the world than was appropriate to its true standing; that it should cast off its inherited finery and go modestly among other nations in plainer, workaday garb. This thesis was argued in a report 442 pages long. Press reaction was practically all critical: Britain's significance on the international scene was not to be measured simply in terms of penny-pinching housekeeping. In no sector was the reaction to the report more consistently adverse than in that concerning culture and education. It was here that the CPRS team took a particularly reductive view. *The Times* wrote in a leader of 3 August 1977, 'The review tends to dismiss too easily the invisibles and intangibles which cannot be measured, such as cultural exports, the cultivation of personal contacts, the informal exchange of views and everything which comes under the vague heading of projecting Britain's image abroad.'

The report recommended that the British Council, as the organization mainly responsible for educational and cultural relations with other countries, should preferably be scrapped altogether or, alternatively, retained in the UK but with no representations abroad; it would then serve simply as an umbrella organization undertaking all recruitment for foreign educational institutions and placement for officially sponsored foreign students. If the former option were followed (about which the authors admittedly foresaw some problems), then a new recruitment and placement agency would have to be created, the Department of Education and Science would develop an overseas capability, all responsibility for educational aid administration work would go to the Overseas Development Ministry, and educational and cultural work abroad would be handled by diplomatic posts and the ministry's Development Divisions. The alternative option foresaw the continuation of the British Council as a Britain-based operation only, incorporating the Technical Education and Training Organisation for Overseas Countries (TETOC) and the Inter-University Council (IUC). British Council representations overseas would be incorporated into diplomatic missions.

In the government's White Paper, *The United Kingdom's Overseas Representation* (Foreign Office, 1978, p. 16), the case for the abolition of the British Council was rejected, although it was agreed that the possibility of closer rationalization of educational and cultural work should be examined. It was also agreed that a Management Review of the British Council should be conducted. TETOC and the IUC were subsequently amalgamated with the British Council. The White Paper by no means filled the gap uniquely existing in Britain, among major countries, by supplying a governmental affirmation of the indispensability of cultural relations as an instrument of policy, but it did say under the heading 'Educational and Cultural Work' (Foreign Office, 1978, p. 16):

> The value of this category of activity cannot be quantified, but the Government believe that it plays a distinctive and valuable role in projecting Britain abroad, in furthering relationships with other countries and in stimulating the use of the English language.

The report's most radical, though not most original, recommendation had nothing directly to do with cultural relations. This was that the Diplomatic Service should be disbanded in favour of a Foreign Service Group, which would bring the combined resources of the Civil Service to bear, both overseas and at home, on foreign policy, political and economic work, export promotion, information and other functions which now fall to the Foreign and Commonwealth Office.

As a final gloss on the report, it will be pertinent to recall two of the many letters that appeared in the British press in controversion of the report's doctrine of self-afflicting puritanism. Several letters published in support of the British Council and cultural relations came from overseas. In *The Times* of 9 August 1977, Professor Hugh Seton-Watson wrote that, although France had, since 1815, not had the resources of a first-rate power at her disposal, 'such she remained for over a century as a result of French diplomatic skill and cultural influence . . . French ability to perform this role was promoted much less by the memory of past glories than by the fact that the French language had become the instrument of civilised men all over the world. This advantage has now passed to the English language'. He went on to compare the political attitudes of France and Britain: 'France has suffered many social changes, often painful, since 1815, and has been torn by factional and ideological disputes, yet all Frenchmen have always shared a pride in French culture. This pride has been a major cause of the relative recovery of France since 1940, which has so strikingly coincided with the steady decline of Britain in the same years'. And in the same issue of *The Times*, W. M. Clarke, Director-General of the Committee on Invisible Exports, takes the report to task for not mentioning invisible exports although these 'are now over £12,800 million gross, one third of our total foreign income and the second largest in the world. The market pattern is different from that of visible exports'.

Prompted by this observation, we might reflect that culture, and especially the English language, is a major invisible export of Britain's and that it is ironic for a country that so depends on invisibles to show such scant appreciation of the returns that derive from foreigners' regard for Britain's culture, language, and values.

The British Council and the BBC External Services are, among their other functions, vehicles for that regard. Here we see in practice the distinction between invisibles, which figure in the economist's vocabulary, and intangibles, which require some imagination if their significance is to be grasped.

Commission of Enquiry of the German Bundestag

Since 1969 the Bundestag (lower house of parliament) has been empowered to appoint Commissions of Enquiry: this, on external cultural policy, was one of the first two to be authorized, in 1971. The Federal Government welcomed the Report and stated in its published comments, *Foreign Cultural Policy* (German Federal Foreign Office, 1978, pp. 5–6):

> The commission's statements and recommendations, divided up into five hundred paragraphs, have been carefully examined and found to correspond largely with the Federal Government's own conceptions. For this reason, they will also serve, beyond the limits of those comments, as an important basis for the formulation of government policy in the future.

As this suggests, the report with its 130 recommendations did not so much break new ground as summarize what was largely accepted wisdom and practice in Germany's conduct of external cultural policy. This degree of common understanding was facilitated by the existence since 1970 of the *Guidelines for Foreign Cultural Policy* (*Leitsätze*), which had been introduced by Ralf Dahrendorf as Minister in the German foreign ministry. Indeed, the only point of open disagreement was semantic. In wishing to avoid the term *Kulturpolitik* with its authoritarian associations, the commission recommended that in future instead of *auswärtige Kulturpolitik* (foreign cultural policy) the term *Kulturelle Aussenpolitik* (cultural foreign policy) should be preferred. But the German government rejected this change of name (German Federal Foreign Office, 1978, p. 13) on the grounds that it 'might lead to speculation that a change in the objectives of and distribution of competences' was proposed. To the non-German, and indeed to many Germans, the distinction seems of minor importance and to be cherished as a touch of Lilliputian humour in a serious work.

The government's publication *Foreign Cultural Policy* is a comprehensive statement of agreed theory and practice as well as a commentary on the report. Some of the report's most significant recommendations are:

- Clear objectives for cultural work are to be set by the foreign ministry.
- There should be a Minister in the foreign ministry charged with the supervision of this work.
- Cultural work is to be considered by German diplomatic missions as equally important as political and economic work.
- Particular importance is to be given to the schools that receive federal government support.
- There should be an annual public forum on foreign cultural policy, comprising experts and representatives of federal and regional government.

The report reaffirms the importance of cultural relations as an aspect of foreign policy. In view of the interdependence of modern states, the principle of mutuality is to be preferred to national self-projection. The different sets of problems that beset cultural relations with both developed and developing countries necessitate an examination of the role and significance of foreign cultural policy. The nature of cultural relations, especially their long-term conception, should be such as to encourage enduring mutual relationships. These relations are not only a third pillar of foreign policy (with politics and economics) but also demonstrate Germany's cultural position in a changing world.

In industrial countries, there is a tension between their culture and their economic competitiveness. After the end of the era of imperialism, culture emerges with growing importance alongside classical foreign policy as an obligation of the state. But cultural and academic institutions, with their programmes of exchanges, are not to be seen simply as a resource for state policies. In the 1950s Germany was burdened with the Nazi legacy and the ravages of war. It made efforts to overcome these handicaps. But it made the wise decision to avoid propaganda. The consequence may be that its cultural policies are based more on means than on aims. It is time to provide more co-ordination for the various agencies. Responsibility for these policies is scattered among ten federal ministries and the government Press and Information Office. The remedy lies in structural changes in the foreign ministry, a committee system, improved information provision and the improvement of work carried out by the overseas representations. While clear policy direction and regional priorities should be determined by the foreign ministry, the autonomy of institutions must be preserved. This must extend to cultural representations abroad, which are not to be subjected to excessive central control. Only local knowledge and experience can make cultural relations work successful. Inevitably differences will arise between representations and their headquarters. When these cannot be resolved by the competent institutions the mediation of the recommended sub-committee for cultural foreign policy of the Bundestag may be invoked.

German is not an international language (though it is the most widespread language in Europe). It is to be furthered wherever it meets a demand, and particularly among multipliers such as teachers. German schools abroad may be for children of expatriates or for those integrated in the local education system. In either case, they should be bilingual and should provide an exemplar of German educational practice. Free places should be available so as to avoid elitism.

This very selective synopsis gives an idea of the scope of the report and of the way it addresses specifically German problems. Its all-party authorship, its backing in parliament, and its support by the government give it an authority that has been of great value to all the organizations involved in cultural relations. The ultimate authority and endorsement consist in the publication, *Foreign Cultural Policy*, already referred to. A quotation from this will make a fitting and, in the eyes of many other countries, an enviable conclusion to this chapter:

> Our foreign cultural policy is essentially international co-operation in the cultural sector. It is a part of our foreign policy, a policy designed to promote the safeguarding of world peace. It must therefore contribute to a mutual understanding of the internal development of individual nations, taking into account social evolution, the rapid development of science and technology, as well as political changes. It must help above all to create ties between peoples of different nationalities . . . All nations are today, more than ever before, dependent on one another for their existence. On an international level, aside from economic achievements, the political weight of the Federal Republic of Germany largely depends upon its cultural accomplishments. In this respect, foreign cultural policy provides a connecting link with other peoples, promoting international understanding and the safeguarding of peace. It is, thus, a mainstay of our foreign policy, not only supplying information about our own culture but also fostering exchange and co-operation. Today, as well as information, we need to offer a realistic image of our country, presenting our accomplishments and potentialities in active exchange with other peoples. The value of what we give is only worth as much as our willingness to take. Thus, an open attitude towards others is a principle of our cultural policy abroad. (German Federal Foreign Office, 1978, p. 7)

14

Activities and Their Planning: Information and Books

The range of activities conducted by a cultural representation in a foreign country will be determined by ten principal factors:

- aims and objectives of its central organization;
- importance of the host country (and its geographical region) in the sending country's international concept (which includes, but also surpasses, current foreign policy as such);
- requirements and receptivity of the host country's institutions, their facilities for exchange and co-operation;
- funds available, from both government and private sources;
- provisions of the sending country's development aid programme that are relevant to cultural relations;
- obligation, for instance, under a cultural agreement or in accordance with agreed reciprocity;
- operations of other countries and of multilateral organizations;
- expertise available in the sending country for specialist work;
- requirements of internal cultural policy;
- traditional patterns followed by the cultural agency, or agencies, concerned (which may be a more dominant factor than they should be).

In the light of policies following from consideration of these factors, the work of a cultural representation will take one or more of these forms, which may in larger, more important countries complement rather than exclude one another:

- the institute: language-teaching, a lending library, a programme of cultural activities on its premises. Sometimes called a cultural centre.

- the office: administration of the sending country's activities and co-ordination between them, with outreach through appropriate institutions of the host country (recruitment of teachers, support of language teaching, lecture series, arts performances), basic information resources.
- support of local institutions, friendly societies and schools.
- use of surrogates and agents.

In many countries there is a thriving nexus of friendly societies. For the cultural agency they can be an economical way of meeting local interest, and they have a surrogate value when, for whatever reason, the country concerned does not maintain a cultural representation. This was the case with the British Council in the three years of its existence before 1938, when its first representation was opened, in Egypt. It used some of its then miniscule budget to foster such societies:

During the first half of 1937 . . . the Council was able to widen and strengthen its work. By now it was giving help to a large number of existing Anglophil societies. While the Council had no representatives of its own overseas, these little groups of enthusiasts for Britain, scattered in all sorts of places from big cities like Buenos Aires to the small Baltic towns like Tartu, were the only network of influence and operational activity (apart of course from Embassies and Consulates) available to the Council. Their officers and members were desperately keen for every sign of interest and support from Britain. In their turn they provided platforms and premises for English language classes, visiting lecturers, libraries, book exhibitions, and so forth. The principal areas in which they were found were Scandinavia, the Baltic States, the Balkans and Latin America. Support to these societies played a major part in the Council's programme, particularly in its earliest days; and it was now able to assist the foundation of new bodies, including the Anglo-Egyptian Union at Cairo, the 'Culturas' at Rio, Sao Paulo, Santiago and Lima, and the Sino-British Cultural Association at Nanking. (White, 1965, pp. 14–15)

We have already seen how France and Italy have developed their own networks of friendly societies, the Alliance Française and the Dante Alighieri Society. Each branch has its own local committee of management but also the benefit of central inspiration, co-ordination and support. Alumni societies for those who have studied at universities in the sending country are essentially an American invention, though they figure under various titles in the programmes of many countries; they can be important instruments for follow-up, a subject which receives more consideration in Chapter 15.

One final general issue, which must determine not only the activities but also the geographical distribution of a cultural agency, is whether it is its policy to concentrate on those countries where receptivity is particularly favourable or to embrace other countries, where conditions are adverse but there may be political or economic imperatives. Beloff (1965, p. 480) uses this image, 'the question of whether one should row with or against the tide is one of the hardest to answer; but the responsibility clearly lies with the policy-making departments . . .' There is little predictability about the shifting of power and influence in the modern world (e.g. the emergence of OPEC countries as arbiters in international affairs after 1973). A country that has traditionally been on the periphery can quite suddenly become the focus of world attention or the fulcrum of great power conflict. If it is part of a country's foreign policy to have friends in sensitive areas abroad, then its cultural presence also has to be planned with this in mind.

It has been said more than once that cultural relations work is long term. It cannot be used with much success as a fire brigade to put out unforeseen conflagrations. An object lesson is contained in the memorandum dated 2 June 1943, from R. T. D. Ledward to Tunnard Moore of the British Council, on British cultural policy in Japan. He wrote:

British cultural policy in Japan prior to December 8th, 1941, may be said to have consisted in a heroic last minute rearguard action . . . against a carefully prepared and skilfully delivered attack. Whereas the foundations of the German cultural institutions in Japan were laid during the immediate post-war years, when Germany was in Japanese eyes politically insignificant yet culturally acceptable, it appears to have been only in the late 1930s that any British cultural policy vis a vis the Japanese was ever seriously considered, and only after the outbreak of war in Europe that it was actively put into effect . . . Our sudden conversion to the idea that cultural interchange might serve a useful purpose at all made it lamentably easy for malicious tongues and pens to attribute our cultural activities in Japan to propagandist motives. (British Council, 1943b)

A cultural agency, whether manifested as an institute or an office, has three basic and irreducible activities in those countries where it is represented:

- Presence
- Information
- Exchange of persons

Presence is more than a self-evident fact. It implies such activities as control of policy, management of programmes, public appearance, cultivating members of target groups, and advising the diplomatic mission. The cultural representative is therefore a resource, perhaps the major resource, especially in posts with small budgets.

Information means dealing with enquiries about the sending country and its institutions (not the projection of a country's image and culture such as the mode of cultural relations that was considered in Chpater 7, p. 58). Information work will be handled in more detail later in the present chapter.

Exchange of persons is an obvious basic requirement, for if cultural relations are conducted through people, there must exist the means of bringing together those who are in key positions.

Wherever there is a cultural representation, there will be those three basic activities. To whatever extent is possible, they may also be practised by surrogacy in countries where there is no resident representative. Other additional activities, depending on local opportunity and on finance, will vary from country to country out of a selection from language-teaching, library and books work, co-operation in science and education, presentation of the arts, and communication with professional elites through exchange programmes, lectures, seminars and the media. The scale of activities is best determined by representatives within the policy and budgetary framework agreed between them and their headquarters. The general experience is that maximum delegation of responsibility by headquarters will conduce to the best results in the field. At the same time, continuity is important; policy changes need to be controlled by headquarters so that there is not a sequence of arbitrary shifts introduced by successive representatives eager to make their mark. The danger of operating without policy guidance and a dialogue with headquarters is explicit in quotations from two French cultural counsellors (Grémion and Chenal, 1980, p. 43 and p. 42):

There is absolutely no policy; if there is one, it is we who make it and it is we who propose it.

If by policy you mean a thought-out, explicit action with its means of realization, I am not sure I notice any. I see rather several levels of bureaucratic inertia which are translated into policy, or rather a policy at the level of control, and difficulties in translating these into administrative facts.

Let it be said that any student of cultural relations has reason to be grateful for the research enshrined in the book, *Une culture tamisée*, from which these quotations are taken, and for the frankness with which reactions are expressed. Voices in the same vein have been, and probably still are, audible in other cultural services, but without the benefaction of public print.

Information as an Activity

Of the two basic activities, information and exchange of persons, it is difficult to bestow primacy on one rather than the other. Information may not produce spectacular success, but it is the bread and butter of cultural relations. Various institutions and individuals – from cabinet ministers to students – turn to cultural agencies for information about their countries. A representation, therefore, needs as a minimum a collection of reference books, including annual handbooks, and hand-out material to satisfy enquiries. Support services from head-quarters should be on tap to meet those demands for information that exceed the competence of representatives in the field. It is the normal practice to provide such information without charge, except where it is agreed that research costs should be reimbursed or when access to an electronic database is requested.

Evidence of being up to date is crucial. It is important to have the most recent newspapers and journals at the cost of receiving them by air rather than by surface mail. Too often, still, one finds a cultural representation caught, as it were, in a time warp, with out-of-date posters and with periodicals that have long been overtaken by the events they record. This is bad not only for the efficiency of the service provided but also for the agency's image.

In representations that run a library, the information work will be located there, desirably under professional direction. Quite often the best and certainly the most economical way to satisfy an enquiry will be to lend a book. Enright (1969) repeats the spoof that appeared in *Punch*:

> a most remarkable piece of equipment, a new aid to rapid learning, which I read about several years ago. This apparatus has no electric circuit to go wrong, it is easy to handle (even a child can use it) and is readily portable. It is known as BUILT-IN ORDERLY ORGANIZED KNOWLEDGE, and in the modern fashion its makers call it by its initials – B-O-O-K. (Enright, 1969, p. 211)

Maheu (1966) compares the book with audio-visual media and comes to the conclusion that:

> The book on the other hand is pre-eminently the working tool for the individual, the source of information which is always and everywhere available, the faithful companion of the personal quest through the collective treasures of knowledge and wisdom which past generations have bequeathed to us. (Maheu, 1966, p. 22)

Hans Arnold, who was at the time head of the Cultural Department of the foreign ministry in Bonn, wrote in the lead article of a number of the *Zeitschrift für Kulturaustausch* devoted to the book in external cultural policy:

> The book is not only the oldest means of communication for international cultural relations; it has also sustained its role as a significant international mediator and especially as a means of promoting one's language abroad, and this at a time when it has received other powerful media as competitors and been partly overshadowed by them. (Arnold, 1976, p. 3)

The book does indeed promote the language in which it is written. The existence of a rich literature is a positive factor for the currency of a language. While the main attraction of a language for the learner is its utility, often as a second language for international use, another is the standing accorded the language on account of the culture it expresses. This means that a library is something of a display of cultural credentials, a show-place of intellectual and artistic achievement.

Libraries with collections of books and audio-visual materials for reference and for borrowing are an important part of the profile of cultural representations that possess them. In societies that respect books and learning, libraries convey a favourable image not only to those who use them, but also to those who simply know that they exist. Cultural representations benefit in their total operations and in their local status if they are seen to offer this benefit.

The British Council received praise for its library work even in the 1950s, before it had won itself an established reputation. A letter in *The Times* of 29 May 1952, admittedly from the President of the Library Association, argued against the cuts then being imposed on the Council:

> Critics of the British Council should understand that today 'trade follows books'. Its direction is largely determined by whence these books come. For example, the engineer or the doctor whose

professional education is based on British books is most likely to favour British methods, apparatus and materials.

The Manchester Guardian wrote on 25 October 1952, 'The Council does no more valuable service than to make available to the foreign reader a good selection of the wealth of British writing'. And *The Sunday Times* on 1 March 1959, 'Books will be the main weapons in Britain's latest drive to win the "Battle for the Mind" in the emerging countries in Africa, Asia and the Middle East'.

French criticisms of some of their institute libraries in Europe illustrate the need for sound policies in the management of what is, in materials, personnel and floor space, often the most expensive single part of a cultural representation. To quote again from Grémion and Chenal (1980, pp. 72–3):

> The libraries actually attract the French colony, very fond of novels; a few Francophiles also come in search of novels or to flip through magazines.
>
> Apart from some brilliant exceptions, the libraries do not generally constitute the most engaging sector of institutes. Somewhat disused in appearance, dependent on a very bureaucratized system of central management, they are as a rule little integrated in the totality of the institute and the other activities. They only marginally come into the debate on the development of the documentation function.

Beloff (1965, p. 486) considered the premises and the impression they make: 'It is no good sending abroad highly talented cultural representatives or well-selected libraries and hiding them away up flights of stairs in dingy and uglily-furnished buildings.' Libraries need to be well-appointed in addition to being well-stocked for their purpose. Inevitably, there is an association in the mind of the observer between the quality of the services and the manner in which they are presented.

The library, because of its costs, is part of a cultural representation much in need of well-formulated policies, and yet it is difficult to apply these consistently. The essence of aiming one's activities at target groups is concentration. But in the usage of libraries there is a high element of self-selection: those who come to seek information or borrow books or other materials may be moved by the need to know, the desire for enjoyment, curiosity, or other motives that have not been deliberately stimulated by the cultural representation. How does one channel one's resources in the desired direction; how does one at least discourage casual expatriates 'very fond of novels'?

The simple answer is – by tailoring the bookstock to target groups.

If one decides it should be the policy in a particular country to concentrate on the applied sciences, for instance, because that is what the government and institutions demand, then the librarian builds up his collection of texts and audio-visual materials in this subject and gives other books away to local libraries; the expatriate and irrelevant readership then withers away, probably under protest. The difficulty is that this degree of concentration can be self-defeating. In any case, there will be a need for a representative collection of reference books, and even the most streamlined library will find it hard to deny the claims of the major classics of national literature and national studies (*Landeskunde*, as the Germans say). Once the door is open to literature, it is difficult to draw the line at the classics or serious fiction; surely, there is a strong case for including more popular novels as an encouragement to those who are learning the language and seek lighter reading matter; it might indeed be argued that Erle Stanley Gardiner, Georges Simenon and Agatha Christie are literary phenomena of our time. Moreover, is it not likely that, among those who are self-motivated to use the library in order to satisfy their various interests, there will be several people who will be, or become, prominent in their own professions and therefore potential mediators between cultures? Should the library not be designed to attract them?

When USIA introduced a policy of drastically reducing library bookstocks to a few restricted subject areas and building up periodicals holdings instead, in order to be able to purvey the latest information and opinion to target groups, it found that this resulted in a loss of visibility and profile. USIA did a reappraisal, and decided it wanted to appeal not only to decision-makers but also to the successor generation and a self-selecting audience in its 130 libraries. When the British Council in India remodelled its Indian library operation in order to focus on developmental subject areas, it encountered criticism from influential Indians that their legitimate preference for English literature was being disregarded. The policy was accordingly modified.

Common experience suggests that a cultural representation will be best advised to pursue positive but balanced policies in its information and library work. Reference and national studies materials are basic. To them are added other subjects in a series of optional areas. The selection is determined by careful analysis of the opinions of target groups and of the local scene. It will heighten the effectiveness of the library if its resources are integrated in those of the host country, for instance, by inclusion in the union catalogue. The size and nature of the library will be factors in the decision whether there should also be a more popular appeal (e.g. light fiction and children's literature).

In spite of the virtues of the library, it does not follow that a cultural representation without a library cannot perform noteworthy services on behalf of the book. As we have seen, the library is normally a feature of the institute model. The office, on the other hand, is unlikely to have either the need or the space for a library; if the office is in an embassy there would in any case be problems of access and security. Even in representations where a library would be possible and desirable, it may be decided, in the formulation of policy with headquarters, that it should be renounced. Typical reasons might be: expense (other activities having higher priority), availability of books in the local library system, control of public access by the authorities – or of course that the local population is not given to reading.

Book Presentation

There are other ways of getting books into the hands of target groups. One is by donation or presentation. If carefully chosen books are presented to educational libraries, as frequently happens with the help of aid money, they will be read by large numbers of students at no administrative cost to the cultural representation. Presentation may well be cheaper than lending. The cost of a textbook with discount will average, let us say, £10. The cost of issuing a book once, calculated as a statistical fraction of the library's total costs with overheads, will vary from country to country on a scale from say £10 to 30 pence. This range from a high-cost West European country to a low-cost developing one is due not only to the difference in running expenses but also to the difference in the size of membership and number of loans.

Having a library or a book presentation programme are not, of course, mutually exclusive alternatives. A representation may maintain a library to serve one set of target groups in the capital city and present books to colleges in the provinces to serve other target groups. Granted, there may not be the same degree of kudos in presenting books as there is lending them from one's own library, but presentation is not a once-for-all act of munificence. It can be a major step in a relationship of mutual interest, which begins with a joint analysis of requirements, meets a specific need, acts as a spur to other activity, attracts publicity, and leads to further co-operation over book needs and perhaps to subsequent presentations in order to update or refurbish the stock.

The donation of books on cultural subjects is a practice of many governments and embassies: anyone on the international circuit will have amassed a collection of illustrated volumes. This is another indication of the way the book is a prestige object embodying cultural values. An example of a country which has a carefully worked-out programme of book presentation is Japan. Japan has obvious difficulties in using its own language as the vehicle for its messages. The Japan Foundation publishes books in English to introduce its culture to other countries, periodicals in both Japanese and English (the *Japan Foundation Newsletter*, for instance) and presents books to libraries and universities according to a programme in two phases:

> Institutions with well-developed Japanese studies programs may apply for donations of books, mainly in Japanese, of their own choice; institutions with programs at relatively early stages of development may receive basic sets of books in other languages, primarily in English, dealing with Japan in ten categories; reference and general works, geography, history, political science and law, economics and business, education, philosophy and religion, literature and language, arts and sociology. (Japan Foundation, 1983, p. 32)

The expense of running libraries can be offset by membership fees, but even then it will remain a major item in any agency's budget. For instance, in its budget for the financial year 1983/84, the British Council calculates a total of £11 million (11.5 per cent of the total budget) on information and books, of which £7.5 million was for 110 libraries. If an agency has extensive operations in the Third World, book presentation is likely to be a major item of expenditure. Again, to quote the example of the British Council, the expenditure in 1983/84 under the Book Presentation Programme alone, which is financed by the British Aid Programme, was £1,350,000.

The sums of money spent on libraries and book presentations in a country's external cultural policy should be seen in relation to the total value of the books that country exports through commercial channels. The purchase of books by individuals and libraries may be assumed to be the most effective way of all to get a particular work into the right hands ('a book bought is a book read' – would it were true!). It also serves the trading interests of the sending country, and reflects credit on those who have assisted the sale. Cultural agencies, therefore, have every reason to help sell their country's books abroad. The British Council, since its inception, has received strong support from the publishers. One-third of the £1,000 million that is the annual value of the British book trade consists of exports.

Book Promotion

The most obvious activity in book promotion is the exhibition. This not only promotes the sale of books but also, in itself, contributes towards the knowledge and appreciation of the sending country's standards of authorship and book production. It is a cultural activity that may be compared, from that point of view, with any other kind of exhibition. The book is a primary tool of cultural policy. A collection of recent publications is a display of creativeness, scholarship and design, qualities that are intrinsic to cultural relations. Book exhibitions are also signposts to greater individual understanding and appreciation. In size, exhibitions range from a stand at an international book fair (Frankfurt, Belgrade, Bahrain, Delhi, Cairo, Moscow, etc.) to a specialized collection of books touring university departments. How far the sale of books is directly promoted through exhibitions has been much debated. Normally, cultural agencies do not sell the books themselves but refer would-be customers to local book shops. The mechanics of the local book trade may then frustrate good intentions. If it is one of the objectives to induce visitors to order books, then it is important to have staff in attendance at exhibitions who can deal with enquiries and provide bibliographical information. Nowadays, it is normal practice to include a visual element, whether in the form of photographs (e.g. of authors), a tape-slide sequence, or a video. This has an eye-catching effect, but the fundamental necessities are that the books should be displayed so that they can be conveniently examined, and that the exhibition should be adequately serviced by people with professional skills.

There are various other devices for promoting the sale of books. The library itself can play a part by periodic displays (e.g. prize-winning books, anniversaries, etc.) and simply by providing a well-appointed collection of books administered by trained staff. If the library is a true showpiece, an exemplar for local librarians, it will create a reputation beneficial for book exports.

Co-operation with local booksellers is advisable. For them, the existence of a foreign library and book exhibitions are major factors in their business. Various activities that help promote the sale of books (e.g. reviews of new publications, dissemination of book lists, lectures by authors) will be of obvious interest to the local book trade. A lecture by a visiting author is enhanced in effect if local bookshops carry his or her photograph and a selection of the author's works in the window.

Both France and Britain produce periodicals with short reviews of new publications. The French periodical, *Bulletin critique du livre français*, is issued monthly; a selection in English, *New French Books*, has been published quarterly since 1983. Both editions appear under the auspices of the Directorate-General for Cultural, Scientific and Technical Relations of the foreign ministry. The British Council publishes *British Book News* monthly, which includes a section on forthcoming books, and also issues a quarterly supplement *Children's Books*. Some countries with book promotion programmes include notices of new publications in other materials they disseminate.

Low-Priced Textbooks

The provision of cheap textbooks for students in the developing world is obviously important. Few if any developing countries have been able to keep pace with the demand for textbooks accompanying the education explosion. Books from the Soviet Union in English and vernacular languages are to be found in some parts of the world at practically give-away prices: it is estimated that since 1980 the Soviet Union has spent £87 million on subsidizing these cheap editions. Some of them are straight textbooks, others have a propaganda content. China has a lesser involvement in the same kind of enterprise. The British aid programme provides more than £1 million a year (£1.2 million, 1985/86) towards the cost of a low-priced textbook scheme called the English Language Book Society, which enables students, predominantly in the Commonwealth, to buy textbooks at between one-third and one-half of the selling price in Britain. Since it started in 1960, some 30 million volumes have been issued in the special paperback edition under the ELBS imprint. There are currently almost 600 titles. This scheme has been enthusiastically supported by the Publishers Association in Britain. One of its not inconsiderable side-effects is to reduce the temptation to bring out cheap pirated editions by offset printing, which is an alarmingly flourishing industry operated from certain notorious centres.

The USIA operates a programme of indirect subsidy by supporting the publication of American books in translation. These are published in Arabic, French, Spanish and Chinese, principally, but also in other languages. The programme started in 1950 and reached the 10 million mark in some of the top production years of the 1960s. In 1982 it had declined to just over half a million. Part of the reason for the reduction is that USIA has devoted more of its books effort to the needs of the Third World and less to its earlier, more political, purpose of projection. But, more recently, USIA has devoted more generous sums to translation and to book promotion. The primary aim remains to win the battle for men's minds rather than to support the book trade.

The increased transfer of knowledge through formal education is one of the most strking phenomena of the second half of the twentieth century. The expansion of education in the Third World has created a demand that is far from being met, in spite of the massive resources devoted to it by governments and multilateral and bilateral aid programmes. Some 40 per cent of the world population are illiterate. Maheu wrote (1966, p. 101), 'At the time when science is opening up the way to the stars, it is unacceptable that two-fifths of humanity remain prisoners of ancestral darkness'. The number of Third World students in higher education increased two and a half times between 1960 and 1970. It has become a common view among aid donors that higher education has received more than its due share of the budget. This proposition can be debated from various points of view. What is certain is that, in higher education particularly, the South looks to the North. Since developed countries are responsible for some 84 per cent of the world's book production, there is a particular need for transfer in this form. The curricula of many Third World colleges are based on those of the developed fraction of the globe and are still dependent on foreign textbooks for the functioning of their system. The flow of books *to* the developing world accompanies the flow of students *from* the developing world, which will be considered in the next chapter. This two-way movement places a heavy obligation on developed countries. An active books programme, with special

Table 14.1   Correlation of Book Publishing and Populations

	Number of titles published 1981	Population 1981 (in thousands)
UK	42,972	55,954 (1980)
USA	76,976	229,805
France	37,308	53,963
Federal Republic of Germany	56,568	61,666
Italy	13,457	57,197
Japan	42,217	117,645
China	22,920	1,007,755
India	11,562	676,218
Indonesia	1,836	150,520
Mexico	2,954	71,193
Nigeria	2,316	79,680 (1980)

Source UNESCO, Statistical Yearbook, 1983: book production, Table 7.4; population, Table 1.1.

emphasis on developmental needs and including libraries, presentations and the subsidization of low-priced textbooks, is the most comprehensive way of discharging this obligation. The point can be illustrated by a comparison of book production and population in the United Kingdom, the analogues and selected developing countries (see Table 14.1).

15

Exchange of Persons

The Foreword suggested that improved cultural relations might have lessened the strains in the Anglo-Egyptian relationship, and it has been said that this aspect of the relationship was neglected from 1882, when Britain assumed power in Egypt, to the run-up to the Second World War. Admittedly, no one can be sure that, as a result, more sympathetic human attitudes would have guided the actions of politicians; however, it is the major thesis of this book that relations between countries in the modern world rest upon a diversity of contacts, and that by the involvement of influential elements in the population one can secure a basis for understanding that puts politics in a positive context, just as the propagation of false stereotypes puts them in a negative context. Indeed, so far as the Suez Crisis of 1956 was concerned, as the nadir of Anglo-Egyptian relations, one of its most unforgivable features was that politicians themselves were constrained by stereotyped perceptions.

The influential elements in the population are the material through which cultural relations principally work. Hence a major feature of external cultural policy is the exchange of persons. With a final reference to Suez, one might quote Michael Adams (1958), who was the Egypt correspondent of *The Manchester Guardian* at the time:

> Instead of princes and sheikhs whose wealth and rigid conservatism set them apart from their peoples, we should be in touch with rising middle classes, the Socialists, the intelligentsia, the radical would-be politicians, the Western-trained economists and technicians, who tend to become, for lack of opportunities in the economic or political life of their own countries, either cynical businessmen or else the angry young men of the Arab world. (Adams, 1958, p. 217)

The exchange of persons is an inelegant expression (with the no better alternative of 'interchange of persons'), which covers a wide range of activity from the individually tailored programme for senior visitors to group programmes for young people. It embraces training and education. The word 'exchange' should be taken to imply movement in both directions rather than reciprocity; strictly speaking, Lilliput's exchanges with Laputa will involve sending Lilliputians and receiving Laputans, regardless of whether, or to what degree, Laputa itself does likewise. Normally, of course, both sides are active in the business, though not necessarily on equal terms: in the aid relationship, the discrepancy of provision is most marked. What compounds the semantic confusion, however, is that an 'exchange scheme' as such, whether of persons or periodicals or whatever, *is* reciprocal. Nevertheless, it is convenient to have a term that covers inward (from abroad to home) and outward (from home to abroad) flows of people. 'Exchange of persons' will be used without further apology; if it requires additional respectability, let it be derived from the fact that the term is enshrined in Article 4 of the European Cultural Convention of 1954.

Exchange of persons ranks with presence and information in the trinity of basic cultural relations activities. Normally, indeed, it will be one of the major activities in any country's programme of cultural relations. Inward flow exceeds outward flow in 'exporting' countries, which are donors in the transfer of experience, and vice versa in 'importing' countries, which are preponderantly on the receiving end. For instance, the British Council spends 22 per cent of its budget on inward flow and 10 per cent on outward flow, Japan 14 per cent and 9.5 per cent, Italy 4.6 per cent and 3.6 per cent. The reason for this emphasis is, of course, that the transfer can best be accomplished in the educational and other institutions of the providing country. The transfer of experience comprises more than a particular skill: it carries with it attitudes, and the appreciation, perhaps adoption, of values.

The balance between inward and outward provides paradigms that can be plotted on the Mutuality Table in Chapter 9 (p. 83). The field B2, 'Mutuality based on co-operation and exchange', is to be preferred, for this as for other activities. Mutuality in the exchange of persons suggests that in a bilateral relationship the official agencies of the two countries will, in accordance with their respective resources, support the traffic between their institutions. In that case, exchange of persons is in the full sense 'exchange'.

When we talk of influential elements in the population (or elites, which are professional groupings of such elements), we have in mind those people who, by virtue of their present achievement or potential, seem most likely to be able to mediate constructively between the two countries. Clearly they should be selected for their personal qualities as well as for their professional standing or scholastic ability. USIA's score card (1983) must be unequalled:

Participants in the program are established or potential foreign leaders in government, politics, media, education, science, labor relations, and other key fields. They are selected by USIA and United States embassies overseas to visit the United States to meet and confer with their colleagues and to have in-depth exposure to this country, its culture and people. Over the years, hundreds of former International Visitors have risen to important positions in their countries. As of September 1983, 44 current heads-of-state and 495 cabinet level ministers round the world have participated in educational and cultural exchange programs sponsored by USIA. (USIA, 1983)

As we have seen, USIA is an official information agency, which also handles educational and cultural exchanges. This double status is reflected in the statistics above. Strictly, cultural agencies do not normally deal in politicians as such, though ministers (of culture and education, for instance) will be included in their programmes, and those who have benefited under them may in time become leading politicians. But the USIA tally is impressive for all that.

A different perspective opens up when we consider the subsequent careers of those who have pursued part of their studies in another country. Whether they are being paid for by their parents or government or by some other agency, or whether they are selected and financed by the country of study, their initial purpose is to further their education, rather than their career. Many of them, however, achieve eminence in politics, especially in developing countries. The Director-General of the British Council included the following statistics in an address at Newcastle:

Thirty-six per cent of the world's heads of government received part or all of their education in countries other than their own. By far the greatest number of these – more than a third – came to Britain. To put it another way 24 overseas countries have leaders who were educated in Britain or one in eight of every leader throughout the world ($12\frac{1}{2}$%). France comes second with 14 heads of government or state representing 7% of all world leaders, the USA is just behind with 6% and the USSR fourth with 2%. (Burgh, 1984, p. 2)

There is, of course, a certain imperial legacy implicit in these statistics. Williams (1982) points out the resultant obligation:

Empire, though more or less defunct, leaves a special legacy of obligations for Britain. Apart from ties of tradition and sentiment many small Commonwealth countries have meshed their education systems in with that of Britain, relying on the UK for specialist provision of education and training that could not be provided economically at home. For some of these countries self-sufficiency may be a matter of time, while for others it may never come. They will inevitably continue to look to Britain for many of their requirements and any British policy must take account of their special needs. (Williams, 1982, p. 5)

Foreign Students

The steady rise of people studying abroad has been a remarkable phenomenon of recent decades. It reflects the exploding demands for education and training in the developing world and also the general increase in student mobility due to easier money and cheaper, more rapid transport. It is reckoned that today there are about one million foreign students in the world, 91 per cent of whom go to developed countries. This annual scholastic migration is a prime factor in the diffusion of knowledge and the transfer of experience. It is not in every respect an efficient means of diffusion. As Brandt points out in writing about the brain drain (1980, p. 109), 'In the early 1960s and 1970s well over 400,000 physicians and surgeons, engineers, scientists and other skilled people have moved from developing countries to more developed ones'. And further (p. 110), 'The brain drain has occurred in part because many students and professionals trained in developing countries have chosen not to return home'. The idea of a 'drain' has emotive connotations of native vigour being sapped. In fact, people have always sought to find the best buyer for their skills on the market, and that has now become a world market. With the rise in unemployment in developed countries it has become very much their interest, as well as that of the developing world, that tighter controls should be exercised to ensure the return of students to the benefit of their own society. As Goodwin and Nacht (1983, p. 41) remark, 'If significant numbers of foreign students remain in the United States and if some of those who return home have acquired training too sophisticated for their more primitive economies, the net effect . . . may be more "brain drain than brain gain" '.

Developed countries finance programmes of training and visits, which redound to their credit in meeting an obligation and to their good by imprinting a favourable disposition on the beneficiaries. This was considered in Chapter 2 (see p. 20), where the burden of proof was left somewhat suspended. Among the now heads of government who have been invited to the United States, at a more senior level, under the International Visitor Program was Mrs Margaret Thatcher, in 1963. It would be a bold and unsubstantiated presumption that Mrs Thatcher's agreement as British Prime Minister with many of President Reagan's policies shows the effects of her exposure to the American scene, in a different political configuration, more than twenty years ago. Yet no one could deny it may have played a part. The disposition in favour of their country of education on the part of those who have spent a prolonged period at one of its schools or colleges ought logically to be considerable. It would clinch the argument if we could point to influential elites who, after their return home, promoted the political and economic interests of their country of education, but this is not clearly in evidence. Indeed, there are striking examples of the opposite. For instance, we could quote the anti-American attitudes prevalent in Iran following the revolution of 1978, in spite of the very large number of Iranians who had studied in the United States in the 1970s (still topping the list in 1979–80 with 53,310 students, or 18.6 per cent of the US foreign student population). Such examples do not disprove the thesis, but they remove any notion of automatic return in political and economic terms.

Familiarity breeds the right to be critical. Foreign students usually find some fault with their host country of education and by so doing they help to maintain their own sense of identity in a status of tutelage. On their return home, their feelings of indebtedness may be overlaid by resentment at the discrepancy between conditions at home and those they knew during their studies abroad. The benefits from study abroad should be sought not so much in minds won over as in the strengthening of academic disciplines and of links between institutions, the increase of enlightenment, the diffusion of skill and expertise, and the promotion of understanding.

The country of education undoubtedly has a certain claim on returned students' gratitude and regard, but it would be mistaken to assume that foreign students always form a better impression of their country of study than they had before. Those who take up awards in communist countries are often desperate to quit before the completion of their studies. And even in Japan, which we might suppose to be a Mecca for people from less advanced Asian countries, experience is by no means always positive. The following quotation draws upon research conducted on students in Japan from other parts of Asia and published in a book with the title *Fat Japanese*:

> out of seventy-one foreign students twenty-five students answered that their image of the Japanese has changed for 'good'. But eleven students answered for 'bad', twenty answered 'no change' and 'no answer' students accounted for fifteen. (Ayabe, 1977, p. 179)

Foreign students may well be victims of culture shock, both on arrival at their place of study and on their return home. They get a double dose, and their recovery on both occasions depends on their own personal qualities most of all. Moore (1985, pp. 109–10) describes three kinds of reaction on the part of Third World students to First World conditions. They either strive to achieve assimilation, at least in outward behaviour, so that they appear like First Worlders; or they 'retreat into their own cultural cocoons and assume that their salvation lies in avoiding all corrupting contact with the host society except in matters purely academic', or, the third and best possibility, they react with 'a critical curiosity about the host culture in which the students acquire some of its norms to conduct a dialogue with it'.

It is perhaps because benefits to countries providing the education cannot be directly measured in political terms that the whole traffic has not become more internationally competitive. Also, the education explosion has meant that there has been an adequate supply of students for all countries in the business. Nevertheless, it is remarkable that there is not more open competition for those students of highest intellectual promise who might be expected to be the greatest asset on the completion of their training. To some extent this is precluded by language. But, just as within countries providing the education (e.g. the United States and Britain) universities have come to vie with one another in their attractions for foreign students, so one can imagine that international competition may become more intense when more . developing countries have evolved their indigenous higher education systems and foreign study is more confined to postgraduates who have survived several stages of selection as a result of outstanding ability. It might then become more evident that such people constitute for the country and institution receiving them not only an investment for future relations but also an input of brain power and innovation.

Where international competition already exists it tends to reflect the East–West divide. Inadequate research has been carried out in the West on the consequences of education of foreign students in the Soviet bloc; reports suggest a high degree of direct or indirect political indoctrination. One remembers Barghoorn's assertion (1960, p. 11), 'Central to Communist cultural diplomacy is the systematic utilization of information, artistic, scientific and other cultural materials, symbols and personnel, and ideas as instruments of foreign policy'. What is certain is that at a time when several of the world's democracies have been limiting their intake of foreign students, the Soviet Union has been dramatically increasing its number of study awards. The report of the US Committee on Foreign Students and Institutional Policy (Berendzen, 1982, p. 23) tells us, 'the Soviet Union rarely shares information on its foreign students with

UNESCO or any other international agency. Thus, figures on actual enrolments are fragmentary, educated guesses made by outsiders. An informal estimate is that, in 1980, there were 80,000 foreign students in Russia. Second, the process whereby a student gets to the Soviet Union is an enigma'. The UNESCO *Statistical Yearbook* for 1981 shows a Soviet growth in foreign student numbers from 27,918 in 1970 to 62,942 in 1978 (125.5 per cent), while the United States increased from 144,708 to 263,900 (82.4 per cent) over the same period. The 1970s were a time of general expansion. The highest rate of increase was France's (213.9 per cent). During the 1980s, when the numbers of foreign students at institutions of some Western democracies declined, the Soviet Union appears to have established an easy lead in the scale of its study awards. *The Times Higher Education Supplement* of 8 March 1985 reported that the United States was to 'increase by 50 per cent to 15,000 the number of scholarships offered to students from third world countries'. The administrator of the Agency for International Development in announcing the increase said it 'was a bid to catch up with Communist bloc countries in training the youth of the developing world'. He stated of the Soviets:

> They are taking full advantage of these scholarships to shape young minds and increase their influence in the developing world. These young people are returning to their countries not only with new skills, but new ideologies as well ... America has some way to catch up, in spite of the latest increase. Its overseas scholarship programme declined by 52 per cent in the decade 1972–82, while Soviet bloc programmes, not including Cuba, tripled. In 1982, seven Communist scholarships were granted for every one of the 8,000 offered by the United States (THES, 8 March, 1985).

Ever since it began to think in Cold War terms, the United States has seen the education of students from other countries 'as an essential element in the worldwide ideological struggle against Communism, especially the totalitarian system of the Soviet Union' (Jenkins, 1983a, p. 310). Writing about Third World students in the Soviet Union, Berendzen (1982, pp. 23–4) says, 'The current annual rate of increase is now in the order of 20 per cent, the highest rate among the major host countries'. Nevertheless, one should not forget the numbers of foreign students at American colleges (98 per cent of their total) whose expenses are met by their own families or sponsoring authorities, and the sheer preponderance of American institutions internationally.

The data reveal that 31% of all foreign students reported by Unesco in 1978 were in the United States, more than twice the share in the next largest country, France. Despite large numbers, foreign students were only 2.3% of the US student population, a much lower proportion than in France (10.6%), the United Kingdom (7.8%), and most other major countries. (Boyan, 1984, p. iii)

It would appear that the Soviet government and its East European partners have followed a consistent policy, in recognition of the likelihood that by opening their educational institutions to students from other countries they were securing an advantage for their own interests. This clarity of perception has not been apparent in all countries. Some of the major centres of foreign student education have passed through a phase of ambivalence. Although in principle acknowledging their obligation to welcome students from other countries, especially from those countries less well endowed with educational facilities, and recognizing the need to maintain their own institutions of higher education as international communities, the authorities have reacted to economic, demographic and social pressures by making it more difficult for foreign students to study at their universities and colleges. This has unleashed a debate that has produced some significant literature.

The title of the report of the International Institute of Education *Absence of Decision* (Goodwin and Nacht, 1983) is in itself indicative. Written in 1983 when there were some 325,000 foreign students in the United States, this work continued the analysis of the *Foreign Students and Institutional Policy* report (Berendzen, 1982), which has been quoted above. The latter report had found:

Although the education of many thousands of foreign scholars, scientists, professionals, and other potential leaders clearly engages vital national interests, a national philosophy or policy on foreign students scarcely exists. Policy is left to be deduced from scattered references in federal exchange program legislation (for example, that governing the Fulbright program), which declare student exchanges to be of national importance, and in the generally facultative policies of the Immigration and Naturalization Service. (Berendzen, 1982, p. 3)

The report stated later (p. 5) 'the Committee also found that foreign students are all too often an unrealized, underutilized, and unintegrated resource for relieving the startling lack of knowledge among domestic students about international matters'.

Absence of Decision comes to the memorable conclusion:

One of the principal assumptions underlying this study was that there was no national policy concerning foreign students. Rather, the aggregate condition reflected thousands of decisions made by many individuals in colleges and universities across the country. In fact, we found the actual scene masked more by an absence of decision than by any distinctive pattern of decision making within or across institutions. In the course of our interviews we were told that the number of foreign students found on a particular college campus was the consequence of 'cumulative incrementalism', 'ad hocism', 'designed ambiguity', 'the virtues of non-policy', the philosophy that 'long-range planning is where you are now', the judgement that 'our greatest reason for our present condition is independent of reason', a process that is 'just sort of going on', 'no policy, no direction, no administration, no staff', or being caught 'with our policy pants down'. (Goodwin and Nacht, 1983, p. 21)

This chaotic picture reflects the multifariousness of the American system and its different levels of academic standard. In 1980/81, 80 per cent of their foreign students came 'from the developing world (of which almost one-half were from OPEC countries); the great majority were privately supported, and only two per cent were supported by programs of the United States government. Two-thirds of the foreign students were undergraduates' (Berendzen, 1982, p. 2). Also, the United States does not have centralized admission procedures.

Britain has traditionally ranked fourth in the Western World in numbers of foreign students, after the United States, France and Germany. Table 15.1 shows how Britain compares with the five analogues.

Table 15.1 Foreign Students in Analogues and USSR, 1970–80

Host country	1970	1975	1979	1980	% increase 1970–80
USA	144,708	179,350	286,340	311,880	215
France	34,500	93,750	112,042	110,763	331
FRG	27,769	53,560	57,421	61,841	207
UK	24,606	49,032	56,774	56,003	228
Italy	14,357	18,921	24,050	29,447	194
Japan	4,447	5,541	5,914	6,543	147
USSR	27,918	43,287	—	—	—

Note According to the UNESCO definition, a foreign student is defined as a person enrolled at an institution of higher education in a country or territory of which he or she is not a permanent resident.

Source *UNESCO Statistical Yearbook*, 1983.

Like the USA, Britain possessed no national policy on foreign students. Universities and colleges absorbed foreign students by in-fill, for the most part, that is by filling vacancies within their existing courses designed for home students. Then, in 1967, the Labour government introduced a fee differential, whereby foreign students had to pay £250 a year as against the £70 paid by home students. This increase of 257 per cent was intended to check the persistent growth of numbers. After some initial success, this regulatory policy was submerged by the continuing flood. Further increase of the differential fee level over the years, and attempts to impose numerical quotas, also failed to stem the tide. Protests at these restrictive policies were belied by the fact that foreign student numbers went up year by year; also, the government had introduced various concessions whereby students from developing countries had the fee differential made up for them out of the aid programme. This went some way towards satisfying Britain's obligations towards the Third World.

The Conservative government that was elected in 1979 made one of its first priorities the reduction of public expenditure. It reckoned that the foreign students then in Britain were being subsidized by the exchequer to the tune of £100 million per annum, that if full-cost fees were introduced this sum would be saved, and that market forces would come into operation as a permanent control mechanism. The government therefore introduced increases in foreign student fees from 1979–80, graduated by subject, up to a maximum of 400 per cent for study, such as medicine, involving laboratory expenses. The effect has been to reduce numbers by some 37 per cent from 1979–80 to 1983–84.

The government had little realization of the likely consequences. There was vehement protest from the higher education sector, informed public opinion, and in parliament. Some of the countries sending students to Britain gave vent to feelings of resentment amounting to outrage. The Eighth Commonwealth Education Conference at Colombo in August 1980 was an opportune sounding-board. Commonwealth countries felt especially aggrieved that such sweeping measures should have been brought in without consultation or even prior warning. The conference report said:

> Two factors made the matter one of Commonwealth concern: first, the value of the mobility of students (and for that matter of staff) in building up links between the citizens of Commonwealth countries and furthering cooperation between the countries themselves; and second, for developing countries the importance of access to the higher education institutions of developed countries. This was one of the most valuable forms of aid, and it was feared that its abrupt curtailment would damage the development plans of developing

countries, perhaps irretrievably. (Commonwealth Secretariat, 1980, p. 56)

The Commonwealth Standing Committee on Student Mobility was set up following this conference. *The Times Higher Education Supplement* of 29 June 1984 said of this committee's third report, 'An analysis of its [Britain's] imposition of full-cost fees shows developing countries, particularly those from the Commonwealth, continuing to be hard hit'. And of the Ninth Commonwealth Education Conference, held in Nicosia in July 1984, the *THES* of 27 July 1984 wrote, 'A succession of ministers from Africa, Asia and the Caribbean accused the Government of endangering the very existence of the Commonwealth by persisting with its policy'.

Malaysia was among the countries that protested most vigorously at the British government's charging of full-cost fees for its foreign students. This is not surprising, because Malaysia headed the list with more than 16 per cent of the total. The Malaysian government, which also had other differences of opinion with Britain, subsequently introduced a 'Buy British last' policy affecting trade (Malaysians were encouraged to 'Look East') as well as the country of overseas study. The strength of feeling was attested by the timing of this policy directive, which was announced in October 1981 when the British Minister of Trade was in Kuala Lumpur with a trade mission. The policy was rescinded eighteen months later. The inclusion of study abroad in a boycott, even if only a partial one, showed how seriously Britain's legacy of obligations was taken in a country where, of the attenuating links with the former imperial power, education still had behind it the strength of tradition and preference. What added irony to the situation was that, by the standards accepted in the world at large, it was greatly to Britain's advantage to provide the disputed facilities. Difficult though it might be to supply conclusive proof of what the *Financial Times* of 23 June 1982 called 'The steel mill theory' (that students return home and eventually repay the benefit of their education by placing handsome industrial orders), it was easy enough to see the ill effects of steely hearts. As the *Financial Times* went on to say, 'Steel mills are probably sold either on merit or on credit. Yet there are other reasons why it might be wise to encourage overseas students to come'.

A major contribution to the lively debate of these reasons was furnished by the study commissioned by the Overseas Students Trust and published in 1981, *The Overseas Student Question*, edited by Peter Williams. The report expressed the essence of the problem, 'Once the cost of educating overseas students stopped being seen as an uncalculated part of the natural order of things, and became instead a matter of cost and choice, the need for "a national policy" was with us' (Williams, 1981, p. 4). The need was defined by the report, *A Policy for Overseas Students*, published in 1982. This, like *The Overseas Student Question*, was an independent study, but it was encouraged and assisted by the government through the Foreign and Commonwealth Office. After a detailed statistical analysis of the situation, it came to the conclusion:

> Britain has numerous interests at stake in this field, with potential benefits to be realised in the areas of diplomacy and cultural relations, trade and commerce, higher education and research. Britain also has responsibilities both as a wealthy nation in a world that is largely poor and as a former colonial power, still the hub of an independent Commonwealth. It is therefore necessary for Britain to recognise and to assert the importance of encouraging overseas students to come to the UK and to adopt a positive, welcoming stance towards them. In this the departments of Government responsible for Britain's overseas relations must give the lead. (Williams, 1982, p. 135)

Following this, the government took various measures, the most important of which was to provide £46 million over a three-year period to finance 5,000 to 6,000 additional study awards a year. The solution, therefore, was not to reduce the fee differential for foreign students but to pay for a larger number of them to study in Britain, wholly or partly at British expense. This was, in effect, control by selection. Those students not benefiting under an award scheme could still come, but they had to pay the high fees. Many did, but the pattern of country representation in the foreign study body changed. What *The Times* of 27 February 1985 wrote of Imperial College, London, seems likely to apply to most British Universities:

> The (very tentative) conclusion is that there is now a much stronger representation from two types of countries – the really poor ones which get a lot of aid and those, like some of the Far East nations, which have rich sub-sections in the population. The losers are those in the middle – like India and Pakistan – neither rich nor sufficiently poor.

Another group of students that increased was that from countries of the European Community, who as a result of pressure from their governments had been granted the concession of paying the same fees in Britain as home students. While there was a 14 per cent drop from the Commonwealth 1981–82 to 1982–83 there was a rise of 4 per cent for the European Community during the same period (Department of Education and Science, 1984, p. 4).

Other countries have applied different forms of control. France, for instance, with the second largest total of foreign students after the United States, was also concerned about the cost of open access and the quality of students, as its numbers swelled to 100,000. The French government introduced centralized admission procedures with tighter quality controls. On the other hand, the Federal Republic of Germany has controlled numbers by quota and operates a 6 per cent limit for reserved (*numerus clausus*) subjects, such as medicine, which require expensive laboratory time and equipment. Both France and Germany have no tuition fees for students, whether home or foreign. Some countries have applied a mixture of financial and other regulating measures.

It is not possible to form any but a subjective assessment of the effects of the British government's policy of charging foreign students 'economic fees'. An extensive field study would be necessary to lay even the basis of any more objective conclusions. The efects are to be measured in various terms, and not the least important are those related to manpower planning, traditions and personal expectations in the countries from which thousands upon thousands of students have been prevented from coming. The drop of 37 per cent means that the numbers were down by some 32,500 in 1983–84, which is in the dimension of five to six medium-sized universities. Some students have gone instead to European countries that charge minimal fees; within the Commonwealth, there has been a boost of admissions to Canadian universities and, within the developing Commonwealth, India has established itself more firmly as a country whose academic resources are comparatively advanced and economic. The continued growth of foreign students in the United States must take account of some of those whose preference for the English language would have taken them to Britain. And some must have gone instead to universities in the communist bloc. Most commentators have concluded that the resulting loss to long-term British interests far exceeds the financial savings that have been achieved. On the other hand, the additional government finance of £46 million for targeted award schemes (plus the special funding of outstanding research students) has been a positive policy; by placing more emphasis on the regulation of admissions through funded selection, the government has both honoured an obligation to the Third World, particularly the developing Commonwealth, and refined the general intake to secure Britain's stake in the most promising minds. One could call this 'scholarship diplomacy'. But this has happened to the prejudice of general mobility. And the principle of market forces, on which the government's policy is based, favours the rich. Those who can pay the increased fees may well sport an OPEC tie.

There is another dimension, which must at least be touched upon. That is the role accorded to higher education in modern society. The way universities and colleges are regarded and funded has a direct bearing on their attractiveness for foreign students. This is another point of intersection between internal and external cultural policy. The British Government's Green Paper of 1985, *Higher Education into the 1990s*, sees higher education very much in relation to the health of the economy; it favours technological and vocational subjects and hard-nosed management. This planning document may prove a milestone in marking the point where the road widened by the Robbins Report (Committee on Higher Education, 1963) narrows in the 1990s to a tollgate of short-sighted utility. The Robbins expansion of higher education to accommodate all those who were qualified and able to benefit from it admittedly produced its excesses, but the Green Paper over-corrects. Already financial reductions of some 10 per cent have cut the universities back. If these policies are implemented, it may well be that Britain is a poor competitor for foreign students, not only because of the fee differential but also because its institutions of higher education will have shrunk into a cautious obsession with their own survival.

Administration of Programmes

The organization of exchanges, whether for students or for more senior visitors, obviously calls for a high degree of professionalism. The programming and care of such visitors are important if their stay is to achieve its effect, and if on their return home they are to be positively disposed towards the host country. Exposure to the way of life is part of the experience. Not all impressions will be favourable; not all encounters will be heart-warming. Receiving countries organize programmes in different ways. What they all have in common is a combination of centralized administration with a regional network for local arrangements, and a combination of the official and the voluntary.

By far the greatest element of voluntary contribution to the programmes of foreign visitors and students is to be found in the United States. The National Council for International Visitors (NCIV), with its headquarters in Meridian House, Washington, comprises eighty-eight community organizations, and five university centres, which all receive visitors, and thirty-nine private national agencies that send visitors up and down the United States. As the NCIV *Fact Sheet* of 15 March 1981 puts it, 'As a result, tens of thousands of influential international visitors are directly exposed to some 725,000 concerned individuals who are directly involved in our public diplomacy as citizen diplomats'. NCIV produces guidance literature for visitor and host, a monthly newsletter and reports on conferences and symposia held for training and the sharing of experience. For students, there is the National Association for Foreign Student Affairs (NAFSA), also with its headquarters in Washington, which 'represents over 1,400 academic institutions, educational associations, local citizens groups active in foreign student affairs, and courtesy associates from embassies and legations in Washington' (*NAFSA*, 1983). This organization also produces a newsletter and co-ordinates work on behalf of foreign students. Its main target is those who are professionally involved, such as the foreign student advisers in universities, but there is also a voluntary element.

Receiving countries with open societies try to integrate foreign students into their institutions. Initial orientation and some degree of continuous counselling will be necessary for many students and especially for those from very different cultures, but in the long run the best induction is through their peers. In France the *Centre national des oeuvres universitaires et scolaires*, with its provincial offshoots, provides services for both French and foreign students. In Britain, the British Council used to employ its extensive regional network for overseas student welfare services, but now that educational institutions themselves have improved their facilities for the welfare of foreign students the British Council services have been reduced. Integration in the student body has obvious advantages provided it is accompanied by the necessary degree of individual support.

One of the special needs many foreign students have is for better language proficiency. That study programmes can be frustrated by inadequate linguistic knowledge is obvious enough. This takes on a particular point when study is lecture-based. Normally, therefore, national agencies in making awards, and individual institutions in granting admission, insist on minimum standards of proficiency. These can be raised by pre-sessional training courses. Germany includes initial language training in its awards and employs the domestic centres of the Goethe Institute for the purpose.

Follow-up should be conceived as an intrinsic element in any exchange of persons programme. It is a way of maximizing the return on the investment made by all parties concerned: the visitors or students themselves, the country providing the facilities, and the institutions in both countries. Germany exceeds other countries in its provision of services to maintain contact with students and researchers on their return to their own countries. The German

Academic Exchange Service (*DAAD*) and the *Alexander von Humboldt Stiftung* are exemplary in this respect. Both devote very considerable resources to this aspect of their work, which they see as an integral part of their operations. The DAAD lists the following activities of a collective nature, which were carried out in 1983 (DAAD, 1983, p. 62):

1　issue of the *DAAD Letter*, a quarterly follow-up periodical, together with a supplement *Letter Literatur* which reports on new publications in all disciplines
2　repeat invitations for 128 foreign scholars to spend three months refreshing their knowledge and contacts
3　supplying some 600 returned award-holders with specialist periodicals and books
4　application of technical co-operation funds to requests put forward by previous award-holders for specialist support of universities in developing countries (*Sachmittelprogramm*)
5　follow-up seminars in specialist areas at which German scholars confer with groups of previous award-holders both on their own subjects and on general questions affecting universities and research.

If it is a cultural agency's policy in a particular country, with the support of the local authorities, to develop co-operation in a certain subject area, this can best be implemented with the help of the exchange of persons. It has already been remarked that the inward and outward concepts tend to be separate and that this is reflected in the structure of cultural organizations. Also, funds are often locked into discrete schemes, which dictate the manner of their administration. The more the two-way principle can be maintained, the greater the chance of being able to follow flexible policies. One outstanding case of a two-way scheme is the Fulbright program. This operates in 120 countries and awards more than 3,500 scholarships annually for Americans to study, research and teach abroad and for foreigners to do likewise in the United States. France and Germany also have a certain degree of inward and outward integration. In Italy, the Directorate-General of Cultural Relations in the foreign ministry includes traffic in both directions in its *Ufficio I*, in addition to inter-university relations and cultural conventions. The British Council makes a clear administrative distinction between inward and outward flows, but this is mitigated in practice by the existence of subject departments, which work in both directions, and by the fact that representatives abroad have the initiative in both kinds of programme and supply the necessary co-ordination between them.

There are three principal ways of measuring success in exchange of persons programmes. An individual achieves a breakthrough in his or her own field, understanding between the two countries is significantly advanced, or lasting and productive relationships between institutions are established. The first two are matters of degree outside the direct control of the agency concerned. The third, however, can be specifically promoted. Moreover, it can be largely self-financing, because the institutions will be pursuing common interests that justify expenditure of their own funds. Links of this kind may be formal, with agreements between universities or departments, or they may be informal, with personal contact and shared facilities between researchers. Most countries possess a clearing-house for such relationships. This may be an association of their universities, a section of the ministry of education or a delegated agency (e.g. *DAAD* in Germany or *NUFFIC* in the Netherlands). Higher education links are an excellent channel for technical co-operation funds in aid programmes, because they involve academic communities. Writing on students from developing countries, Jenkins (1983b, p. 21) comes to the conclusion, 'The further building of cooperative linkages, at the level of individuals and institutions, is a necessary concomitant to education and training in the United States'.

Links between civic authorities (twinnings, sister cities, *jumelages, Partnerschaften*) have more than a purely civic role in relations between countries. They also enhance trade and media connections. They therefore have significant implications for diplomacy. They impinge on cultural relations in varying degrees. They often open doors to cultural activity in provincial locations and so help reduce the concentration on major cities. There may well be a cultural element in activities conducted by twinned local authorities (e.g. exhibitions, choirs, folk dancing, etc.), appealing to members of a community who would not otherwise have much international involvement. Large numbers of citizens participate. For instance, Bristol's links with Bordeaux and Hanover, to mention one British city with well-established twinnings, have had a considerable effect on the public's international awareness. Breitenstein (1974, p. 48) gives another example:

> Exchange visits between Bath and Brunswick (Braunschweig) go back to 1951 and over 10,000 people have taken part in them. Between Easter and September hardly a week passes by without one or more Brunswick families visiting Bath. There have been a number of marriages, too, between Brunswick and Bath people – and no divorce or separation has been registered to date.

Twinnings are frequently a focus for youth exchanges. This is another activity that in most countries has no direct organizational connection with cultural relations; in Britain it has, because the British Council is the channel of government funds for both links and youth exchanges. There is a considerable relevance in youth exchanges for cultural relations in the wider community. Young people who have participated in such exchanges are likely to play some mediating role in later life between theirs and the country they visited; they may well become active in cultural relations activities. A lively policy of youth exchanges is one of the most fundamental ways of opening horizons, breaking down prejudice and building friendships.

Two outstanding schemes of youth exchange are the Franco-German Youth Exchange Programme and President Reagan's International Youth Exchange Initiative. The first was one of the effects of the treaty signed between de Gaulle and Adenauer in January 1963, which was seen by de Gaulle as a step towards a treaty of union (Frank, 1982, p. 12). A Franco-German Youth office was set up, with administrations in both countries. By 1980, an exchange of 100,000 young people was taking place each year on a joint budget of £8 million. As Ardagh writes (1982, p. 464), 'Over six hundred French towns are now happily twinned with German ones, while scores of thousands of young French and Germans cross the Rhine each year in youth exchanges, and for this newer generation the old fear of *les Boches* has faded into history'. President Reagan's initiative was announced at the Versailles Summit of Spring 1982. The NCIV *Newsletter* of September 1983 gives this summary:

> The program is designed to increase the number of exchanges of young people between the ages of 15 and 19 (slightly older in a few cases) among the United States and its six principal economic partners, which participate in the annual economic summit meetings. Its purpose is to foster improved international communication among young people, especially those of high school age, as a step toward restoring the bonds among the United States, its allies, and its former enemies ... Announcing the Initiative at the White House on May 24, 1982, the President said: 'There is a flickering spark in us all, which, if struck at the right age ... can light the rest of our lives ... Education and cultural exchanges, especially among our young people, provide a perfect opportunity for this precious spark to grow ...'

This programme is the third in a series of American presidential initiatives aimed at increasing international understanding through young people. The previous ones were Eisenhower's People to People International and Kennedy's Peace Corps.

There are many more workaday youth exchanges, especially between European countries. Their main purpose lies outside the formal education system (e.g. young workers, youth clubs, Scouts, sports) but one scheme inside the education system which has been effective in an area of particular need is the Language Assistant Exchanges. More than 2,500 students from Britain served as English Language Assistants in schools and colleges abroad in 1982/83 and about the same number from twenty-three countries taught six languages in Britain (Central Bureau, 1983, p. 17).

The range of the exchange of persons is apparent from the number of different schemes and activities outlined in this chapter. Another very important scheme, which must at least be mentioned, is teacher exchange. Probably no single phenomenon since the Second World War has played as great a part in furthering understanding across frontiers as the various bilateral and multilateral exchange programmes that have grown up. They are now a common form of international co-operation, responsible for the constructive move-ment of people outside the frontiers of their own countries and beyond the horizons of their habitual attitudes. Tourists travel in their millions today, and there are certainly benefits for international understanding in this traffic, although the nature of tourism does not always conduce to their realization. But the more formal and purposeful organization of exchange programmes produces direct results in the participants, which, moreover, are then disseminated among much larger numbers of people. This 'trickle-down effect' works with people in a way it has not always been found to work in programmes of development aid, the area to which the term is often applied. The exchange of persons brings direct and indirect returns which give it a high place among the less proclaimed postwar developments.

One of the most obvious priorities is to boost student mobility. Even within the European Community, with its high level of pro-vision and expectation, the Commission estimates that of the 6 million students at 3,000 tertiary institutions, less than 1 per cent is studying abroad. In order to raise this meagre portion tenfold by 1992, the Commission has launched ERASMUS, an acronym which stands for European Community Action Scheme for the Mobility of University Students and also signifies international scholarship by invoking the mediaeval Dutch theologian.

16

Languages and
Language-Teaching

We have seen that a prime motive in the projection of national cultures during the past century has been the desire to extend the currency of European languages. But it would be mistaken to suppose that cultural relations work depends intrinsically upon the diffusion of language. Two countries may share the same language (like Britain and the United States) and yet find scope for lively cultural exchange; countries with languages little in demand internationally may nevertheless be active in cultural relations by relying on the language of the host country (or a *lingua franca* such as English or French) as the vehicle for their work. Language-teaching and support for language-teaching is an optional activity, which will be appropriate in many situations but not in all.

Yet language is the expression of a culture as well as being a medium; it is a component of cultural and national identity. Translation from one language to another soon reveals that exact equivalence of word and phrase by no means always obtains. Each language is a distinct thought system. Countries that need to use foreign languages internationally, such as those whose own languages are little known beyond their frontiers, have the burden of acquisition, whereas the international use of one's national language confers prestige as well as material benefits. Hence, the insistence on multilingualism in international organizations; hence, also, the recurrence of language questions, often taking the form of demands for reciprocity, in Mixed Commission meetings.

Without doubt, countries whose languages are widely spoken have the advantage of possessing a ready means of international communication. But, if the consequence for them is that foreign languages are insufficiently taught in their own schools, for lack of incentive, then their politicians, intellectuals and exporters will have a limited ability to penetrate other thought systems, to understand other peoples and cultures. The advantage is by no means all on the side of the big battalions. This is just as well, for equality of treatment between languages is obviously out of the question. It is practised for political reasons in some multilateral organizations. For instance, the Commission of the European Community in Brussels attempts parity for seven languages. This means that each language translates into six others, or $7 \times 6 = 42$ transactions each time there is an utterance. When Portuguese and Spanish are added in 1986, this will become $9 \times 8 = 72$ transactions each time. By contrast, the Council of Europe, with its 21 member states, has from the beginning confined its official languages to French and English.

From a cultural point of view, the world's language pattern is one of its greatest, and most amazing, riches. Participation in other cultures entails a readiness to learn the languages that are inseparably bound up with them. A first step in emancipation from one's native cultural confines is to learn a foreign language. Every citizen of the world needs to be able to operate within at least one thought-pattern different from his or her own. Assisting the process by language teaching and support facilities is a major contribution for cultural relations to make.

English as a World Language

The status that English has won is the result of happy accident rather than any particular merit. It has the advantage of a grammar simpler than that of other major European languages. It is written in the most widespread form of alphabet, and is able to assimilate linguistic items from any source. On the other hand, its enormous vocabulary of half a million words appears daunting to learners, even when they are assured that the educated native speaker does not know more than 15,000 of them. Its spelling is notoriously inconsistent. Its vowel system, with 20 different sounds in the standard British pronunciation, brings an element of risk into comprehension between non-native speakers, and indeed between native speakers.

It is usually reckoned that 300 million people speak English as their mother tongue, another 300 million as their second language (that is, for purposes of communication, for instance where English is an official language in their countries) and 100 million as a foreign language (for its educational value or cultural content). Crystal (1985, p. 7) points out that the total is much greater if a partial knowledge and localized forms of English (e.g. pidgin) are added, and settles for 1,000 million. How many millions are learning English in the world's schools and colleges, or non-formally by radio and television, is incalculable, but the total must be several hundred million. Crystal (1985, p. 9) says that in 1983 the BBC television series on English, *Follow Me*, was watched by around 100 million Chinese. English is certainly sufficiently widespread among elites and professional groups to meet the need for a language that can be used for those purposes that have become international: travel, politics, business, defence, technology and science (50 per cent of the world's scientific literature is published in English).

French has been displaced from the linguistic primacy it enjoyed until 1919. The Treaty of Versailles was the first major international treaty in the modern era not to be in French only. French policy, as expressed in the Rigaud Report of 1980 and *Le projet culturel extérieur de la France* (Ministère des relations extérieures, 1984, p. 30) no longer makes a main objective 'the maintenance of the position occupied in the world by the French language' (*DGRCST*, 1974, p. 3) as stated by the then Foreign Minister, but seeks to encourage linguistic plurality: 'the refusal of the supremacy of one single language of international communication corresponds to the refusal of the political supremacy of one group of nations on our culture' (Ministère des relations extérieures, 1984, p. 30).

For some French commentators, it is not only the dominance but the nature of 'Anglo-Saxon' or 'Anglo-American' linguistic hegemony that is repugnant, with words like 'Coca-Cola' being employed in a derogatively generic sense. Sometimes the argument is more philosophical, as in the book with the expressive title, *La France colonisée*, by a former head of the *Direction générale des relations culturelles, scientifiques et techniques* (Thibau, 1980, p. 247): 'Finally there comes a moment when the colonized intellectual loses confidence in the prime instrument of his identity – his language'. *Le Monde Diplomatique* carried five articles in its number of July 1984 on the status of French. One, by the President of the Association for the Defence of French and the Languages of Europe (*ADFLE*), said of English 'it tends ... to become an element of levelling, of uniformity, indeed of alienation. We Europeans should begin to understand, to quote the celebrated remark by Valéry, "that our civilizations are mortal" '. Another article considered the alien identity imported with English, and made the philosophical point that Europe, rich in the diversity of its concept of *being* (*l'être*) was being overwhelmed by trans-Atlantic obsession with *doing* (*le faire*).

Multilingualism, the policy of teaching a variety of languages, is difficult to sustain in any education system for structural reasons as well as those of learner preference. Zapp (1979, p. 19) shows that in the school year 1977–78 in France, 81 per cent of the pupils learnt English, 15.7 per cent German, 2.6 per cent Spanish, 0.3 per cent Italian and 0.2 per cent Russian as their first foreign language. This preponderance of English is certainly unbalanced, as indeed is the preponderance of French in British schools. The percentages for the study of second foreign languages in France, 1977–78, restore the balance somewhat: English 20.9, German 33.8, Spanish 37, Italian 7.0 and Russian 1.0. Multilingualism in education will depend very much on whether the policy of learning more than one foreign language is fully introduced, as advocated by the Education Committee of the European Community in 1984.

Meanwhile, the sheer utility of English grows by what it feeds on, that is, the overriding requirement for an established, adaptable international language. After independence, Malaysia introduced a policy of concentrating on its own most spoken language, Bahasa Malaysia, as a means of heightening national cultural identity and reducing the reliance on English, which was seen as a vestige of the former colonial status. But this policy was found to put Malaysians at such a disadvantage in various international connections that English has been rehabilitated: an intensive recruitment programme was introduced for British teachers of English in Malaysian secondary schools to reverse its decline. In Singapore, the Prime Minister has announced that, from 1986, English will be the sole language of instruction in all sectors of education, while Mandarin will remain the national language. In India, English and Hindi are the two official national languages. Although there is opposition to the continuation of this status for English, the violent reactions – the language riots – have come from those who feared the imposition of Hindi.

In addition to the proven utility of English, there are other, less definable factors that lead to learner preference in its favour. The language opens the way to values and to literatures that have a great appeal, especially in those parts of the world where freedom of expression is denied. English also bestows a second identity, a persona, which appeals particularly to the young in other cultures. It provides an escape from social constraints and artificial boundaries into the wider world of brand names, pop music, glossy magazines and television soap opera, where collective dreams move towards realization. It is a world that owes more to American than to British models, more to *Dallas* than to *Coronation Street*. There is a temptation in Britain to assume more benefit to its national interests from the spread of English than actually accrues. The means of international communication are successfully exploited by those who have most to offer and know how to present it. English as a second language has lost much of its association with its place of origin.

There is even more truth in this today than there was twenty years ago, when Max Beloff wrote:

> It is worth reminding oneself, when people talk of British influence 'east of Suez' or of reviving our links with Latin America, that for a large proportion of the people whose interest or support we wish to attract, what they know about Britain is what *Time* magazine can find room for, that any voice that Britain may have independent of America's in world affairs must be a muffled one. (Beloff, 1965, p. 482)

The extent to which countries benefit from having their languages taught abroad leads to a consideration of language promotion. On 24 September 1936, the Director of the British Institute of Florence wrote to the Secretary-General of the infant British Council: 'everywhere German is taking the place of English; German books are in the shops and German tourists crowd the pensions and trams. Evidently for business purposes their language is more important than ours, as it was before our Institute existed'. And on 18 November in the same year he told the same correspondent that there were ten full professorial chairs for German at Italian universities as against only two for English (British Council, 1936). But the British Council grew. Its budget increased from £5,000 in 1935/36 to £330,000 in 1939/40. Institutes were set up in the Near East and Europe, mainly the Balkans, regions where hostile cultural propaganda was particularly intense. The first purpose of an institute was to teach English; the second to diffuse a knowledge of Britain, and its way of life. Added to this was a library and often a programme of lectures, play-readings and other offerings. The British Council's Annual Report for 1940/41 says, in quaintly pedantic idiom, 'At its most complete a British Institute becomes a centre of British studies, of necessity giving a first place to the study of the English language, and a social and cultural centre for the friends of this country. So far as possible, it should form a microcosm of England and be the projector of English culture and ideas in the country where it is situate' (British Council, 1941, p. 23). Fees were collected from the students of English, but they were modest: the idea was to lure people in and win them over. It was even truer in those days of slower and dearer travel, though it remains true today, that the classroom relationship is often the first, and closest, which students experience with the country whose language they are learning, and that thought should be given to the social as well as to the didactic aspect of the relationship if feelings of friendship are to evolve. There are thousands of people in high places who have learnt English and affection for Britain from teachers to whom they are still devoted. The British Council continued the teaching of English along these lines after the Second World War.

This policy was modified, however, in 1947, when the British Council decided that a short-cut to the minds and sympathies of foreigners lay through adult education. The direct teaching of English was to be cut back, especially at the elementary level, and the resources put into running discussion groups in which various aspects of the British way of life would be dwelt upon. This represented a move not only away from language-teaching but away from the institutes in which it took place. The population at large, rather than the spoilt intelligentsia of the capital city, was to be the target, 'by making an immediate approach to the people down to as low a social and cultural level as possible' (White, 1965, p. 67). In those postwar years it did not seem so overweening as it would now to suppose that foreigners should want to come together to talk about the British way of life. Objections from British Council representatives to this change of policy were many. They thought it misguided to throw away a 'priceless asset' in the English language; they doubted whether enough of the right people had sufficient English to conduct thoughtful discussions; they questioned the capacity of their staff to master the art of animating the discussion. And indeed the new policy was not pushed through consistently. The Council's representative in Italy wrote to London (British Council, 1947) in reply to a circular letter from the Council's Chairman of January 1947 and argued cogently against the modishness of the new policy:

> It is the permanence of our work that matters and we cannot afford to take short-term risks. Transitory pageants may score journalistic successes, but it is the continuous day-to-day effort that in the end produces results which justify our expenditure of the British tax-payer's money. This is the great argument in favour of Institutes in Italy. They are always present, instilling their lessons drop by drop, whereas even the most brilliant dramatic or pictorial success is here today and gone tomorrow – at the best the table-talk of a week – unless the implications of it are developed and the memory of it kept alive by a permanent centre. (British Council, 1947)

Institutes were thought to be expensive, anyway, because they were heavily subsidized. When they were given up, others made money out of them. In Italy, for example, former British Council staff took over the Institutes in Rome and Turin, charged market fees, and made a small fortune.

The second reason for reducing direct teaching of English was perceived in the early 1960s. This was that, as the effects of the postwar explosion of English-teaching became manifest, it was more productive to feed the British Council's expertise into the improvement of national teaching rather than into the institute classroom. When the Council took over the Aid to Commonwealth English scheme it seemed obvious that, with vast numbers of young people hungry for learning and for access to it through English, a maximum multiplier effect must be achieved. The most economical way was through supporting the training of teachers and the trainers of teachers.

Direct teaching did continue. In countries such as Spain and Portugal, where native facilities could not cope with the demand for English, it went on being taught in the old institute style, that is as a foreign language with a good deal of cultural reinforcement to emphasize things British. Later, it was realized that direct teaching could be made profitable and that students' fees could be used to cover costs and even to finance other activities. After the oil crisis of 1973 and the shift of wealth to oil-exporting countries, it became the norm for European countries and the United States to charge for educational services to those parts of the world that could afford them. The idea of charging the going rate for English-teaching, as a paid educational service, received new impetus. In this situation, the main need was for English as a second language, as a vehicle of communication without any necessary reference to Britain. So it was entirely reasonable that the service should be charged at the market rate. Thus began for the British Council a second and differently conceived programme of direct teaching, which aims at covering its costs, and in some countries produces a surplus, which goes towards the financing of other activities. The position now is that the Council is teaching more than 50,000 students of English at any one time and adapting the curriculum and methodology to their particular requirements. English for Special Purposes (ESP) courses have evolved as a way of meeting these requirements.

One task for the English-speaking nations is to defend their language against the tendency to fragmentation into vernaculars that are no more mutually intelligible than, say, Italian and Portuguese. They probably best discharge this by exporting their newspapers, periodicals and books. The availability of English in print has been a prime factor in maintaining the currency of the language as a common vehicle in so many remote and different parts of the world. Today, other forms of communication also play their part. Above all, the current requirement for international communication through English is so great and so generally accepted that any parallels with the linguistic fragmentation of Latin after the fall of the Roman empire have become unrealistic.

'My Fatherland is the French Language'

Albert Camus would presumably not have expressed this sentiment if he had spent his early years in France rather than in Algeria. The identification of language and culture is a common theme in France, however, and one that has conditioned French external cultural policy to an unusual degree. Salon (1983, p. 68) refers to the mystical regard that French enjoys:

> the French language was and remains in France a work of art, consciously and patiently constructed, a protected national institution, an affair of state, a subject and object of constant care, even of cult, on the part of very many French people – all of which the English language is not in either England or the United States. If French culture comes close to a religion, the French language is its holy text, rather as classical Arabic is the language of Islam.

Certainly, one could hardly imagine the British Prime Minister or the American President employing the exalted tone of the speech made by President Mitterand at the World Congress for the Centenary of the Alliance Française in October 1983, when he said: 'It is with admiration and pride that I speak to you on this anniversary, admiration before so much work accomplished, pride at hearing, thanks to you, the beautiful language (*la belle langue*) of my country sound throughout the world'.

With its base of 53 million native speakers in Europe and another 15 million elsewhere, and with a further 130 million who can use it, French remains a major vehicle for international communication (Salon, 1983, p. 72). The propagation of French is of long history. It can be traced back to the Crusades (*Gesta Dei per Francos*), to the work of the religious orders, and to overseas expansion under Louis XIII and Louis XIV. The Lay Mission (*la Mission laïque*) joined the religious orders in running French schools overseas. The Alliance Française, founded in 1883, now has 300,000 students each year throughout the world. There are 327 French schools abroad with 1,500 teachers, and 600 French lectors at foreign universities. French cultural institutes have the teaching of French language and literature as one of their main tasks. The Directorate for French (*Direction du français*) is one of the main divisions in the *Direction générale des relations culturelles scientifiques et techniques* in the foreign ministry.

The decline of French is not so much in its standing as a foreign language: it still enjoys a high regard for its qualities as a language of precision and elegance and as a vehicle of cultural values. Its decline is much more as a second language, as a means of international communication. Before the First World War, it was after all the undisputed medium of diplomacy and civilization. A successful attempt has been made in former French and Belgian dependencies to give it new impetus. Léopold Senghor, when he was President of Senegal, referred to French as 'the marvellous instrument found in the rubble of the colonial régime'. The attempt has led to the phenomenon of *Francophonie*.

This concept was invented by the French geographer Onésime Reclus (1837–1916). It was revived with a more linguistic reference in the 1960s as a response to the British Commonwealth. Just as the Commonwealth is an association of states linked by, among other factors, the English tongue, so the concept of *Francophonie* should link Francophone countries. A meeting of French-speaking nations was held at Niamey in 1970, and President Hamani of Niger announced the establishment of the *agence de coopération culturelle et technique*, which by 1984 had a budget of 100 million francs. A variety of official and unofficial organizations are involved in maintaining the links between the Francophone states. Regular ministerial meetings are held. One important effect of this network is that it facilitates regional South-to-South communication, just as English does within the Commonwealth. This contact between developing countries, based upon their sharing the same language and concepts, is one of the less proclaimed advantages in the legacy of colonialism.

Francophone countries seem to find it less alienating to express their cultural identity through the use of French than do former British possessions through the use of English. The French made much more effort than the British to have their language well taught in their dependencies. We find, for instance, that Senegal, which exercises an active cultural role (and hosts a regional office of UNESCO and the African Cultural Institute) with a pan-African tendency, has no qualms about using French as the means of expressing its cultural heritage and of conducting cultural exchanges with countries such as Tunisia and Morocco.

The effect on North–South cultural relations of using languages of former colonial rulers as the means of communication internally and externally has not been adequately researched. Having a language available that is widely intelligible and possesses an extensive specialist literature is, on the face of it, a cause for rejoicing. For that matter, such languages play a part in the political unity of many newly independent countries. Several states in this category show a degree of linguistic diversity that can be understood only in tribal terms. For instance, in West Africa the Ivory Coast has over two score languages or distinct dialects for a population of 7 million; in East

Africa, Tanzania has many more for a population of 18 million. The Ivory Coast uses French as its official language; Tanzania uses Swahili but is heavily dependent also on English. The former colonial languages are cultural as well as functional vehicles of communication with the outside world. African and Asian writers who have expressed themselves in English or French have been able to reach a much larger public than would have been conceivable in their mother tongue or a regional *lingua franca*. Nevertheless, a language brings with it a way of thought, and for many who use English or French this is not their native way of thought. A writer from Zaïre made the point at the First International Conference on Cultural Identity held in Paris:

> How to liberate our speech from Western norms erected as absolute and universal principles, and how to bring this speech to signify, in their totality and diversity, our historical condition and our natural and technical spatio-temporal and mystical environment, if the ideological and political apparatus (education, mass media, administrative and socio-cultural structures) . . . continue to perpetuate, inherited as they are from colonization, the hold of the West upon us. (Kadima-Nzuji, 1982, p. 32)

Moreover, any language is organically changing, and the changes are introduced mainly at the centre. When words like Reaganomics or Thatcherism emerge from America or Britain, they will find their way into the media and challenge the non-native speaker with unfamiliar concepts.

The number of world languages is small. Apart from English and French, there are Spanish (215 million speakers) and Portuguese (100 million), both of which span nations and continents. Arabic qualifies on the same terms, with more than 100 million; Saudi Arabia, by virtue of its oil wealth and custodianship of Islam's holy places, takes on the cultural role of actively promoting Arabic. Russian is spoken by more than 140 million, but does not qualify as a world language because it is confined to one land mass. We should note, however, that the Soviet Union's expanding programme of study awards to students from the Third World is precipitating a great number of Russian-speakers in the Middle East and Asia and in Latin America. Hausa and Kiswahili are spoken in extensive regions of West and East Africa respectively. Chinese is spoken by more people than any other language (a billion) and forms of it are in use by the overseas Chinese, but it cannot be considered a world language, because only the Chinese use it. The fact that it is one common language in its written form gives its speakers a potential coherence, which could be significant in the future. Some 120 million people speak Japanese. It might appear that Japanese should play a greater part in the Pacific century, which we are told is about to dawn, with that ocean becoming a focus of trade and travel like the Mediterranean in the late Middle Ages. If the Japanese could get over the difficulty of their language's written form, this would be more conceivable. Foreign students now take more interest in technology and industrial management than in classical Japanese culture. If the government's plan is realised and the present small number of foreign students is increased tenfold, i.e. to 100,000 by the end of the century, this will in itself be a significant way of spreading a knowledge of the language.

German is spoken in four European countries. It is not a world language but a leading European language, and the only one that takes in both sides of the East–West divide. The West and East versions have slightly diverged, as can be seen in the Mannheim and Leipzig editions of Duden, a long-established dictionary. There is little collaboration between the West and East German states about the evolution or teaching abroad of their common language. In the Federal Republic, which has, as we saw in Chapter 13 (p. 127), one of the best articulated policies for its cultural relations, there has long been a debate whether German should be taught for its own sake or simply as a means to an end, a cultural property or a vehicle for specific messages – in scientific and technical collaboration, for instance. The Guidelines (*Leitsätze*) say:

> The German language is the vehicle not the target of our overseas operations. There are traditional German-speaking areas where the promotion of German can be strengthened, but in other parts of the world it will be more appropriate for the aims of exchange and collaboration to use the most current language as a means of communication. (Bretzler, 1976, p. 52)

This divorce between language and culture perturbed the Goethe Institute in particular, since German-teaching was the main concern of their staff in many overseas posts. The new policy was endorsed by Hansgert Peisert (1978, p. 295), the academic sociologist who was commissioned to examine Germany's external cultural policy. The Goethe Institute countered by drawing up and agreeing with the foreign ministry a set of its own 'Guidelines for the German Language Abroad', which redefined the relation between language and culture. The Commission of Enquiry of the German *Bundestag* also rehabilitated the role of the German language in cultural policy. Then the German Foreign Office published in its policy statement (German Federal Foreign Office, 1978, p. 14):

The German language is and remains a central component of our culture and an important instrument for achieving understanding between peoples. Its significance as a literary, scientific and technological language reflects this importance. Thus, in the opinion of the Federal Government, there can be no cultural policy abroad without a meaningful language policy. This is one of the most important tasks of foreign cultural policy.

Germany has thus found a rational balance in language policy. German is taught by the Goethe Institute abroad mainly to target groups, among which teachers of the language figure largely; in its teaching centres within Germany the Goethe Institute gives pre-sessional instruction to those who require German for study or training in the Federal Republic. The cultural programme abroad supplements the teaching programme by means of libraries, lectures and audio-visual facilities; it also operates in the language of the country or a third language, usually English or French, when the local partners do not have sufficient German for the purposes of collaboration.

Italian policy follows the French model in considering its language and the teaching thereof to be an intrinsic task of cultural relations. Like France, Italy runs schools abroad and recruits teachers from the domestic education system (also for the 80 Italian cultural institutes). Although Italy does not share with the French their more mystical concepts of the way language informs the national culture, it is certainly conscious of the linguistic heritage from the Roman Empire. Ten universities run courses for foreigners in Italian language and culture. The most famous and longest established of these is the one at Perugia (instituted in 1925), which is entirely devoted to foreign students and exists side by side with the state university in the same town. The Dante Alighieri Society, founded in 1889, resembles the Alliance Française in having a world-wide membership (125,000 people) most of it abroad, and being mainly focused on the language in its cultural and (as its name implies) literary context. Yet in spite of this extensive language-teaching programme, there is much dissatisfaction in official and public quarters at its rate of success. The congress held in December 1983, on Italian cultural policy abroad, was mentioned in Chapter 12 (p. 111). In essence, Italians feel that they, with their abundant treasures, are suffering the irony of becoming a cultural colony of the United States, and part of the reason for this is their linguistic submergence.

According to speeches made by Sergio Romano, then Director General of Cultural Relations at the Foreign Ministry, at congresses in 1981 and 1982, Italy has been prevented from following a clear linguistic policy by the turmoil and disunity through which the state and the national consciousness have passed (Romano, 1982a). First of all, the fascist past has been a constraint. Then there is the impediment of regionalism, which is a strong cultural factor in Italy. Romano calculated that the number of people studying Italian abroad was one million and pleaded for up-dating of foreign teachers of the language. Italy also adopts a similar viewpoint to France's over the steamroller effect of English. In 1982 the two countries held a conference on their cultural co-operation, including the mutual promotion of their languages. The menace of Anglo-American monolingualism was held in general abhorrence. In his introduction to the report on the conference, Romano (1982b) takes up the French idea of *plurilingualisme* and makes the profound remark: 'we should take comfort in the apparently paradoxical conviction that the only way to defend and conserve one's own language today is to learn another one.' One of the proposals discussed was that French and Italian should be given mutual preference in the respective education systems.

In view of the fears of creeping Anglo-American monolingualism and the subversion of other linguistic cultures, the question has to be asked whether there is an alternative. Of artificial languages only Esperanto has achieved much currency and that is too European in conception to answer the problem world-wide. Perhaps electronic data processing will eventually provide a solution, though here too much of the software is English-based, at least in the present generation.

Further thought might be given to Basic English or an adapted form of it. Basic was derived from word frequency lists elaborated by American and British researchers between the wars. Finally, C. K. Ogden and I. A. Richards evolved the Basic vocabulary, predicated on function rather than frequency alone, consisting of 850 words to cover ordinary needs. Churchill lent his weight to Basic during the war. He set up a Cabinet Committee with the idea of getting it adopted as an 'auxiliary international language', and there was even a debate in the House of Commons in 1944, in which it was announced that the British Council should teach Basic, various kinds of literature should be translated into it, and the BBC was asked to consider including the use of Basic in its overseas programmes (Hansard, 1944, p. 2189).

Basic petered out except as an academic curiosity. The diffusion of normal English overtook it. One particular disadvantage was that native-speakers would have found it unnatural to confine themselves to its restricted vocabulary. But one might wonder what would have been its fate if the Group of 77 or UNESCO had espoused the Basic cause. Basic might have received a good deal of support as a second language for the Third World if its propagation had happened two or three decades later. Certainly it is a language in which the cultural content has been neutralized to some extent. As a medium with fewer overtones, it might find favour for purposes of international communication. But the same disincentive to its use still applies, except indeed that there are now many more speakers of normal English, who would have to distort their linguistic habits to fit the limited vocabulary.

17

The Arts

Probably most observers who take an informed but outside interest in cultural relations would place the arts right at their very core. For the politician, journalist or diplomat, presentations of the arts are the most manifest sign of a cultural presence; they appear to be the hallmark of a cultural relationship. They not only achieve publicity and bring prestige, they reach audiences containing those with the greatest power to influence relations between the participating countries. If in this book the arts are placed among the optional rather than among the basic activities of a cultural representation, this does not derogate from their importance.

In more sophisticated countries, arts imports from other countries are an essential part of the cultural scene, and foreign cultural agencies are expected to make their contribution. But there are other parts of the world where, for reasons of receptivity, expense or security, the arts may hardly figure at all in a cultural agency's priorities. 'The arts' is, of course, a comprehensive term which embraces such diverse aspects as music, drama, dance, opera, film, video, folklore, television, and exhibitions of painting, sculpture, photography and graphics. Out of this variety it is usually possible for something to be included, however irregularly, in the programme of any cultural representation. Clearly, any cultural programme that did not include the arts in some form would present an impoverished picture, but in some representations the arts necessarily take second place.

Another reason why the arts are not considered to be organizationally part of the basic activities in cultural relations is that they frequently take place without official support. It would be arbitrary to consider the performances by an officially supported quartet playing contemporary music to minority audiences more significant than those of a symphony orchestra touring at the invitation of the host country with a repertoire of international classical favourites; both have their part in the interplay of cultures. But the one could not happen without the mediation and probably subsidy of the cultural agency, whereas the other belongs in the area of open exchange through commercial channels where pop music and television soap opera are also to be found. They are all part of culture and, in an extended sense, may therefore be regarded as becoming part of cultural relations when they are exported to another country; however, they are not part of the policy determining cultural relations on behalf of governments and their agencies.

Another general feature of the arts is that their availability for export depends on the extent to which they are fostered under internal cultural policy. It is here that internal and external cultural policies are most closely intertwined. And the effects are felt by artists, as well as audiences, in other countries. As Towse (1984, p. 150) says:

> the fact that there is a well-established European (and inter-national) market for the services of artists as well as for their products, such as paintings and recordings, means that the policies of one country about levels of provision and subsidy of the arts can have considerable effect on prices and earnings paid to artists in other countries. Therefore, no one country can afford to ignore what is taking place elsewhere in this international market if it wants to understand its own internal situation. In addition, tourism has an impact on the level of demand for many cultural items, the economic implications of which cannot be revealed without the collection of the requisite data.

The same source, *Funding the Arts in Europe*, a collection of papers from a Research Workshop on the Financing of Cultural Policy, held in Munich in 1983, provides (see Table 17.1) this comparison of public expenditure on the arts per head of population in selected European countries (which it says should be used 'with the utmost caution').

Table 17.1   Public Expenditure on the Arts

	Year	£
Austria	1980	18.61
France	1982	22.55
West Germany	1981	15.77
Italy	1980–1	7.54
Sweden	1980–1	24.82
UK	1981–2	5.80

Source   Myerscough, 1984, p. xvi

Even granted the notorious difficulty of making exact comparisons between cultural budgets, the discrepancy to a factor of four between the maximum (Sweden) and the minimum (UK) illustrates the bearing of internal cultural policy on the arts and artists in other countries. Countries that are well endowed attract artists from elsewhere. They offer more engagements (especially in those performing arts that are not language-based, such as music), more chances to play in orchestras or sing in operas. In Germany, particularly, there is a high proportion of foreign performers employed in its musical life.

The arts have in recent decades, and especially at the grander symphony orchestra end of the spectrum, become remarkably internationalized. National cultural policies have become correspondingly international in their effect. As *The Times* wrote in a leading article 'Arts in a cold climate' on 6 March 1985, 'Britain must operate in a context where the pound buys steadily fewer and fewer square millimetres of export-threatened Mantegna and ever more momentary fragments of Pavorotti hours, and in which the going rate is frequently inflated by the readiness of other countries to subsidize the arts at far higher rates (four times as high per head, in Germany; six times as high in France)'. The fact that these proportions do not correspond to the statistics in Table 17.1 will surprise no one who has wrestled with the comparison of cultural budgets.

If we turn from the variety in official subsidy to the diversity of organizational structures, we find a wide range from the centralized to the federalized. Fohrbeck (1981, p. 12) classifies them thus:

1   Centrally organized with state finance and predominantly state characteristics (France and most Eastern European countries).
2   Predominantly centrally organized, financed by the state or a funding organization, characterized by cultural associations and institutions (Denmark, Sweden, Norway, the Netherlands, Poland).
3   Sub-centrally organized, predominantly financed centrally by public or private money, characterized by relatively independent Arts Councils and large foundations, associations and industry USA, Britain, Australia).
4   Federally organized, predominantly financed by the state centrally and regionally, characterized by central and regional state institutions (Austria, Canada, Yugoslavia).
5   Federally organized, predominantly decentralized public finance, characterized by public and private bodies (Federal Republic of Germany, Switzerland).

Another factor, the diversity of ministerial responsibility, is an additional complication. When, in this classification, the state is referred to, this means a variety of different ministries with different competences. The performing arts are financed by a combination of four sources of funds: box-office takings, sponsorship, local authority support, and subsidy from central or regional government. The figures in Table 17.1 comprise the last two items. Comparisons of national arts budgets sometimes refer to the last item only.

The interrelation between internal and external cultural policies also has social implications. In some societies the 'democratization of culture' means not only that everyone should have access but also, according to the consensus of the ministers of culture of the Council of Europe (Depaigne, 1978, p. 21), that 'every individual should be encouraged to create. What is important is not consumption but cultural production, individual creative action'. The formulation of the concept of 'cultural democracy' seems to date from the cultural conference organized by UNESCO at Helsinki in 1972. It was spelt out by the Conference of Local and Regional Authorities, in the framework of the Council of Europe, as quoted by Weber (1981, p. 35):

> Cultural development means the creation of conditions allowing each individual to express himself, to develop and find his own identity, individually and in a group or association. It is a matter of helping individuals to regain the capacity for communication, often lost owing to the development of a consumption culture passively imbibed and encouraged by television, by the use of individual media and by large scale anonymous housing.

It is a question for external cultural policy, therefore, how far it should take it upon itself to represent cultural democracy. It is one thing to show this as a social phenomenon, but it would be another to include its products in a programme of artistic exports. Possibly cultural agencies of countries favouring cultural democracy will not in future be able to observe a clear distinction between the professional and the amateur.

It is the first business of cultural agencies in the arts to encourage and support those events that will have the desired effect in the host country. How the desired effect is conceived will depend on aims, policies and objectives. For instance, if the representation's aim is 'To promote mutual understanding by exchanges in the arts, etc.', then policies will be framed so as to give priority to those events that coincide with the cultural predilections of the host country. Objectives for a particular event have in mind targets (audiences and media reaction) that are most likely to be instrumental in their fulfilment. The second business of cultural agencies is to help the institutions and artists of the host country to export their arts in return, either with advice and introductions or with funds, or with both. Evaluation of one's own activities is, as we have seen, of great importance and will be facilitated if it is conducted in collaboration with partner organizations of the host country.

It not infrequently happens that what is on offer from an agency's headquarters corresponds to the preferences of neither the host country nor the cultural representation. It is only in countries in Karla Fohrbeck's first category that the cultural representation can call the tune, and then only if it finds an echo in the headquarters organization.

It is also a matter of policy decision whether arts events should be arranged on a representation's own premises or in a local institution. The institute model described early (p. 128) typically assumes performance on the premises. This gives the institute more profile and exploits a captive audience that expects cultural as well as educational activities. When this model was the norm, each national institute in a major capital city would run a varied programme of attractions that were tacitly competitive. Its members (even if some individuals were in common) represented a corps of supporters for the culture of the country in question. This model has not become extinct but, so far as the arts are concerned, it has been largely over-taken by the internationalization of the arts scene and the greater sophistication of audiences. Nevertheless, there are still advantages in having certain events on one's own premises. The occasional attraction of a wider public by a presentation at a cultural institute, or centre, maintains the agency's visibility and reinforces the country's cultural identity.

An article by Terence Mullaly in *The Daily Telegraph* of 26 May 1984 praises the Polish Cultural Institute and Canada House in London for their in-house activities in the visual arts. Both institutions are situated in prominent, attractive buildings and Canada House has considerable hanging space. Not all of what they show could easily be housed in public or commercial galleries, which in any case require very long lead times. By using their cultural centres in London (as in Paris), the Canadians have won an enhanced reputation for their art. Mullaly says, 'No one here interested in the arts is unaware of what is happening in Canada. At Canada House on Trafalgar Square there is a continuing series of Canadian exhibitions, many of which then go on tour, along with concerts and recitals. At the same time a stream of information goes to those who are interested.' He contrasts this with the less frequent and less visible activities of Australia and New Zealand. He quotes the words of a public-spirited Australian, ' "I don't understand it, we have much better artists than the Canadians, but everybody in Paris and London talks about Canadian Art" '.

It is perhaps not a profitable pursuit to make theoretical comparisons of the impact of different arts media. But, for each country, it is a matter that must inform policies. Given a limited amount of money, should a cultural agency prefer an art exhibition, a drama company or an orchestra? The answer will depend on policy and on a careful assessment of local needs and interests – and on what is available. Nevertheless, it is a reasonable generalization to say that the visual arts have tended to be most successful in making a striking impression or, in the language of cultural relations, 'a big splash'. A major exhibition lasts for some weeks, appeals to anyone with cultural awareness (whereas orchestras and theatre companies have a more limited public), announces itself through prominent posters, which are part of its total effect and seen by many more than the exhibition itself, and leaves a tangible legacy in the form of catalogues and reproductions. So far as the wider, rather than the specialized, public is concerned, an exhibition can touch the sensitivities with more enduring effect. For this reason the visual arts are perhaps the most potent means of putting across a national image or changing that image.

A good instance is the Great Japan Exhibition organized by the Japan Foundation at the Royal Academy in London: some 500 national treasures were included, and the exhibition was shown in two phases between October 1981 and February 1982. Attendance exceeded half a million. The art of the Edo period was known to sections of the public from public collections, but the exhibition had a magnificence and richness that made it unusually memorable. It is thought to have changed British attitudes towards Japan and helped to overcome residual wartime bitterness. It inspired a boost in activities in Britain involving the arts of Japan. The striking visual images conveyed by those arts leave a strong imprint on the spectator, incomparably greater for a Western audience than that created by the performing arts. Indeed, when Japan and South Korea inaugurated full-scale cultural exchanges in 1981, it was again an exhibition – of contemporary Japanese art – that was selected to make the initial breakthrough of the barriers of distrust. Several Japanese feel that, in spite of such successes, their country needs to redress its international image as an industrial power-house decorated with ancient art treasures.

In an article in the *Japan Times* of 20 December 1984, Reijiro Hattori, a leading company president, says, 'what we would truly like a larger number of Europeans to understand at present is the real picture of the ordinary social life and the economic activities of the Japanese who are devoted to making a contribution to the maintenance of peaceful co-existence . . .' The author makes a distinction between 'those activities which introduce traditional or classical subjects from Japan, and the activities which introduce the contemporary situation in Japan', and thinks that the emphasis needs to be adjusted in favour of the latter.

This is a recurrent controversy in cultural relations work. Of course, one must agree with him. A realistic, up-to-date picture of a society should be put across and not just cultural highlights or items of folklore that may strike the uninitiated foreigner as quaint or amusing (e.g. tea ceremony, thatched cottages, yodelling and the like). Nevertheless, there is a timelessness about great art, which makes it an enduring epitome of a nation's genius. Every now and again this needs demonstration by a grand gesture. Cultural relations should be capable of the grand gesture as well as the effect achieved by an accretion of more restrained expressions.

Grand gestures can elicit grand responses. The exhibition arranged by the British Council in Caracas, the capital of Venezuela, in March 1983, one year after the Falklands campaign, of some 260 works by Henry Moore (sculpture, drawings and graphics) was a success in more than artistic terms. It is of incidental interest that Moore has on many occasions shown his warmth of feeling towards the British Council. He wrote to the Prime Minister, Mrs Thatcher, 'All these large one-man shows of my work could not have taken place without the essential help given by the British Council – in consequence, and fortunately for me, my work is well-known outside England' (British Council, 1982, p. 24), giving a remarkable example of the symbiotic relationship between an artist and a cultural agency.

The Moore exhibition had previously received great acclaim in Mexico City. In Venezuela, it formed part of Britain's contribution to the celebration of the Simon Bolivar Bicentenary, and was accompanied by a smaller travelling exhibition of Moore's work, which was shown at six venues. The total impact was beyond expectations. At the main exhibition, there was a record attendance of more than 200,000 visitors in eight weeks. It was remarked that 'only the Beatles at their height could have created a comparable stir'. In a letter to the Director-General of the British Council (from which this is quoted) the Director of the Museum wrote of a housewife from a provincial town who had seen the travelling exhibition there and flew 600 miles to Caracas to see the main one: 'She was almost in tears. She said she had to bring her husband and children to see this, even if it meant (plane tickets being too expensive) driving 14 hours and sleeping in the car before going back.' (The British Council, 1983).

The Venezuelan media gave the event full treatment. The President spoke at the opening. The political results were more immediately visible than the cultural. The temper of Anglo-Venezuelan relations, precarious after the Falklands, became sounder. Within the context of the Bicentenary and other activities in its celebration, this exhibition proved conclusively the positive effects of well-timed and well-executed cultural presentations in reaching a profounder level of appreciation between two peoples. But, of course, the whole enterprise depended on the appeal and renown of Moore's works.

Another instance of the 'big splash' in the visual arts was the Turner exhibition at the Grand Palais in Paris from October 1983 to January 1984. Like Moore, Turner is an eminently appealing export. Indeed this was the twelfth Turner exhibition, including the 1948 Venice Biennale (when he and Moore were shown together), that the British Council had arranged. All the same, the success was of triumphal proportions, whether measured by the 600,000 visitors (third in Paris only to Tutankhamen and Monet) or by the extensive media coverage (*Le Figaro* called Turner 'the Shakespeare of Painting').

It is hard to imagine an impact comparable to these being achieved by the performing arts. But, inevitably, such monumental exhibitions are rare, and may well become even rarer in view of the reluctance of collections to lend priceless works. The choice for cultural agencies is not normally between Turner, a symphony orchestra and a national drama company. It is more likely to be between, say, the graphics of an artist who has not yet achieved an international reputation, a far from famous string quartet and a provincial theatre with an unsuitable repertoire. And the choice often turns out to be Hobson's choice. One sensible basis of selection is to give preference to artists of high promise who have not yet established themselves internationally, and to those who are extending the frontiers of their particular art by avant-garde innovation. Both categories are unlikely to be able to pay their way without subsidy; by providing this, the cultural agency fulfils its role as a mediator between cultures at their creative fringes.

Assisting experiment engages the participation of those people in both countries who are exploring the boundaries of their art form. This involves a dimension of intellectual as well as artistic encounter. The inclusion of some workshop sessions provides an element of discovery that is exciting in itself and creates openings for co-operation in the future. One of the ultimate reasons for maintaining cultural representations abroad, as opposed to using embassy staff or relying on specialists sent out for special events from arts organizations at home, is that they possess the local familiarity and insight that make it possible for them to penetrate the local scene, to identify counterparts and to bring them together.

An active arts programme will be measured not only by the number of events from the sending country but also by the frequency with which its music and drama, etc., are included in the repertoire of the host country, not only by the number of exhibitions mounted by the sending country itself but also by the representation of its visual arts in collections and exhibitions of the host country. Given the internationalization of art, quality will often prove its own best promoter and salesman. But it is part of the mediator role of a cultural agency to assist the process. The exchange of persons programme can be invoked to arrange visits by impresarios, musical and theatrical directors so that they can attend performances in the sending country; texts of new plays (nowadays increasingly supplemented by video tapes) and music scores and recordings can be made available to them in their own institutions. Conductors, singers and soloists on contract are well placed to introduce their own country's music into the repertoire of orchestras and opera houses. A theatrical director who is contracted from the sending country to produce a play with a local company does more than introduce his own style and interpretation: he creates valuable links in the acting professions of the two countries. Ignorance of the local language has been found to be remarkably unimportant. Theatrical directors from Britain have produced Shakespeare in languages as diverse and, to them, unfamiliar as Serbo-Croat and Korean with outstanding success.

A Shakespeare (or Mozart or Michelangelo) is an endorsement of the cultural credentials of the country that produced him. It is true, of course, that such great masters have long become the property of the world, but they bring inalienable associations with their places of origin. It is a great advantage for the standing of Britain in the world that the works of Shakespeare are not only known in most countries, but that his language has become international to the extent that British companies performing his work in English are in great demand as the authentic voice. The language carries overtones that are in themselves an important cultural and human message. As Wordsworth wrote:

> We must be free or die, who speak the tongue
> That Shakespeare spake...

It was no wonder then that, in arranging a major drama tour in commemoration of its fiftieth anniversary, the British Council should have organized an extensive European tour by the Royal Shakespeare Company. This took place for five weeks between March and April 1984 and embraced France, Germany, Austria, Czechoslovakia and Spain. The plays were *Much Ado about Nothing* and Edward Bond's *Lear*, both of which had previously been running at the Barbican in London. In some venues both plays were shown, in others one or the other. The reaction both of audiences and reviewers was unanimously favourable. In Paris, the *Magazine Hebdo* of 29 March 1984 wrote of the English, 'Not only are they lucky in having been given Shakespeare, the greatest poet ever, they do their best to deserve him'. The *Financial Times* of 6 April 1984 reported *Le Parisien* as saying, 'Since the Iron Lady said no in Brussels, we say yes in Paris on a matter which has every chance of uniting Europe'. But the reception was probably the most moving in Prague. For Czechs, theatre is particularly important as a route below the surface of life. Members of the audience said the performance had been an escape into a magic world; many were in tears. The players themselves said they had never encountered a more intense audience.

In January 1985, the Royal Shakespeare Company took *The Winter's Tale* and Arthur Miller's *The Crucible* to Poland, where each play was performed in Warsaw and Wroclaw. Seminars on the texts and aspects of interpretation were held in both venues. This tour was accounted not only an artistic success but also a notable political event, being the first major artistic offering from Britain since the imposition of military rule in Poland and coming as it did between the visits to Poland of a Foreign Office minister and the Secretary of State. It would have been impossible indeed to silence the political echoes aroused by *The Crucible*. *The Sunday Times* wrote on 20 January 1985:

> As the elite of Warsaw sat on the floor of the student's club at the Technical University ... watching the Royal Shakespeare Company perform a play about false witness, dictatorship and terrorism by an informer, 100 miles away in Torun three secret policemen were being tried for their lives for the murder of a dissident priest.

The Times of 19 January 1985 wrote more provocatively:

> the Royal Shakespeare Company is giving Poles an object lesson in how to stage a witch-hunt. Nerves are exposed, faces flushed by the search for the shadowy figures behind the murder of Father Jerzy Popieluszko, the pro-Solidarity priest murdered three months ago by secret police agents.

We have already seen the difficulty that exists in assessing the returns on cultural expenditure. The European tour by the Royal Shakespeare Company in 1984 cost the British Council about £250,000 and the Polish tour £75,000. What did the British taxpayer get out of them? As always the question cannot be answered in measurable terms. But several thousand people, consisting largely of members of influential elites, and their eventual successors, witnessed performances of a high standard; they were moved by stirring drama in English; they ended up with a favourable regard for the country that had sent these fine specimens of its dramatic art. That may not sound to the unconverted like an adequate reply. Nor is it complete, for it omits the benefit to the British actors from meeting their opposite numbers from several countries, from the employment provided (if not to them, then to other actors at home who were taking their places), from what the Applebaum Report (1982, p. 335) postulated for Canadian artists: 'They need international experience to advance their careers artistically and financially'.

Having the English language as the vehicle of cultural relations in itself represents a great asset and a great economy. It is primarily because English is easily the first foreign language in Germany that the costs of staging 'The British Scene' in Cologne were predominantly borne by the German side. *The Times* of 31 December 1984 wrote: 'But what the Scrooges in Whitehall will probably find most impressive about this outpouring is that the West Germans paid for 90 per cent of it.' 'The British Scene' was organized by the British Council in the Federal Republic from September to December 1984 as its contribution to the Council's fiftieth anniversary celebrations and as a commemoration of the Council's twenty-fifth year in Germany. German partners, especially the City of Cologne, were generous in their co-operation. A comparison with the German Month of 1974 in London is revealing. The activities of both were similar. Both events covered art, literature, theatre, music and film. The German Month ('Germany – Facets, Faces, Facts') additionally included a large book exhibition in the Festival Hall. But a comparison of costs immediately shows up a striking difference. The then director of the Goethe Institute in London, Klaus Schulz, calculated the total cost of the German Month at one million German marks, 'of which about DM 180,000 were contributed by our English partners, that is, almost 20 per cent of the overall costs' (Schulz, 1976, p. 40). The difference between 90 and 20 per cent is due not only to the relative appeal of English and German as cultural vehicles (there are other factors, such as the public subsidy of the arts in Britain and Germany, which have been considered above, and there is the health of the economy of the two countries at the time), but the fact remains that, in this comparison, the greater market value of British cultural exports has less to do with superior quality than with language. The German weekly *Die Zeit* of 8 November 1974 wrote about language difficulties in the German Month:

> So the notion was abandoned of inviting the production of Schiller's *Maiden of Orleans* of the *Deutsches Schauspielhaus* in Hamburg. For 160,000 marks it would have been possible in London to attract an audience for at most three or four performances in the German language. There is likely to be more success in commissioning a successful young director, Hovannes Pilikian, to work on Schiller's *The Robbers* as an English premiere under the title *The Highwaymen* with an English company. Together with commissioning a new translation (Gail Rademacher), sixteen performances in the Roundhouse (950 seats) can be scheduled at a cost of about 100,000 marks.

Clearly, the cultural balance of trade, so to say, is very much in Britain's favour and particularly in the arts. If the investment of £1 sterling is going to attract the equivalent of £9 contribution from countries such as Germany, then this might be an answer for the 'Scrooges in Whitehall' to the question that was posed earlier. It might be said that countries with English as their native language, but particularly Britain, have an invaluable opportunity to spread their influence internationally at a cost that is well below the market price.

It is easier, as well as cheaper, for countries with dominant languages to export their cultures. It has already been shown that the concept of mutuality, the highest expression of a bilateral cultural relationship, places an obligation on such countries to smooth the way for imports in return. It is important, therefore, that there should be a system in each country for the assistance of cultural imports. It may depend on a central organization, such as the French *Association française d'action artistique* or Britain's Visiting Arts Unit, or it may be decentralized, as in Germany, where internal cultural budgets are primarily in the hands of the *Länder* and municipalities. There is a particular need to encourage arts imports from the developing world. The advantage of committing a small proportion of aid budgets to this purpose is not universally appreciated. Aid without understanding seems like perfunctory alms-giving, whereas aid based on understanding is a contribution towards a common humanity.

Germany, in its publication *Ten Principles for Cultural Encounter and Co-operation with Countries of the Third World* emphasizes the importance of sociocultural processes in development (German Federal Foreign Office, 1982, p. 13). Principle no. 5 is indeed concerned with the promotion of cultural identity. The Federal Republic makes a special point of supporting cultural presentations from Third World countries, both as a form of aid and as an instrument of education for Germans in development matters. At its Overseas Briefing Centre in Bad Honnef, the Foundation for International Development (*DSE*) hosts artistic performances from the Third World. In London, the Commonwealth Institute is a sounding-board for the wide variety of cultures that make up the Commonwealth; the regular visits of schoolchildren give it an educational function. Also, the Africa Centre in London is a focus for various artistic and intellectual activities from that continent. Many such institutions throughout the world serve as a focus for its cultural diversity, which is also its common heritage.

Leading culture-exporting countries, especially those possessing a dominant language as their vehicle, need to be especially alert to the claims of reciprocity. *The Guardian* published an article on 28 January 1985 telling of the difficulty foreign companies have in appearing in Britain after British companies have played in their countries. The particular instance given is of the Peking Opera's proposed visit to the London International Festival of Theatre (LIFT) in the summer of 1985. It seems that there was no lack of receptivity and goodwill. The problem was simply that whereas the British Council had funds to subsidize tours like those of the Royal Shakespeare Company or the Ballet Rambert to China, there was no pocket to defray a comparable proportion of the expenses of incoming events. The Visiting Arts Unit provides an excellent advisory service but its operational funds (contributed by the British Council, the Foreign and Commonwealth Office and the Arts Council) amount to no more than £100,000, which even with scrupulous management is exiguous in the face of the demand from so many countries to appear before British audiences. The imbalance between grants for exports and grants for imports is an expression of the division of competences between outward and inward that was considered earlier (see pp. 68–70). The organizer of LIFT is quoted as saying, ' "The Chinese are extremely annoyed" . . . Wherever we go in the world there is this same anger: why isn't Britain reciprocating?' The answer is that there is money available but not on a reciprocal basis, except with East European countries where there is an exchange programme. Funds have to be dug for in a variety of sources, some of them national, some of them local. One source of growing importance is business sponsorship.

In Europe there is still some opposition to sponsorship on the part of purists or puritans. For some people the idea of dependence on private patronage is unattractive. They forget the part that princely, noble and bourgeois patronage has played in the past; they ignore the practical impossibility, and in free societies indeed the undesirability, that public authorities should be monopolist paymasters. The Scandinavian countries have long been active in business sponsorship. 'Support by commerce and industry given to culture and the arts has a long history in Nordic countries' (Wisti, 1981, p. 731). In the United States and Japan, business sponsorship has a well-established tradition. Indeed, the US National Endowment for the Arts is responsible for seeing that most federal grants are matched by private sources. The American tax system encourages contributions to arts expenditure. In Britain the Conservative government has made business sponsorship a matter of deliberate policy, to the point where it now brings in £15 million a year. In 1984 the Minister for the Arts announced a new Business Sponsorship Incentive Scheme, whereby the government matches certain business sponsorship contributions.

Business sponsorship benefits external cultural policy indirectly because it strengthens the home base for the arts; it can also make a direct contribution to the costs of cultural exports. The advantage to the business, of course, is publicity, first and foremost, but also the prestige that rubs off on associates when a first-class event is presented abroad, receptions are held and the richest and most influential forgather. As a government booklet says, 'Artistic performances and projects can receive considerable coverage in the local and national press and other media and provide a subtle and cost-effective means of reaching the informed general public' (Office of Arts and Libraries, 1981). In the twelve-month period from July 1982 to June 1983 the British Council raised almost £600,000 for business sponsorship of its programmes, mainly in exports of the arts, which represented some 25 per cent of its Arts Division's budget for that period. Most of this money was raised in the countries where the events took place.

There are several disputed areas in the arts side of cultural relations work. Should, for instance, the popular arts be supported or left to commercial channels? How far can one go in shocking the locals, one's paymasters, or home opinion, by avant-garde exports? How nationalistic should one be in insisting on including native compositions in orchestral programmes? How contemporary and how traditional should arts programmes be? How should funds be apportioned between the arts?

These and many other questions arise repeatedly. The existence of well-formulated policies makes it easier to handle such questions. But a cultural agency is best equipped to frame policies if it has advisers to turn to for specialist advice. Hence the existence of advisory committees, which have been considered more generally above. Ideally, in view of the specialization involved, it is desirable to have one committee for each broad sector of the arts. Members should be recognized as authorities; chairmen should be persons of sufficient distinction to be taken seriously by government and specialists. Committees of this kind can serve as a guarantee of the agency's soundness of judgement and as its champions against criticism.

The proliferation of festivals since the war has brought an enormous enrichment of the arts scene. They range from the great international occasions of world quality (e.g. Salzburg, Osaka, Berlin, Edinburgh) to small-scale celebrations of the significance and creativeness of particular localities. The *British Music Yearbook* of 1984 lists some 220 festivals in Britain 'wholly or considerably devoted to musical performance'; another sixty-odd folk and jazz festivals; just short of one hundred overseas festivals 'which have music as a principal feature', and about 275 competitive festivals in Britain, not including brass band championships and highland bagpipe competitions (Barton, 1984, pp. 387–419). In addition, there are festivals in celebration of events and anniversaries (e.g. 'Britain Salutes New York' of 1983, the Los Angeles Olympic Arts Festival of 1984, the Australian Bicentennial of 1988, and the William and Mary Tercentenary of 1988–9). Furthermore, there are drama festivals, film festivals and other more specialized festivals by the hundred.

It would be easy enough for any cultural agency to use up all its funds for the arts on sending performers and exhibitions to such festivals. The temptation consists not only in the prestige of the occasion but in the availability of money: ninety-six commercial companies and individual donors helped fund the Edinburgh International Festival of 1984, in addition to its grants from the City of Edinburgh District Council and the Scottish Arts Council. The first question an agency needs to ask itself is whether the expense of representation at international festivals is justified in comparison with other opportunities; for even if the money available to festivals is comparatively bountiful it is never enough, and costs are high because of the premium on world quality. The second question is whether the occasion is in line with the agency's objectives in the arts: is the audience compatible with one's targets, or is it too diffuse, too international, too blasé? An international audience may sound a perfect captive for the presentation of a country's best and boldest, but would one's objectives be better fulfilled by serving target audiences such as other artists, academics, students, officials and politicians? Obviously it depends on *ad hoc* factors as well as policy.

Frequently, there will be diplomatic pressure in favour of flying the flag at major festivals. In other words, the criteria of cultural diplomacy will be invoked. And some special festivals are too much like landmarks to be missed. The programme information of the Olympic Arts Festival of 1984 contained this mouth-watering statement:

> Variety abounds: clowns from Italy and Australia, giant puppets from Quebec, acrobats and musicians from the People's Republic of China. Discovery awaits: the white-powdered dancers of Sankaijuku, demon drummers of Kodo, the winners of the world's major chamber music competitions. Placido Domingo stars in the Royal Opera's stunning new production of *Turandot*, Jon Vickers sings *Peter Grimes*; and Derek Jacobi headlines the Royal Shakespeare Company's production of *Much Ado About Nothing*. France's celebrated director Ariane Mnouchkine presents *Richard II* in the Kabuki Tradition and Giorgio Strehler puts his distinctive directorial stamp on Shakespeare's *The Tempest* for Italy's renowned Piccolo Teatro di Milano.

Film, television and video have the capability of reaching vastly greater audiences than live arts performances. They have tended to figure peripherally in cultural relations work because their own prescribed channels of diffusion are commercial. Film distributors and television companies are anxious to receive revenue from abroad, and this can put restrictions even on non-theatric showing. For these reasons, the potential of the moving image has tended to be confined, mainly in institutes, to showing older feature films and screen versions of classic literature, together with documentary appetizers. The Goethe Institute in London, for instance, runs a valuable series of films for A-level examination pupils taking German.

But there are potential opportunities, which in terms of audience size far exceed these applications. A documentary or drama series on television, or a prize-winner at a film festival, can reach millions, often with an effect well adapted to the purposes of cultural relations. In many systems, it will fall to the embassy rather than the cultural representation to provide any services that are needed to smooth commercial channels, but there are various ways in which representations can be associated. Above all, they can invoke their other programmes in support, notably the exchange of persons.

Video also has many uses that make it an invaluable accession to cultural relations. The rapid expansion of software makes it possible for cultural representations to show material to small specialized groups. The availability of video tapes of very recent television programmes from home is one possible basis for the intellectual encounter that will be studied in the next chapter.

18
Schools, Science, Universities, Literature and Multilateralism

The purpose of this multifarious chapter will be to pursue the principle of exchange and co-operation in international cultural relations into other areas of activity. This will involve a consideration of target groups and the institutions to which they belong, the emphasis on communication in the mediator role of cultural representations, and the relationship between bilateral and multilateral functions.

Schools

Overseas schools are a starting point in the process of cultivating target groups for countries such as France, Germany and Italy, which maintain or support large numbers of schools abroad. If foreign children with academic potential attend such schools and acquire a grounding in the language, they represent a valuable reservoir for bilateral relations in subsequent stages of their careers. They can be encouraged to follow higher education in the sending country (at undergraduate or postgraduate level) and to become points of contact and influence on their return. Their diffusion throughout the professions builds up a nexus in such areas as government and public administration, the education system, science and technology, the arts, and various aspects of the media.

This strategy is obviously less necessary for the external cultural policy of countries that can rely on foreign education systems to produce, at the active professional stage, a goodly supply of their nationals already possessing a command of the target language. This is the case with English and, especially in Francophone regions, with

French. English demonstrates the point fairly conclusively. It is possible for cultural representations of English-speaking countries to select from a wide cross-section of 'successors' when they are looking for the most promising candidates to receive scholarship awards or to participate in youth programmes; in most parts of the world, they can depend on the availability of a basic, if not always adequate, knowledge of English, which has been inculcated by the local education system. Their choice, therefore, will be socially wider than that of cultural representations which depend on their own schools in the host country to produce successors with a knowledge of their language, for such schools inevitably attract the better-off and already internationally minded.

There are also other ways of dealing with the fundamental question of language in the selection of successors to target groups. The Soviet Union and East European countries give scholarship awards which are generous enough in their duration to include lengthy pre-sessional language study. As was said above, there is little information available about the success of the massive scholarship programmes of communist countries, but there is evidence that several award-holders never acquire a linguistic knowledge sufficient for the understanding of lectures. Another question that calls for some evaluative data is what the effect of study in Soviet-bloc countries may be on award-holders after their return home. After spending many years learning, and learning in, a difficult Slav language for instance, how are they encouraged to maintain contact with its source and with professional literature published there? Politically coloured friendship societies can be only part of the answer.

A different strategy is to employ the language of the host country for communication with target groups. It presupposes an advanced knowledge of that language on the part of cultural representatives; for this reason, it is not likely to be successful in countries whose languages are little-learnt elsewhere. Another strategy is for the cultural representative to communicate with target groups in a common language, which will usually be a world language but may be one that has currency locally for historical and geographical reasons (e.g. German in Hungary). Cultural representatives of the Federal Republic of Germany, for instance, find it practical in many countries to use English as the main vehicle of their cultural relations work to a degree that their French colleagues would find unacceptable. Moreover, German cultural representatives display an above-average ability to operate in the language of the host country.

Most countries' cultural representatives, in fact, will follow a combination of these strategies in communicating with their target groups. Again, it can be seen that English-speaking countries enjoy great advantages: not only do they have the benefit of a world language at their disposal but they save themselves the very considerable expense of supporting a considerable number of schools abroad in order to create the linguistic reservoir from which successors can be drawn.

Schools do more than turn out people with potential as successors to target groups. They instil the values and perspectives of the cultural base that informs their curriculum. They should therefore also be seen as an activity in cultural relations. They are indeed a first step in the sequence of intellectual encounter. The establishment of schools abroad was originally intended to meet the educational needs of expatriate communities abroad. Towards the end of the nineteenth century, European countries such as France, Germany and Italy were exporting their population at a vigorous rate. The reasons were partly commercial, partly demographic and partly colonial. Schools were set up initially to retain the national allegiance of emigrant families: the title of the private organization created in 1881 in Germany, the *Allgemeine Deutsche Schulverein zur Erhaltung des Deutschtums im Auslande* (the German Schools Association for the Preservation of Germanism Abroad), is itself a summary of this development. Alongside it, and sometimes interlocking with it, there were mission schools (also hospitals and, of course, churches), which were concerned with christianizing local people. By the twentieth century, and particularly during the turbulent years between the two World Wars, the lay schools also opened their doors to local children and, with the encouragement and support of home governments, sought to establish a basis for national influence by providing a subsidized education of a higher standard than in local schools.

The position now is that France has 174 *lycées* (secondary schools) and colleges, and 187 other schools, making a total of 361; Italy 373; Germany 507, of which, however, 284 are part-time. These figures will not be totally comparable, because they include schools of different types, private and state for instance, which have different bases of subsidization. But they give an idea of the scope. The geographical distribution tends to correspond more to historical causes than to current political shifts; there is clearly an obligation to maintain continuity in a matter so long-term as education. Both France and Germany have a wide spread of schools in Latin America. France also has a concentration in Francophone Africa and especially in North Africa. The financial commitment is heavy. About 38 per cent of the budget of the French foreign ministry in 1983 was spent on its cultural relations (that is, by the *Direction générale des relations culturelles scientifiques et techniques* – DGRCST) and of this the greater part in 1984 (54.8 per cent) was earmarked for the promotion of the French language (at the disposal of one of the four departments in the DGRCST, the *Direction du français*) (DGRCST, 1984, p. 18). Roughly two-thirds of this total has been devoted to schools. According to the German foreign ministry publication on its schools policy (*Auswärtiges Amt*, 1980, p. 5) about 40 per cent of its budget for external cultural policy in 1978 was spent on about 500 schools and minor support for some 1,000 other schools. Seen in these terms, the burden is heavy indeed. There is an obvious necessity to consider the priority that should be accorded to schools overseas.

The fact that they consume so large a proportion of the budgets of France and Germany, countries that have traditionally given due weight to the place of culture in society and to the demands of external cultural policies, poses the question whether the returns are commensurate with the expenditure. Obviously, these returns are to be assessed not only in strictly cultural relations terms (preparation of promising individuals as partners in co-operation) but also according to broader concepts of long-term political and economic advantage. Again, there exists no accurate means of measurement. It might be supposed that those who are brought under the educational and moral influence of another country during their formative school years make a greater return in goodwill than do those who spend a year or two at one of that country's universities at a later stage. There is no firm evidence either way. But from the point of view of backing winners, it is a more dependable strategy to devote one's resources to the further education and training of those who have emerged with distinction from their own national education system.

Since schools have such preponderance in the programmes of some major countries, it will be worth considering the matter more closely in relation to one practitioner. Germany offers extensive documentation. The publication of 1980 referred to above, *Auswärtige Kulturpolitik im Schulwesen* ('Schools in External Cultural Policy'), draws upon the Bundestag Report outlined in Chapter 13 (p. 125f), the study by Professor Peisert (p. 171), and a report of 1978 approved by the Federal Government, *Rahmenplan für die auswärtige Kulturpolitik im Schulwesen* ('Outline Plan for Schools in External Cultural Policy'), which coincided with the hundredth anniversary of the creation of the *Reich* School Fund in 1878 for the support of German schools abroad. The following classification of schools is described:

Begegnungsschulen ('encounter schools'), which cater for both German and local children and lead to examinations valid in both countries for entrance to universities. Such schools are subject to legal provisions of the host country. Schools of this type also exist in Germany itself: for example, the Franco-German schools in Saarbrücken and Freiburg. They are supported by the foreign ministry.

Expertenschulen ('expert schools'), which are intended primarily for the children of German experts resident abroad, have similar curricula to schools at home, and have German as the medium of instruction and the local language as preferred foreign language. A sub-category consists of *Firmenschulen* ('company schools'), which cater for the more transient population of children whose parents are required by their company to spend a limited time abroad. The main costs of these do not fall to the foreign ministry.

Schulen mit verstärktem Deutschunterricht ('schools with intensified German teaching'), are for non-German-speaking children being educated either in German as the medium of instruction or with a concentration on learning German.

Sprachgruppenschulen ('language group schools') are mainly the result of initiatives by German immigrants in Southern Africa and East and South-East Europe. Not all of them are supported by the foreign ministry. Their purpose is the maintenance of the mother tongue in German communities.

Sprachkurse ('language courses'), are mainly for children of German descent in local schools. In North America they are sometimes called *Sonnabendschulen* ('Saturday schools').

Then there are the European Schools, nine of them, which were originally for children of officials of member countries of the European Community but now also accept other pupils. German, with other languages, figures prominently in their teaching, both as a first and as a foreign language. In the Federal Republic, education is the responsibility of the *Länder*. The administration of overseas schools, therefore, is shared by central and regional governments, of which recruited teachers remain seconded employees. A central office in Cologne recruits and co-ordinates.

This panorama illustrates the demands and complexity of an overseas schools system, which from historical roots has extended and adapted to meet evolving needs. For completeness, we must also take into account the more general requirement of external cultural policy to assist the teaching of German in the schools of foreign education systems. This takes on a particular significance for Germany in view of the large number of children of foreign workers

(*Gastarbeiter*) who have returned to their own countries with a good knowledge of German.

It is not surprising that many Germans reflecting on their external cultural policy should express concern at the heavy commitment that is represented by the support of overseas schools. Is it still necessary to maintain *Deutschtum* (Germanism) at this high cost? The Federal Government's *Foreign Cultural Policy* (German Federal Foreign Office, 1978, p. 19), says, 'The federal financing of schools abroad raises numerous problems. Expenditures for educational services have risen enormously since 1967 . . .' and illustrates this point by showing the growth of school expenditure from DM 68.4 million in 1967 to an estimated DM 189 million in ten years to 1977. The then head of the foreign ministry's Cultural Department wrote (Arnold, 1979, p. 54):

> If however the number of German pupils at the German schools abroad should continue to rise exponentially then inevitably in many places, and ultimately also fundamentally, the question would arise about the conception, that is, whom and for what purpose the German schools abroad are meant to serve and how this aim could be integrated into foreign cultural policy.

There is also the question of the education of one's own nationals (essentially in the type of school the Germans call *Expertschulen*). It is desirable that any country with widespread overseas commitments should have the benefit of a network of schools for the use of its citizens working abroad; indeed, it can be argued that the absence of such schools can have an inhibiting effect on the country's commercial representation abroad and on the willingness of its enterprises to bid for contracts. Since Britain does not support schools abroad in the way of France, Germany and Italy, it is not easy for British subjects to find schools for their children. The US Department of State assists some 150 private schools around the world, which follow an American curriculum and have some American teachers. Many of them are called International Schools and have about half non-American pupils (Shriver, 1979, p. 101). Sometimes British children can attend these or other English-medium schools.

The schooling requirements of British subjects abroad is more a matter of educational than of external cultural policy, but there is clearly a connection between the two. Many British people working abroad feel at a disadvantage compared with those from countries that maintain networks of overseas schools. They normally have an allowance from their employer so that they can send their children to boarding schools in Britain. But this does not suit all families as a form of education and hardly meets the needs of the early school years. This is again a situation where the division of ministerial competence creates inflexibility. The Foreign and Commonwealth Office and the Overseas Development Administration have no general responsibility for the education of British children; the Department of Education and Science bears this responsibility at home, but not abroad. No part of government, therefore, can be expected to fund British schools abroad. The British Council has always given the support it can – for the sake of the foreign rather than the British pupils in such schools – but this rarely takes a financial form nowadays. Where they exist, schools are privately managed and financed. The realization that this puts British people at a disadvantage and the schools themselves under strain has been emphasized by the campaigns of such bodies as the Conference of Head Teachers of British Schools in the Middle East and the Council of British Independent Schools in the European Community. Essentially, the problem exists because, for Britain, there is a divorce between external cultural policy and education policy. But the underlying cause is that the spread of English as a world language has obviated the need to give official backing to English-medium schools as a means of diffusion; also, there is the tradition of private boarding school education in Britain. For France, Germany and Italy the two strands of policy coincide, but at a heavy cost in money and, arguably, in missed alternative opportunities for expenditure under external cultural budgets.

Science

Science, medicine and technology are obviously important areas of activity for the engagement of target groups in cultural relations. The sciences have their own long-established patterns of bilateral and multilateral co-operation; there is an abundance of agreements between governments and institutions. To a surprising extent, considering the jealous protection of military and industrial secrets, it is accepted that the fruits of research should be made available in print, that minds should meet at conferences, that students should seek out the most renowned exponents of their speciality, and that projects of common interest should be jointly pursued. This recognition of the universality of science is a positive factor, and has been strengthened by what one might call an environmental coming-of-age. It is not so much new as a re-assertion of earlier good sense. When Britain and France were embattled in the Napoleonic Wars, Sir Humphry Davy was enabled to visit Paris and lecture to the

Institut de France, and the American navy agreed not to impede Captain Cook's voyages of discovery during the War of Independence.

The governmental involvement in this universality means that science has become an ingredient of diplomacy and, because of its socio-economic effects, of cultural diplomacy. We shall consider later the need for non-governmental mediation at the level of cultural relations. But first it is necessary to have regard to the 'size' of science, in international matters. Science is big when it is a field of high priority and heavily funded by participating governments. CERN (the European Organization for Nuclear Research), which is the major focus for non-military nuclear research, is an obvious example; so is ESA (the European Space Agency). There is also a great deal of scientific co-operation which rests on inter-governmental agreements and finance but which does not qualify in the general estimation as big. Whatever its size, inter-governmental science has a predominantly practical purpose. This is a point of difference between joint programmes and projects in the postwar world and their more exploratory forerunners at the time of initiation in the nineteenth century. This practical element, often tending towards the technological, is evident in the world-wide context in the United Nations specialized agencies, for instance, UNESCO, FAO (the Food and Agriculture Organization), WHO (the World Health Organisation) and IAEA (the International Atomic Energy Agency), whose predominant concern is indeed not only practical but developmental.

The characteristic of inter-governmental science of any size is that it is based on agreements, paid for by national contributions and subject to national and international control. The representation of national interest is the business of the organizations' own mechanisms and of diplomatic staff. Many embassies now carry a scientific attaché to act as a regular channel for this purpose and, of course, to report on scientific developments in the host country. Such functions are properly seen as belonging to diplomacy. When they touch directly on the non-governmental sector (for instance, research institutes and universities) or when they have a wider socioeconomic effect, they become cultural diplomacy. As a rule, science is explicitly included in Cultural Agreements and Conventions: Appendix B (p. 235) gives an example in quoting the part of the Agreement between the United Kingdom and the USSR concerned with 'Exchanges in the Field of Science'. Basket III of the Helsinki Agreement of 1975 has already been adduced as a manifestation of cultural diplomacy. Under the overall rubric, *Co-operation and Exchanges in the Field of Education*, this engages the signatories,

'Within their competence to broaden and improve co-operation and exchanges in the field of science . . .' with particular reference to the sharing of information, contacts between scientists and institutions, and co-ordinated or joint programmes (Conference on Security and Co-operation in Europe, 1975, p. 47).

The fact that the Helsinki Agreement puts science under the heading of education is more logical than might at first appear. Although inter-governmental agreements are normally concerned with the productive or industrial end of the scientific process, this process has its roots and sustenance in education, training, research, information, visits, and links. From these spring the scientific potential of any country; without the development of this and its injection into the institutions that apply it, the whole process would atrophy. It is relevant to this theme that the Commission of the European Communities has put forward a proposal for setting up an action programme of the Community in education and training for technology (Comett) which in the period 1986–92 is intended to bring about closer harmonization of training between universities and industry, and in its initial phase to create a European network of University–Industry Training Partnerships.

For all the universality of science, the greatest number of trained scientists enters the national system of each country and is enclosed there. International contact is far from automatic, nor is it envisaged by government programmes. It is here, and particularly on the educational side of the national system, that cultural relations have their part to play. For cultural agencies possess the wherewithal to foster valuable exchanges in the sciences. By the provision of scholarships they give able students the opportunity of study and research; by inward and outward visits they bring together the key people in particular specializations; by arranging seminars in partnership with local institutions they highlight areas of common interest; by their library and information services they lay a basis for the sharing of knowledge; by their language-teaching they open the way to more effective assimilation, especially if the language in question is one that has an international scientific literature, such as English, French and German.

We have already seen that cultural agencies achieve their greatest success if they direct their efforts at target groups. This applies *par excellence* to work in the sciences (even if we accept that the isolated action may prove an imaginative first step towards the opening-up of new vistas, and that the inspired award of a scholarship may indeed turn out to be a triumph of serendipity; in these cases, if the recipient is outstanding there may be benefits in personal terms, or the dream of the 'Einstein in Chad' might be realized). But as a matter of general priority, it is desirable to concentrate resources on target groups according to those subjects that promise the greatest scope for co-operation and the building of long-term relationships.

The fostering of links between university departments or research institutes is the pre-eminent way of helping such relationships to grow and flourish. After the identification of the partners, the cultural agency injects funds, which facilitate the overtures and mutual familiarization, and thereafter applies its exchange of persons programme and other resources to maintain the vigour of the connection. Otherwise, the linked institutions provide the administration and the bulk of the resources, which is natural because they are the beneficiaries. Some examples from the British experience will serve as illustrations. The Chinese National Research Centre for Science and Technology for Development entered into an arrangement with the Science Policy Research Unit of Sussex University in 1983. This covered the exchange of research fellows and the development of joint research projects. This collaboration, financially supported by the British Council, led to an agreement on the theme of technology transfer in the offshore oil industry. Another link supported by the British Council was initiated in 1980–1 between the Centre for Water Resources in Madras and Birmingham University, on groundwater modelling. Between developed countries links are legion, and often require no outside help. One striking initiative is that undertaken by the Spanish government in its wish to encourage cultural and educational relations with Britain. In 1983 a Spanish Joint Co-ordinating Committee selected the initial thirty-six inter-departmental joint research projects between Spanish and British universities and polytechnics. This programme is jointly funded by the Spanish Ministry of Education and Science and the British Council. It is interesting, and an example of flexibility in cultural relations work, that the British Council's contribution came from the earnings of its direct teaching of English in Spain.

Of even greater importance than individual links is the network of learned societies and national research councils. Against a background of longer history, the International Association of Academies was founded in 1899 to co-ordinate the work of learned societies and the international unions devoted to particular sciences. After the First World War, the International Research Council was set up as its successor, only to be succeeded in turn, in 1931, by the International Council of Scientific Unions (ICSU). Obviously, learned societies and academies have many functions besides the international one, but they are powerful and prestigious components of bilateral and multilateral co-operation. Moreover, they have the authority to launch important initiatives. It was, for instance, at the suggestion of the Royal Society of London, in 1982, that the European Science Foundation (ESF) was set up at Strasbourg, with the objects of promoting co-operation in fundamental research, the free movement of research workers, the exchange of ideas and knowledge, and the harmonization of research programmes.

Organizations such as ICSU and ESF perform at the macro level the co-operative functions that cultural agencies further at the micro level. And, because cultural agencies operate mainly bilaterally rather than multilaterally, the scope as well as the scale of their work in the sciences is less. But the exchange of persons programmes are of real significance. The British Council, for instance, which has some thirty specialist posts abroad occupied by scientifically qualified staff, states that of the foreigners for whom it arranged programmes in Britain during the financial year 1984/85 'approximately half (some 10,000 people) were in the subject areas of science and technology' (British Council, 1985, p. 50). In the same annual report the Council says, 'the commercial benefits to Britain from promoting a wider knowledge and understanding of our scientific and technological advances are considerable'.

The exploitation of these commercial benefits and the representation of national interest in inter-governmental science falls to the diplomatic mission. But in each country there needs to be a co-ordination point, whether in a cultural agency or at the embassy, where an up-to-date conspectus is available of all the various governmental and non-governmental inputs. And, of course, in science as in the arts there is an intimate relation between external and internal policies. To take the British example again, the development of the Nuffield Science Programme at home had a considerable influence on teaching methods in other, especially developing, countries. The funding and furtherance of science at home will have an inevitable effect on international co-operation. When it was said in the presidential address at the 147th annual meeting of the British Association for the Advancement of Science, in 1985, that industry should make up the deficit in the funding of basic research, with reference to the example of Germany, this pointed also perhaps towards new or extended forms of international co-operation.

The indispensability of co-operation through science and technology for the solution of the world's material problems is obvious enough. But scientists are also among the leading thinkers of their generation. Beyond the empirical, they are contributors to the philosophical, moral and futurological debate. Out of their intellectual encounters arise the ideas and formulations that will shape the context of politics and determine our way of life. It is significant that the most high-ranking, non-official action to safeguard world peace, the Pugwash Movement, which began its meetings in 1957, is composed predominantly of eminent scientists.

Target Groups and Communication

In accordance with its agreed objectives, the cultural representation works with target groups through whatever activities are included in its programmes. Members of these groups are people who are in a position to carry out exchanges as the executors of co-operative programmes. They may be academics in university departments, scientists, arts administrators, or whatever. There are various ways in which they can be addressed and cultivated (gifts of materials, specialist information, invitations, honours) but the main attraction will be professional opportunity. The emphasis is on mutual communication between these groups and counterparts in the sending country. We must now consider how this communication can best be achieved and how it relates to intellectual encounter.

Most of the activity areas to which intellectual encounter applies clearly call for the support of the exchange of persons programme. The areas are, for instance: science, medicine and technology, in which, as we have seen, clear identification of subjects of common priority is an essential starting-point; education, where changes in theory and practice create a background of mutual interest; information and libraries, which we have seen to be a basic activity; language teaching and learning, which are of general concern and in some relationships will have a policy dynamic behind them (as in the European Community); social sciences, which in most countries' cultural relations programmes receive less attention than they should as one of the principal interfaces; literature, which is one of the most obviously exposed fringes of national consciousness and creativity; the arts, which require contact between people as well as perform-ance and the presentation of artefacts.

In the institute model, the lecture has been the preferred means of communication. The programmes of activities of cultural representations still tend to bill the lecture as a hallmark of serious intent. And yet there are two substantial objections to it. First, it is not really an effective means of communication: unless the speaker happens to be famous, brilliant or in some other way memorable, his remarks will be only half absorbed and rapidly forgotten. Secondly, the lecture is a one-way activity; it dates, in concept, from earlier forms of cultural relations work. Apart from a few, usually rather peripheral, questions at the end, the lecture is by its nature a piece of exposition without discussion; it scores few marks for mutuality.

True, it gives the audience the chance to follow native speech, but there are more effective audio-visual alternatives.

Lectures designed for target audiences are much more likely to attract a good attendance if they are given in the local institutions. Lectures held at cultural institutes seldom attract the active, professional audience that would best assist the process of understanding. It is the lecture that seems most to beguile those scapegoats of communication failure whom the French call 'old ladies' and whom the Germans embellish as 'old ladies with hats'. Grémion and Chenal (1980, p. 102) report the reaction of a seconded teacher in a French institute, which reflects the need to drum up audiences, 'As for lectures, when the hall is empty we drive the students up to fill it. All the same, one lecture a month is not enormous'. The director of one institute said (p. 102), 'It's free here. We would pay people to come'. And another seconded teacher went so far as to say (p. 104), 'The lecture is a ridiculous piece of sclerosis. This formula should be given up – it's a waste of money. You get the impression that the lecturers come to sell their books. And we are forced to attend.'

A more successful alternative is the kind of discussion that goes under various titles – seminar, symposium, colloquium. The essential point is that it should involve participants from both countries, deal with a subject of common interest and be an exchange rather than a one-way transfer. Seminars (to choose one name for them) are best organized in co-operation with a local institution such as a university department; costs can be shared in this way and one is assured of the right kind of participation. Often the sharing is done by the cultural representation bringing out specialists from its own country and the local partner providing venue and publicity. The Austrian Institute in London has run a series of seminars on this basis. One, held in May 1984, a 'Symposium on the Viennese Popular Theatre', illustrates the methodology. There was an opening lecture at the Austrian Institute; then there were lectures and discussion at Bedford College of London University, where theatrical performances of Nestroy and Raimund were given by a visiting Viennese company. Another example, which also included artistic performances, was the four-day symposium 'City Culture: Cultured City' organized by the Goethe Institute in Hong Kong in October 1984. The theme, which was concerned with the role of culture in an urban society, had a particular appropriateness to Hong Kong. In addition to the actual performances, there were exhibitions, experimental films and a film workshop as part of the programme. Papers were read by invited speakers from Britain, Germany and Hong Kong. Each of these was followed by a response from one of the Hong Kong participants as a way of launching a discussion.

Universities

Any consideration of intellectual encounter as a theme in cultural relations must include, however superficially, some reflections on the role of the university. Of the institutions outlined in Chapter 8 (p. 68) as making up the Constituency (that aggregate of resources and interests on which cultural agencies draw), the university is the most obvious power-house and co-operant. It is remarkable how much universities in different countries and different thought-systems have in common, both in concept and in structure. The university is one of the least acclaimed European exports. Yet it has exercised a normative function throughout the world in propagating techniques for national progress and models for international co-operation. Just as from its beginnings in twelfth-century Bologna, Paris and Oxford, the university broke through self-validating preconceptions and diffused the new learning of the Renaissance, and in the nineteenth century applied the lessons of industrialization, so in our time it has driven a highway through wastelands to the shared attainments of modern thought and technology. Moreover, the university is a means of social as well as educational evolution, for it disseminates ideas, and ideologies, across traditional barriers; in the process it creates elites, which give their own particular focus to accumulated learning and experience. It creates these elites not only by teaching but also by bestowing qualifications which distinguish those who are predictably going to occupy leading positions in research, education, communication, administration, the professions and the bureaucracy.

It follows that universities are natural partners in the activities of cultural relations. They are uniquely equipped to co-operate with like and other institutions in three capacities. First, as concentrations of thinkers, researchers and administrators; secondly, as places where minds are trained and skills imparted; thirdly, as corporations possessing their own organizational features. More briefly, university staff can perform as specialists, teachers, and academics. And one of the common features universities share is a dedication to values as well as to products. One of these values is a respect for learning as something that transcends political frontiers: the frontiers of the mind are undrawn.

There are divers forms of association in which this internationalism finds expression. The International Association of Universities (IAU) was founded in 1950 and embraces 100 countries all over the world, with a secretariat in Paris. Within the European context there is the Liaison Committee of the Rectors' Conferences of the European Community (LC), founded in 1973 to co-ordinate relations between national conferences and with the European

Community. The European Community itself finances schemes such as the 'joint programmes of study' and 'short study visits' and publishes the *Student Handbook*. Although the Treaty of Rome made no specific mention of education at any level, the EC has meetings of Education Ministers and an Education Committee. The EC Commission's Directorate-General XII (Science, Research and Development) has an important involvement in higher education, and to a lesser extent so have DG V (Employment, Social Affairs and Education) and DG VIII (Development). The Standing Conference of Rectors, Presidents and Vice-Chancellors of the European Universities (CRE) is a product of the Brussels Treaty of 1948 and took its current shape in 1964. The secretariat is in Geneva.

The Council of Europe has a Standing Conference on University Problems (CCPU), which is a committee of the Steering Council for Cultural Co-operation and evolved from the now defunct Committee for Higher Education and Research. UNESCO runs the European Centre for Higher Education (CEPES), established in Bucharest in 1972 for co-operation and innovation. Of wider geographical scope are the Education Committee and the Centre for Educational Research and Innovation (CERI), run by the Organization for Economic Co-operation and Development (OECD), in Paris. Even wider are the bounds of the Association of Commonwealth Universities (ACU), which was founded by the universities themselves in 1913. One major South–South forum, to which we shall recur later in this chapter, is the South East Asian Ministers of Education Organization (SEAMEO), whose collaborative programmes include higher education.

Three international university institutions have come into existence since the war. The oldest is the College of Europe at Bruges, founded in 1949, which offers a one-year course for graduates on different aspects of European integration. The University Institute at Florence, created in 1972, provides study and research facilities for postgraduate work on European themes. Unlike these, the United Nations University set up in 1975 in Tokyo, has no campus, for it has no student body. It is an autonomous academic institution that operates through more than 120 institutions in over 60 countries. It runs a decentralized system of co-ordinated research networks, 'which bring the scientific and intellectual resources of academic institutions and research centres round the world to bear on practical problems of global significance, such as nutritional deficiency, the effect of sudden oil wealth, or international migration' (Newland, 1984, p. 1).

This by no means exhaustive tally indicates the scale of multilateral co-operation that exists. But, important though this is for establishing principles of common interest and concerting their application, much of the more practical co-operative work is done between universities or their individual departments. Links of this kind are, as we have seen in Chapter 15, a productive way of focusing effort, whether through staff interchange, enrolment of foreign students, shared research or integrated courses. Moreover, links can often overcome the chronic problems of equivalence of qualifications, still one of the major obstacles to greater student mobility, through courses with built-in mutual recognition. Russo (1982, p. 59) gives the example of a joint engineering course, which is trilateral, involving the University of Essex, Karlsruhe University and the *École Supérieure d'Ingénieurs en Electrotechnique et Electronique* in Paris. Each student follows a course that includes all three institutions and provision is made for language training. One of the objects is stated as being, 'Total integration of the students into the host institution both scientifically, linguistically and culturally' (Russo, p. 60). In Britain, the division of study time between the foreign and the British University has become a growing pattern for postgraduates taking higher degrees, especially those from the developing Commonwealth. The North–South axis of university co-operation produces a major flow for the transfer of skills and experience. Although this attracts large sums of educational aid funds, the universities themselves operate in free association; their independence is not the least of the lessons they have to teach.

These arrangements and the courses of study that are part of them are normally set up by the institutions themselves. The capacity for independent initiative is one of the strengths of the higher education system. But there is frequently a role for cultural agencies to play in helping to identify opportunities for inter-university collaboration and injecting the sums of money that get them launched. Selective pump-priming has become all the more necessary with the increase of financial stringency and administrative obstacles affecting university management.

In addition to reciprocal activity of this kind, there is a range of schemes and programmes operated by cultural agencies in which university staff are the principal participants. In many parts of the world research in subjects of international interest is based predominantly on university departments, on a gamut from science and technology to philosophy and art history. Creative as well as scholarly writers are often also academics. The university is therefore commonly the most important single resource for cultural agencies in their work, and a prime focus for intellectual encounter.

Whether the university is currently able to realize its international potential to the full is questionable. Its main purpose must lie within the domestic education system. The fulfilment of this is often adversely affected by restrictive and regulatory government policies and the resultant bureaucratization. Furthermore, the function of the university in the community at large has been modified by social and institutional change, so that the university today is increasingly perceived as one component of a congeries of bodies for further and higher education. No wonder, then, if universities have suffered an erosion of confidence, which impairs their international vision and might even bring about an inward-looking preoccupation with their own problems. The remedy for this is less likely to be forthcoming from governments than from themselves. And, in Britain, universities are making a notable effort towards self-help. There has been an increased emphasis on public relations work so as to raise the level of general awareness as well as to attract financial support from industry and well-wishers, and to earn more revenue from their own facilities. Universities are after all institutions with historically proven powers of resilience and adaptation. And part of the remedy must surely be sought in the international dimension. Not only are the difficulties common to other countries. At a higher level, the capacity of universities to address overriding problems, such as those presented in the Brandt Report, is a measure of their intellectual and moral vigour, and of their power to contribute to the policy formulation of governments.

It is an almost self-evident fact, but one that bears assertion in this context, that cultural representatives need to have a real familiarity with the universities of the countries in which they work and a sound knowledge of those at home. For them, the universities and other institutions of higher education are a vital part of the home constituency they represent. The more this can be recognized by training attachments of career staff to these institutions and by the secondment of academics to cultural representations abroad, the better for the fostering of inter-university relationships.

In his *Notes Towards a Definition of Culture*, T. S. Eliot (1948, p. 123) said of the universities, 'they should stand for the preservation of learning, for the pursuit of truth, and in so far as men are capable of it, the attainment of wisdom'. The last of these is a quality that is not included in link agreements and aid programmes. Most people would consider that wisdom is in short supply. There is no obvious reservoir of it in modern societies, but it is to the university rather than anywhere else that the questor might turn to find out where, and where not, to start looking for it.

The Involvement of Writers

The role of literature as a bridge between nations has found many advocates. Authors probably have more regard and sympathy for their foreign counterparts than members of other professions. Since its inception in 1921, PEN has been a forum for this solidarity, especially in respect of writers oppressed by totalitarian regimes. These words of Storm Jameson, the first woman president of PEN, appeared in *PEN News* of October 1938:

> We of the P.E.N. believe that the intellect can, and indeed must, ignore frontiers. The man of letters has two mother countries, the one he entered at his birth, and the other that he entered on the day he recognized, in a writer of another nation, a friend or teacher whose written words became part of his own experience.

The international-mindedness of writers has long been a factor in their attraction to cultural relations work, whether as representatives, contract teachers or visiting lecturers. The cultural institute, with its library and programme of events, is a natural focus for the sharing of literary interests. Cultural agencies, therefore, regard writers as an important resource. The Canada Council and the Scottish Arts Council even run an annual exchange of Canadian and Scottish writers, who are attached to universities for the duration of their award.

Writers are among the most rewarding participants in intellectual encounter, which often appears to score its greatest successes when the dialogue is between writers on opposite sides of a political barrier. The successful efforts of the Goethe Institute to bring local writers together with their German opposite numbers in Salazar's Portugal, which has been mentioned above (p. 76), is an example. PEN itself exists to provide this kind of communication. The *Frankfurter Allgemeine Zeitung* of 11 January 1975 carried an interview with the German novelist Heinrich Böll, recently returned from a PEN Congress in Jerusalem, in which he reported the view of the chargé d'affaires of the German embassy that the presence of German writers at the congress had done more for Israel–German relations than two years of routine cultural work.

The most successful way of transferring experience through literature is in the form of books. Since the number of people who can read books in the original is small, and in some languages very small indeed, translation is necessary, which in many countries is left more or less to commercial channels. Some countries subsidize the translation of their literature into other languages; fewer do the same with translations into their own languages. Again, the inward-and-outward syndrome shows itself. The translation of significant works of literature, especially contemporary literature, is highly germane to the concerns of cultural relations. Hungary is one of the few countries that have an active subsidized programme of translation in both directions. There could well be some future in the French proposal, advanced at a symposium at the German–French Institute at Ludwigsburg in October 1984, that special scholarship awards for translators should be given to enable them to spend some time gaining more knowledge and insight at one of the universities of the partner country.

The Multilateral Challenge

If the promotion of understanding between two nations is good, is not the same between several nations even better? And, if enduring links of co-operation between two countries are the desirable product of cultural relations, what of links between many countries? How does one in any case exploit the funds that member states make available through international organizations?

Bilateral cultural relations are conducted today in a context where myriad international organizations, many of them concerned with subjects of direct interest to cultural agencies, are at work. Archer (1983, p. 29) refers to the *Yearbook of International Organisations* in saying, 'Even excluding the INGOs [international non-governmental organizations] associated with the European Community and EFTA, the total number of these organizations has mushroomed from 176 in 1902 to 1,253 in 1960, 1,993 in 1970 and now stands at well over 2,000'. Archer also makes the point that international organizations have an important role in communication and information:

> The more traditional approach towards transmitting ideas and messages in the system was through national governments with the help of their diplomatic services. The growth in international organizations together with the increased and easier use of the media of communications has meant that sovereign states can no longer pretend to be dominant in the exchange of international information. (Archer, 1983, p. 168)

Also, as we have seen earlier, international organizations have a particular relevance to the North–South dialogue because they are not so readily associated with propaganda or cultural imperialism. A transfer from a developed to a developing country may be less effective than the same transfer filtered through an international organization of which both countries are members.

Yet, in general, international organizations are likely to remain a context and not to become a principal focus in cultural relations. A dialogue between two parties is more conducive to understanding than is a debate between several. An umbrella organization such as UNESCO, quite apart from its present administrative problems, is no more capable of subsuming cultural relations work between states than the UN would be of supplanting diplomacy. International organizations can direct world attention and resources to global needs, as in the campaign against illiteracy, but they are too diffuse to concentrate on more nationally specific questions. Bilateral relations would hardly be furthered if they were approached through multi-lateralism, whereas multilateralism acquires practicality from the bilateral experience of participating states. Moreover, relationships of partnership and co-operation, such as can with some professional ingenuity and adequate resources be developed between two countries, would be diluted and depersonalized – and almost certainly bureaucratized – if they were attenuated to an international dimension. The language problem would be another impediment.

Regional multilateralism provides a more unitary context. The meetings of ministers of culture and education of the Council of Europe and, since 1984, meetings of the ministers of culture of the European Community (EC), launch initiatives and release resources that can be of use to cultural agencies in their bilateral work. We have seen how difficult it is for some governments to justify expenditure on cultural relations when domestic necessities are so clamant. The agreement on priorities at an international level, and the obligation on governments to follow positive policies, may therefore be beneficial. When ministers from a variety of countries come together to discuss culture there is a tendency for the discussions to take on an elevated tone – in which admittedly individual national interest may also be audible. For instance, the EC ministers of culture at their meeting in November 1984 discussed the intensification of cultural co-operation. One of the matters debated under this heading was the Greek initiative that Athens should be designated European Cultural City for 1985, with a concentration of Greek and other European cultural events. The Greek minister of culture, Melina Mercouri, has represented the view that the EC is also a cultural community and that this aspect of its identity is more fundamental than the economic. Yet at little as 0.0007 per cent of the EC budget is devoted to culture.

Other cities proposed for the title in subsequent years are Florence (1986), Amsterdam (1987) and London (1988). This is an example of the way a collective initiative can involve the participation of govern-ments and lead to greater public awareness of a common cultural base. The effect of this initiative on bilateral cultural relations between EC countries cannot be foretold but, as the series of European Cultural Cities unfolds, it may be anticipated that these relations will be intensified between the countries hosting the occasions and their partners. The idea of having a European showcase erected in major cultural centres is appealing. The Council of Europe's art exhibitions, which have been held regularly since 1955, have a similar purpose but do not embrace other accompanying activities in the same way.

Europe has been described – perhaps inanely – as a 'cultural super-power'. One question arising from this imputed status is how to exercise it effectively on the world stage; another is how to employ it as a unifying force for member states. So far as the EC is concerned, the second question takes on new compulsions with expanding membership. From time to time the idea of advancing European union is mentioned – and researched. The Catholic University of Louvain (1985) catalogues 1,786 works of university research on European integration. The Solemn Declaration on European Union, which was signed by the EC heads of government at their European summit meeting in Stuttgart in 1983, includes a chapter on cultural co-operation where member governments are urged to seek closer co-operation in youth exchanges, language teaching, artistic contact and conservation, as well as improving the level of knowledge about Europe as a whole in individual countries and promoting Community cultural activities in third countries. Linked with this is the Tindemans proposal of a European Foundation for the purpose of improving understanding among peoples of member states and promoting a better understanding of the European cultural heritage. The European Foundation will be sited in Paris and financed by EC contributions. It is not to be confused with the non-governmental European Cultural Foundation (ECF), which has existed in Amsterdam since 1960 to promote cultural, social, educational and scientific activities of European interest; the membership of the ECF goes beyond the EC and its funds have come largely from Dutch lottery and football pool proceeds. The ECF has set up a network of institutions and centres for scientific and research and policy studies.

Multilateral v. Bilateral

It is clear that, in the future, West European governments are going to be confronted with a more compelling choice between multilateral and bilateral options in executing their external cultural policy. The choice will pose some fundamental questions, the answers to which will condition policies over a wide area of activities. At present governments still favour bilateral channels – overwhelmingly so far as their budgetary allocations are concerned. But it can be debated whether this is because these have been found more effective or because external cultural policies are still conditioned by the concept of national self-projection, or even cultural propaganda. If the principle of mutual benefit were to be fully developed, might it not be considered more appropriate to broaden the scope of mutuality more extensively into the multilateral dimension? Probably not, at least not at present. Dread of international bureaucracy has been exacerbated by the UNESCO scandal. And yet multilateralism has already proved its advantages in the sciences, where many programmes of study and research are by their nature international. As we have seen, the European Science Foundation at Strasbourg is an invaluable focus of co-operation and the International Council of Scientific Unions (ICSU) provides a forum not only for programmes of co-operation but also for new ideas that open up perspectives for the future.

UNESCO is so central to the themes under consideration in this chapter that it calls for closer treatment. So far as the 'S' for science is concerned, UNESCO has maintained its value more persuasively than in some of its other, more politicized areas. It is easier for politicians to ride their hobby-horses over the downland of education and culture than up the crags of scientific specialization. From a Western point of view, the essence of the UNESCO aberration is expressed in an article in *Encounter* of December 1984:

> The 161-member organization, founded by some 20 post-war constitutional democracies, now serves the majority of anti-democratic countries, ruled by unrepresentative and unelected leaders, running the modern government gamut from tin-pot-authoritarian to iron-walled totalitarian. The mid-century's unlearned lesson – although taught by savants from Tocqueville to Aron – is that the special interest among these ruling political classes is holding on to state power, frustrating the aspirations of citizens for genuine self-determination. (Crovitz, 1984, pp. 9–18)

It was no doubt inevitable that UNESCO should in some measure fall victim to the East–West divide and the North–South gap. In sober retrospect, we can see that the often quoted proposition in the preamble to its constitution begged the question: 'Since wars begin in the minds of men, it is in the minds of men that the defences of peace must be constructed, and peace must be founded on the intellectual and moral solidarity of mankind'. The withdrawal of the United States and Britain and the threatened withdrawal of other countries from UNESCO make sense as a condemnation of the abuses that have reportedly permeated its administration and attitudes. Lord Vaizey summed up the argument when he said in a debate in the House of Lords, 'It has been allowed to become a major centre of anti-Western agitation and propaganda' (Hansard, 1984, p. 304). Nevertheless, it is also true that the differences dividing the four parts of the world-compass exist and that they require a forum for their expression. That UNESCO should take on that function is a corruption of its idealistic, universalist purpose. But this is not in every sense a negative development. There are worse ways in which the opposing interests could be manifested. And there is, as has been shown, a cultural (and an educational and scientific) dimension to the East–West and North–South axes. UNESCO can hardly solve, but it can vocalize these problems. By so doing, it is a mouthpiece for the dynamic engendered by these cardinal tensions.

The Commonwealth has succeeded surprisingly well in coping with North–South tensions. The fact that its now forty-nine member countries, with their great variety, have voluntarily and comparatively informally maintained their mutual connection, in spite of the fundamental differences that occasionally arise between them, speaks for the vigour of their cultural bonds. They share a language, certain institutional models, and an approach. The Commonwealth has been likened to a club: its members are equal, respect one another's right to be different, can resign whenever they feel like it, and accept the club rules. The relationship is an example of implicit cultural diplomacy, which is reinforced by co-operative programmes but draws its real strength from like-mindedness and goodwill.

Regional co-operation which does not attempt to span one of the great divides has better chances of success than essays in universalism. The West European mechanisms referred to above achieve undramatic but valuable progress. The Organization for Economic Co-operation and Development (OECD) also has an involvement in culture and education. On a more limited scale, Denmark, Finland, Iceland, Norway and Sweden collaborate as members of the Nordic Council in the spirit of the Nordic Cultural Agreement, which they signed in Helsinki in 1971. The object is to strengthen co-operation between them and 'create a basis for a co-ordinated Nordic contribution in international cultural co-operation' (Lyche, 1974, p. 115). There is a Nordic Cultural Secretariat in Copenhagen and a joint cultural budget (Nordic Cultural Fund). Three regional associations of states concerned with intra-Third World development are the Arab League Educational, Cultural and Scientific Organization (ALECSO), based in Tunis, which maintains links with UNESCO and has the promotion of intellectual unity of the Arab countries as one of its aims; the Association of South East Asian

Nations (ASEAN), which has strong cultural objects, thanks in part to the ASEAN Cultural Fund of US $25 million set up by Japan in 1978; the South East Asian Ministers of Education Organization (SEAMEO), based in Bangkok, which promotes co-operative projects and programmes in education, science and culture, and maintains regional centres for their execution.

This by no means completes the list of regional associations between states that have some bearing on cultural co-operation. The scene is a variegated one. The debate on bilateral and multilateral alternatives in cultural relations would benefit from more evaluation of their respective cost-effectiveness. Indeed, a world conspectus of activities, budgets and results would be invaluable. It would make it possible to assess comparative value, and value for money.

Co-operation between Cultural Agencies

Co-operation between like-minded cultural agencies is already practised informally in many parts of the world. It has been suggested that this might be more structured. Institutes would perhaps best lend themselves to any experiment of this nature because they have in common a high degree of public access through language-teaching, libraries, and cultural programmes. In this spirit, the Council of Europe commissioned the Goethe Institute to investigate the possibility of closer co-operation between European cultural institutes. The result was a 1983 publication, *Jeder für sich oder gemeinsam?* ('Every one for himself or together?') This contemplates some Asian country, as suggested by the Council of Europe in 1971, as the possible site for the experimental creation of a European Cultural Institute (Triesch and Deutschmann, 1983, p. 31).

Such an experiment would bring not only valuable lessons but would be a manifestation of the common elements in European culture. The EC has political and economic representations overseas; why not a cultural one? If Europe is indeed a 'cultural super-power' should it not occasionally display itself in its full majesty rather than in national fragments? After all, Tindemans (1976, p. 28) foresaw that the European Foundation he recommended would 'have a role to play in presenting abroad the image of a United Europe'. There would be advantages for the local citizenry in being able to go to one establishment to learn different languages, read books and periodicals from different countries, and choose between cultural offerings. Moreover, having premises in common and using expensive public and teaching rooms by rota would bring a financial saving. As Efinger (1976, p. 89) pointed out, this could also be more minimally achieved by the sharing of premises without any surrender of national identity. Already cultural representations of the Western democracies liaise and co-operate in some of their programmes (e.g. by combining over European film festivals) and have succeeded in playing down the earlier spirit of rivalry. It would not be a tremendous step to set up shop together in one capital city and see the effect on their business.

Europe possesses a more unitary culture than other continents. Its cultural divisions are more linguistic than anything else. A European Cultural Institute with a sophisticated teaching programme in at least the main European languages and a European emphasis in its other activities would be an interesting departure for Europe and stimulating for the country chosen for the experiment. There would be advantages in selecting a country with a living cultural tradition of its own and without a recent colonial history. Michael Freiherr Marschall von Biberstein, a proponent of this notion, wrote in an article in *Die Zeit* of 7 December, 1973: 'As executive organs of a common cultural policy, institutes should be established, first in other parts of the world and then in Community countries. It will be their task to analyse the needs of the host countries and accordingly to establish as far as possible long-term programmes.' The time is ripe for the experiment.

19

External Broadcasting and the New Technology

External broadcasting is not normally considered in connection with cultural relations (or even cultural diplomacy). The literature on the two subjects tends to be discrete, and there is little connection in the minds of governments which engage in both activities. There have been several reasons for maintaining a conceptual distinction. Cultural relations had already established their pattern of operation before external broadcasting became widespread in the 1930s; radio quickly became an instrument of propaganda and counter-propaganda in the period before, during and after the Second World War. Both subjects, however, reflect the foreign policy and domestic attitudes of countries concerned, and both of them depend for their success on their sensitiveness to receptivity in the countries addressed. Sometimes external broadcasting is, like cultural relations, the business of the foreign ministry, sometimes of another ministry, such as the ministry of information. Programme emphasis is on the presentation of news and political comment, with other material to attract audiences and create a favourable image. Culture, especially popular culture, is often used to take away the bitter taste of the doctrinaire pill.

There are important common factors, then, and these have indeed led to some consideration of external broadcasting in earlier chapters. These factors are perhaps a matter of alignment rather than of similarity. This alignment will probably increase in importance with the development of new technologies. Certainly, the traditional activities of cultural relations agencies would diminish in impact if they failed to take account of technological innovation. At a time when the means of communication are so rapidly expanding, external cultural policies must be open to these new opportunities. If they were not, they would be in danger of becoming peripheral to major changes in the way cultures and societies interact.

New Technology

The use of satellites (of which there were about 270 in orbit in 1984) has initiated a revolution in communications technology. According to Ingberg (1984, p. 5) some 2,100 satellites were put into orbit between 1957 and 1979. They were used for radio and television transmissions and telecommunications for various users. World-wide management of satellite systems is shared between Intelstat and Intersputnik. Intelstat has 106 member countries. Its 1982 report 'shows an increase of 24 per cent in telecommunications traffic in 1981 and estimates that this figure will double by 1985'. The great variety of programme choice afforded by cable television (whether fed by satellite or not) and the prospect of direct broadcasting by satellite (DBS) to individual television receivers open up momentous possibilities. According to the *UK Press Gazette* of 19 August 1985, the French government has approved an ambitious European television channel devoted to educational and cultural programmes, which will use a French satellite and is due to begin broadcasting to some 100 million households at the beginning of 1987. Whereas external broadcasting has so far been directed at a mass audience, the introduction of these technologies in the future will facilitate the direction of cultural messages at more specialized publics: the process that Borelli (1984, p. 9) has summed up as 'From broad-casting to narrowcasting'.

Already in the domestic provision in certain countries there has been a progression beyond the mass television audience to smaller publics satisfying their interests by pay-cable and video; the inter-nationalization of this development will in itself bring a new range of facilities into home viewing. Among these, the scope for education (the teaching of languages, for instance) and the presentation of arts and documentary programmes will be of immediate interest to cultural agencies. Moreover, such agencies can make a very desirable contribution to the cultural level of programme availability: one possible defence against the danger of quality decline, with the proliferation of material, will be the competitive element between international sources. Add to this the 'new literacy' of the post-Gutenberg era, with the use of the domestic TV screen for videotex and teletext, and even general worldwide interaction through 'integrated services digital networks' (ISDN), and a scenario emerges that may eventually turn the lecture, the language class, the reference library, and perhaps even in some degree the live arts show into anachronisms. Nor need these new processes be one-way: the postulate of mutuality could be to some extent satisfied by the bilateral and multilateral production of programmes and by the individual's power of interactive response. The effects would be far-reaching. Many people think they would inevitably be to dilute and trivialize content: they point the finger of alarm at the example of pay-cable in the United States. Clearly, there is a danger that the elaboration of medium sophistication would dissipate the message. But the future is clear and ineluctable. As the Commission of the European Communities says in its Green Paper (1984, p. 25): 'Radio has already become an international medium. Television will move towards becoming one through the use of direct satellite broadcasting and cable relay systems.'

The effects on cultural agencies themselves will be incalculable. One might predict that they would need to devote more resources to the production or subsidy of programmes for target publics and correspondingly fewer resources to the maintenance of staff and materials (libraries, film and teaching equipment) in foreign countries. But one can hardly imagine that the basic activities (presence, information and exchange of persons) would be dispensed with, though the information services in particular would greatly change their methods. The exchange of persons would not be basically affected, though where the purpose is the transfer of professional experience or the inculcation of a specific skill (as on a short course, for instance) it is foreseeable that cable TV programmes in the home country would play a greater part, presumably as a preparation or follow-up rather than as a substitute. Such refinements might lead to a reduction of the proportion of cultural budgets spent on exchanges of persons. When the individual recipient can dial a number from a catalogue and then view on his home television screen programmes or indeed series of programmes for his enlightenment as well as for his entertainment, the potential for increasing the availability of foreign cultural and educational materials of all kinds is prodigious; when the same recipient can also tune in to a variety of national transmissions by DBS, the need to visit foreign cultural institutes to taste their offerings must be reduced. The institute will predictably complete its process of gradual replacement by other modes, at least in the developed world. Thus will be phased out and eventually terminated a device that has served international relations for some hundred years with sensitivity and humanity, the foreign cultural institute.

Alignment with External Cultural Policy

The alignment between cultural relations and external (and internal) broadcasting will therefore be emphasized by technological advances. But there is another, more basic, form of alignment in their purposes. This also applies historically. Just as in the last quarter of the nineteenth century the governments of France, Italy and Germany involved themselves in the welfare of their exile populations overseas by providing schools and other services for them, which then came to embrace indigenous elites, so it was the major colonial powers (Holland 1927, France 1931, Britain 1932) that first used the ether to address their compatriots overseas and then, together with other countries, found a wider audience for their broadcasts. As Sir William Haley (1950, p. 13), then Director-General of the BBC, said in his Montague Burton International Relations Lecture of 1950, 'Their purpose was to use this latest, swiftest, and perhaps most personal means of communication to forge a link between the homeland and the pioneers in voluntary exile overseas'.

The scope of external broadcasting between 1950 and 1983 is shown in Appendix C (p. 237). It can be seen that most countries registered a growth in programme hours per week during this period. In the same period the number of radio sets in the world increased from 150 million to 1.3 billion. Before the transistor revolution, listening to the radio was an elitist pursuit, in world terms. The BBC started external broadcasting to the Empire in 1932. Then it followed the British government's request to broadcast in other languages, as a response to the propaganda transmissions of the Axis powers. So the Arabic service began in 1938, followed in the same year by Spanish and Portuguese services for Latin America, and then by German, French and Italian. The BBC emerged from the Second World War as the dominant external broadcaster, with programmes in English and 44 foreign languages, and with an unequalled reputation for veracity and independence. Now the BBC has been relegated to fifth place in the world league, after the USSR, the USA, the Chinese People's Republic and the Federal Republic of Germany. It broadcasts in English and 36 foreign languages and reckons its audience during any one day of transmission at 100 million.

'It was that technician of power Lenin who first realised the potentialities of international broadcasting. He called radio "a newspaper without paper and without frontiers" ' (Muggeridge, 1982, p. 3). And it was the Soviet Union that first exploited radio in this way. Haley (1950, p. 2) tells us:

> The earliest services of international voice broadcasting which can be traced are the Comintern broadcasts put out by Russia in English, French and German in 1924. The first use of Broadcasting as an offensive weapon aimed at one particular country was also by

Russia. This was against Rumania during the dispute over Bessarabia in 1926.

The total cost of the BBC External Services (including the Monitoring Service) is estimated at £99 million for 1985–86. If this may be taken as a benchmark, it would follow that the USSR and the USA are spending three times as much and China twice as much. What are the returns? Audience research goes a long way towards providing an answer, but in the longer term this is not conclusive. Certainly radio broadcasts contribute to the formation of attitudes in the countries to which they are beamed, but it is no more possible than it is with cultural relations to say what the ultimate consequence is or what is its benefit to the transmitting country. We can accumulate evidence, of course, and make the safe deduction, for instance, that the BBC's high reputation internationally redounds to Britain's general advantage. But there is no way of making a cost-benefit analysis. There are many instances of short-term effects, especially when the message has been aimed at them, as in time of war. It was a short-term achievement of Radio Free Europe to encourage the Hungarian uprising of 1956, but how far this was to the ultimate benefit of the United States is highly debatable. Perhaps the costs of jamming practised at various times by the Soviet Union and other communist countries may for them have a more tangible justification, in a negative sense. To maintain a monopoly of information is vital to any closed society. Since jamming costs at least as much as the broadcasts it is intended to render inaudible, the total expense for such countries is considerable. More positively, the returns, at the most obvious level, are in telling your version of the facts, in accordance with your ideology, and transmitting this message direct to the individual listener; if you are successful you will make your world-view more attractive and credible than the world-views which rival or oppose it.

Abshire (1979, p. 24) is writing from a Western, post-Helsinki point of view when he says:

The significance of international broadcasting is not that it can say things over greater distances, or say them to more people, or say them more loudly. Each new medium of communication has brought new possibilities for the creation of human community, expanding the common store of human knowledge, and of people's knowledge of each other and of themselves. The importance of international broadcasting is that it offers a major channel for establishing that communication between nations and people necessary to a reliable structure of peace.

But we could extend the argument to cover all forms and directions of external broadcasting, and see them all as communications between nations across the divides of hostility, prejudice and ignorance. And we could see the involvement of opposing governments as a ritualization of fear and aggression, a display of habitual postures as an alternative to belligerency. In this optimistic interpretation, international broadcasting does indeed play a part, even if deviously, in bringing home the returns of stability and peace.

The importance of radio as a means of alternative information and of breaking down monopoly in the presentation of facts emerges from the following two quotations, both of the same year and requiring no further commentary.

> As a consequence of the transistor revolution, radio is more than ever the principal means of nourishing the people in the East, who are fed a daily diet of selected, filtered, edited and censored information. (Lendvai, 1981, p. 141)

> Just as nobody has ever succeeded in covering the sun with the palm of his hand and plunging the world into darkness, so nobody will succeed in blocking the way to truth about real socialism, about the Soviet people and their way of life. (Belyayev, 1981, p. 75)

A government's aim in external broadcasting is likely to be similar in spirit to its aim in external cultural policy. The convergence will be closest when both are funded from the same source. This is the case with the BBC and the British Council. The BBC External Services are paid for by the Foreign and Commonwealth Office, which with its aid wing (the Overseas Development Administration) provides the grant for the British Council. A recent review of the BBC External Services summed up their objectives thus: 'The salient point is that the BBC External Services should enhance Britain's standing abroad and form among listeners a better understanding of the UK.' (Perry, 1984, p. 16) This does not differ in spirit from the British Council's aim, 'to promote an enduring understanding and appreciation of Britain in other countries through cultural, educational and cultural cooperation'. The Central Policy Review Staff (1977, p. 227) said:

> The BBC has two main objectives:
> a)   to provide an unbiased source of world news and information;
> b)   to convey information about Britain and its culture.

The Review endorsed both objectives, with some reservations about the 'projection' aspect of the second. It is precisely this that most obviously aligns the External Services with the work of the British Council, about which the CPRS was extremely negative.

The BBC External Services and the British Council complement one another in providing information about Britain and its culture. Their co-operation is close in English language teaching, but extends to a range of measures of mutual support. They have been fellow sufferers in the government's economies on several occasions. Simon Jenkins in the *Listener* of 28 March 1985 treats them both as exponents of 'alternative diplomacy': 'Those prime agents of alternative diplomacy – the British Council and the BBC's External Services – are cut and cut again.' And he says of the External Services of the BBC:

> This extraordinary British institution now reaches into virtually every corner of the globe with still the best news and current affairs service on the air. The very desperation with which some totalitarian regimes seek to suppress it – and others to emulate it – is a testament to its quality. In my view it transcends every other aspect of Britain's overseas projection, at less than 15 per cent of the Foreign Office budget.

The BBC's motto is 'Nation Shall Speak Peace Unto Nation'. The message bears thinking about. How does a broadcasting service speak peace? The optimist might say that simply by speaking to one another over the air nations are committing an act of communication, which must help to bridge frontiers and bring about greater convergence of thinking between them. Obviously, even the most sanguine could not believe this of outright propaganda and incitement to civil disorder. But this is not the pattern of the major part of external broadcasting. Manifest propaganda is less effective in an age of alternative information; broadcasting depends for its success on being sensitive to the receptivity of its audience. Broadcasts from communist countries, for instance, are much more likely to win listeners over if they play upon dissatisfactions and trade on the idea of humane fellow-feeling than if they relentlessly pour forth the turgidities of Marxism.

The BBC motto's use of the word 'nation' raises similar questions to those we have considered earlier. Just as cultural relations, in general, strike deeper and in a wider range of institutions if they are not tied to political purposes, so broadcasting too is more persuasive if its agencies are not seen as government spokesmen. And yet, no one doubts that governments pay for external broadcasting because they expect some benefit to their own national interests. External broadcasting purely for the purpose of international understanding, with no national motivation, not only does not exist but can hardly be expected to exist. The medium is self-seeking. Possibly, when television becomes international to a similar degree to radio, but with its greater immediacy of appeal, the pressure of competing channels will have the effect of making national interest less evident – and therefore more subtle. It is, of course, not unlikely that its place might be taken by trans-national commercial promotion. As to that prospect, some might argue that consumerism is a force for cross-frontier convergence.

External radio services are not, then, ostensibly the voice of governments. An appearance of impartiality is normal. The typical announcer's style is dispassionate and elevated. The listener should feel he is being sympathetically addressed rather than harangued or suborned. The notion of the independence of external broadcasting is therefore important, and the existence of exemplars of that independence is also important. The BBC's well-established reputation for independence suffered a blow in August 1985. Although the cause lay with domestic television, which is financed by the individual citizen's TV and radio licence fee, the effect was felt on the external services too.

Britain's Home Secretary, who licenses broadcasting, felt that he had reason to caution the chairman of the BBC's independent governors about the projected showing of a television programme, *At the Edge of the Union*, concerned with Northern Ireland and containing an allegedly too sympathetic interview with an IRA leader. The programme was thereupon screened for the governors, who decided that it should not be sent out, as scheduled, in its then form. The fact that the BBC's top officials had not been duly consulted about the content of a programme on such a sensitive theme was an anomaly in itself; moreover, several people who had the chance of seeing it found nothing objectionable. But the important point is that the government had apparently interfered with the BBC's independence. In a day of protest, not only the BBC's own staff went on strike but most of the independent television and radio stations joined them out of sympathy for the cause. There was a virtual twenty-four-hour media shut-down.

The day's strike also put the BBC External Services out of action. It is an unusual organizational feature of the BBC that its internal and external services are under the same overall management. The fact that the World Service and the foreign language broadcasts should go off the air in this way excited much comment. Would this protest against government intervention on the domestic front damage the BBC's undoubted reputation abroad as a vehicle of impartial news and objective comment? Would unfriendly governments be able to make capital out of this really rather unnecessary crisis? After all,

BBC Television intended to use the programme, not to scrap it; indeed, it was transmitted two months later with minimal alterations. Or would listeners in such countries, where government control of the media is axiomatic, marvel at the freedom and compulsion of BBC personnel to express their indignation, and would this carry final conviction, if any were needed, that a service in which such independence of mind is possible must indeed be independent? As *The Sunday Times* leader said on 11 August 1985 'No other public broadcasting system would have reacted so fiercely to official attempts to influence its programmes'. For it is the listeners' reactions that matter. Illiberal states are going to be equally opposed to alternative sources of information, whether they are concocted or ventriloquized by governments or genuinely free of editorial control. Sir Anthony Parsons gave the fruits of his diplomatic experience when he wrote in *The Times* of 8 August 1985, 'nothing will convince governments with an unbroken tradition of absolute control and unfettered power of manipulation over their own public media that, in the case of the BBC, the Foreign Office, payer of the piper, does not call the BBC tune'.

The system whereby both the domestic and the foreign transmissions of the BBC (although they are separately funded) are overseen by the same independent governors has always been a guarantee of credence to the listeners abroad. The guarantee may seem to be less persuasive in view of this furore. The case was aggravated by the coincidental revelations that MI5 (the Security Service) vets senior appointments to the BBC, and that the Foreign and Commonwealth Office regularly supplies confidential reports on foreign affairs to External Services for their information. But none of this invalidates the BBC's refusal to accept government direction on programme content on several recorded occasions. To accept editorial control would mean something even more insidious than subjection to a particular view of the national interest; it would mean subjection to changing attitudes as governments change and, in an elective democracy, to the vicissitudes of party politics. Immunity from any such contagion is essential for all forms of cultural relations, and certainly not least for an instrument with the power and the potential for cross-frontier communication possessed by broadcasting. The prospects considered above for the expansion of communication across frontiers as well as within individual countries make it more desirable than ever that objectivity should be generally observed. The same spirit of reconciliation and honesty that has led to textbook revision between previously antagonistic countries can be invoked to purify at least cultural and educational broadcasts. Then it would become apparent that the greatest national advantage lies in encouraging and being a part of a world network constructed on mutual communication and respect. That is the way of effective cultural relations and that is a practical way of speaking peace, by dialogue.

In conclusion, we can see that external broadcasting is closely related to external cultural policy without being intrinsically part of it. Their purpose and objectives are likely to be subject to similar policy directions in individual countries. They share an involvement in communications technology. Their alignment will be encouraged, and their mutual support furthered, by the development of this technology.

Picasso's peace dove may yet take wing, as a communications satellite.

20

Thematic Propositions

The purpose of the present chapter will be to outline the major propositions that emerge from this study. As was stated in the beginning, the approach is thematic. It is appropriate, therefore, to conclude with a recapitulation of themes that have been examined historically, organizationally and functionally, and to consider what pointers they provide for the policies of governments engaging in cultural relations. Given the diversity of aims and practices, it will be preferable to employ the form of propositions rather than recommendations.

Cultural relations have evolved from being a vehicle of national projection and propaganda to assuming a specific role in the mutual communication between modern societies. The term 'cultural diplomacy' is sometimes used as though it were a synonym; in fact, it more exactly refers to the inclusion of cultural activity in international agreements and to the conduct of cultural relations for diplomatic purposes. For all the importance of diplomacy in international affairs, especially in the preservation of peace, its remit is at the governmental level. At this level an opposition of interests frequently obtains, even between like-minded states, which hinders the realization of closer and more harmonious relations between peoples. Cultural relations can, on the other hand, advance *beyond diplomacy*, and create a context of understanding and co-operation between institutions and elites in a bilateral (or multilateral) relationship. This context has an intrinsic value because it encourages exchanges across frontiers to the general benefit; it also encourages factors in the climate of opinion, and in attitudes, which are themselves conducive to positive foreign policies.

External cultural policy is part of foreign policy as a whole in so far as this is seen as the national concept in relation to the world and individual countries rather than as the reaction to transient political and economic situations. Culture requires state finance and justifies it by its works. These, however, are hard to evaluate in their consequences. They cannot always be justified on the time-scale of politics and diplomacy because their practices and effects are conceived in the longer term. Nevertheless, external cultural policy and the cultural relations by which it is executed serve foreign policy in accordance with the broader concept of a country's geopolitical and economic aims. The budgets and geographical distribution of cultural agencies will accord with these aims. But here again the dispositions should not reflect short-term political priorities. Cultural relations, being concerned with relationships and co-operation, require continuity of pursuit. A 'stop-go' approach to work in individual countries undermines efficacy. Withdrawing representations from victim countries for budgetary reasons wipes out the accretion of goodwill, and negates the investment of work and resources in the past. Moreover, even from a purely political point of view, it is advantageous to spread the net of friendship wide over the globe in order to take account of the vicissitudes that may unpredictably elevate countries to positions of influence or threat.

Although external cultural policy is part of foreign policy as a whole, it operates not only on a different time-scale from that of diplomacy but also by different methods. For this reason, agencies conducting cultural relations should be independent of their diplomatic service. This can be most consistently achieved if they are non-governmental; but it is also feasible to build this independence into a cultural service that is a branch of the foreign ministry, so long as the essential differences are observed and the right personnel are selected. However, the diplomatic connection is likely to be a limiting factor in work abroad. Being part of an embassy may be helpful in the operation of official programmes, but it is likely to hinder access to the more original creators and alternative thinkers as well as to dissident intellectuals. These are the people who constitute the avant-garde in a society's cultural evolution. Mediation between them and their counterparts in the home country is one of the distinctive tasks of a forward-looking cultural agency. It belongs to the category known as intellectual encounter, which takes place within a variety of activities involving people of two or more countries. The essence of it is that minds are brought together for the purposeful consideration of questions of common interest.

When a country's cultural services do not themselves enjoy the degree of independence necessary for this role, or when their staff are not qualified for it, they may delegate it to others. For instance, they can subsidize teaching or advisory posts that place the incumbents in a key position for intellectual encounter and afford them freedom of manoeuvre, or they can apply their exchange of persons programme to ensure that contacts are explored between innovators in the two countries.

Another reason why it is desirable that cultural relations should be independent of direct government control is that their clients are not necessarily all in sympathy with their government, and with the system that sustains it. The acknowledgement that truth does not exist exclusively under any one system and the entitlement to alternative information are in harmony with various international declarations – the Atlantic Charter, the Declaration of the United Nations, the European Conference on Security and Cooperation, for instance. But, in practice, governments, even on occasion in democratic countries, have their reasons for applying restrictions. If it is the policy of another country to break through these restrictions, whether by external broadcasting or by cultural contacts, it will be easier to implement if the services carrying out these measures are not themselves government organs. The liberal notion of peoples speaking to one another across frontiers carries more conviction if the voice is not ventriloquized by the political will of governments.

Cultural relations have at their disposal various activities and programmes. Some of these are basic, while others are optional. Several of them are time-honoured and date from the first engagement of governments and public finance in this work. Among them are language-teaching, the maintenance of reference and lending libraries, lectures, film-shows, play-readings, and the other cultural activities that belong to the institute model. Others are arranged in collaboration with institutions in the host country. These include tours of the performing arts and exhibitions. Such events involve considerable expenditure but reach a wider public, though seldom a mass public. By displaying the achievements of the sending country they raise its prestige, and this in turn furthers its national interests as well as enriching the soil in which more routine activities are cultivated.

There are less conventional activities, which are evolving in accordance with contemporary change. Intellectual encounter, for instance, can take many forms, some of them innovatory and avant-garde. Its exponents belong to elite groups, even if they feel intensely individual. One of a cultural agency's major tasks is to identify and cultivate target groups. By this means it is enabled to encourage counterpart elites to engage in exchange and co-operation. Cultural agencies are well placed to do this, because they possess both the resources to facilitate such encounter and the inside knowledge that enables them to relate these elites, and the structure on which they depend, to one another.

Intellectual encounter exceeds in scope the more conventional areas of culture and education. How far it exceeds them will depend on the policies of the agencies concerned, but nowadays cultural relations are normally understood to embrace societies at large, with the exclusion of such subjects as religion, politics, commerce, defence, and political journalism. Modern communications make it possible as never before to bring about the relation of elites in different countries to one another. Cultural agencies can set up the connection.

Another activity, which is less conventional (although no doubt it will soon come to be regarded as conventional) is the exploitation of advanced communications technology. How these techniques will be applied to the messages of cultural relations is as yet unknown, but it seems certain that a cornucopia of live broadcasts, recorded programmes and information data-bases will be available in people's homes. It is a safe prediction that this development will shift the emphasis from on-site resources such as libraries to the provision of facilities electronically to individual or group recipients. At first sight this might seem to imply reaching mass audiences, and no doubt this can be one consequence for certain types of programme. Activities conducted heretofore according to the institute model – such as language instruction and the provision of information – will, presumably, be available on tap for all those who summon them to their television receivers. But more specialized programmes will also be available to target groups and can be prepared with their specific interests in view.

In all the activities of cultural relations, the practice of mutuality conduces to the more effective establishment of relationships. Mutuality has two aspects: it means collaboration between cultural agencies and local institutions abroad, in recognition of the fact that the benefit from the activities is common to both countries, and it also means helping the institutions of the host country to conduct their cultural relations work in the sending country. Both aspects serve to underline one of the basic tenets behind successful cultural relations, namely that they are a two-way process.

There is little standardization in the manner of organizing cultural relations. More might be achieved if responsibility for inward and outward traffic were bestowed upon a comparable body in each country, such as a ministry of culture. There is little standardization either in the staff structure for conducting cultural relations. Historically, different countries have evolved structures that suit their policies and the competencies they consign to their cultural agencies. The developments that have been considered above, and especially the fostering of intellectual encounter, put a premium on the employment of persons with a high degree of language proficiency and understanding of the societies in which they serve. These desiderata cannot be unfailingly met within a career service.

There is therefore an advantage, especially in the more sensitive and innovative areas of work, in recruiting people on contract from home institutions.

By whatever method they are recruited, staff need to be highly trained. In view of the position that cultural relations have come to occupy in world affairs, and prospects for the future, it would be appropriate if professional training courses were organized at an international centre. Cultural relations are the most effective and least controversial way for nations and societies to attain an active and co-operative understanding of one another. They are also an essential dimension of the aid relationship, for they cater for the human element, which is so essential to manpower development and cultural identity. They are, of course, no panacea for the world's ills, but they offer potential for their reduction and manageability. It would be superfluous to employ idealistic phrases to reinforce the thesis. But one should not, for the sake of balanced assessment, baulk the fact that many of those who engage in and support this work are motivated by ideals. To provide a focus for rallying these people at a time of world tensions is no mean role in itself.

In conclusion, one might adapt the phrase of Satow's (Gore-Booth, 1979, p. 3) in his famous work on diplomatic practice: 'Diplomacy is in fact, as the Duc de Broglie remarked, the best means devised by civilisation for preventing international relations from being governed by force alone'. And make of it:

> Cultural relations are . . . the best means devised by civilisation for preventing international affairs from being governed by politics alone.

APPENDIX A   *Cultural convention between the government of the United Kingdom . . . and the government of the French Republic*

Paris, 2 March 1948

Treaty Series No. 36 (1948)

Cmd 7450 London: HMSO
(*Reproduced with the permission of Her Majesty's Stationery Office*)

[*Author's Note* These Articles 1–6 contain the gist of the Convention and illustrate its permissive, facilitating nature. The are followed by the text of the Protocol in full, which defines the composition and functions of the Mixed Commission.]

ARTICLE 1

Each Contracting Party shall encourage the creation at Universities and other Institutions for higher education in its territory of Professorial Chairs, Readerships, Lectureships and courses in the language, literature, social studies and history of the other country and in other cultural subjects concerning that country.

ARTICLE 2

Each Contracting Party shall be permitted to establish cultural Institutes in the Territory of the other provided that the requirements of the local law with regard to the establishment of such institutes are complied with. The term 'Institute' shall include schools, libraries and cultural centres dedicated to the purpose which the present Convention has in view.

ARTICLE 3

Each Contracting Party shall encourage visits and exchanges of students, schoolchildren, professors, teachers and all other groups likely to profit from such cultural exchanges.

It shall facilitate the organisation in the territory of the other of exhibitions, lectures, broadcasts and musical and theatrical performances, and the distribution of books, periodicals and other publications, printed and recorded music and films.

ARTICLE 4

The Contracting Parties shall consider how far and under what conditions degrees, diplomas and certificates of one territory may be accepted as equivalent to corresponding degrees, diplomas and certificates of the other for academic purposes and, in appropriate cases, for professional purposes.

ARTICLE 5

For the purpose of close and continuous consultation between the two Parties in the field of cultural relations, a permanent Mixed Commission consisting of fourteen members, shall be set up. This Mixed Commission shall meet when necessary and at least once a year in France and in the United Kingdom alternately.

ARTICLE 6

Each Contracting Party may designate organisations to ensure the execution of the above or any other measures falling within the scope of the present Convention, and more particularly those measures detailed in the Protocol annexed hereto which shall have force and effect as an integral part of the Convention.

PROTOCOL

On the signature of this Convention between the Government of the United Kingdom of Great Britain and Northern Ireland and the Government of the French Republic the undersigned Plenipotentiaries have agreed as follows:

1.   The Permanent Mixed Commission set up under Article 5 of the Convention will be divided into two sections, one composed of

French members sitting in France and the other of British members sitting in the United Kingdom, the complete Commission meeting according to the provisions of Article 5 of the Convention. The Foreign Office, in agreement with the competent Departments of the Government of the United Kingdom, shall nominate the members of the British section and the French Ministry of Foreign Affairs and the French Ministry of Education in agreement with the competent Departments of the Government of the French Republic shall nominate the members of the French section. Each Contracting Party shall fix the terms under which the members of its own section are appointed and will have the power to nominate alternative members. The Mixed Commission and each section thereof shall be authorised to co-opt additional members without voting powers as specialist advisers.

2.   The meetings of the Mixed Commission shall be presided over by a Member nominated by the Contracting Party in whose country the meeting is to take place and the Secretary shall be nominated by the other Contracting Party.

3.   At its first meeting the Mixed Commission shall draw up detailed proposals for the application of the Convention, which will then be considered by the Contracting Parties. At its further meetings the Commission shall review the position and draw up further proposals or suggest modifications to its previous recommendations, for consideration by the Contracting Parties.

4.   The Contracting Parties shall consider any proposals for the implementation of the Convention which may be submitted to them by the Mixed Commission. They shall also agree to encourage by all means in their power, within the limits set by local law, the following activities:

(a)   the interchange between their territories of members of technical institutions, heads of schools and colleges, school teachers, pupils, students, research workers, librarians and persons engaged in the other activities mentioned in the preamble to the Convention;

(b)   the development by invitation or subsidy, of reciprocal visits of selected groups for the purpose of creating or increasing cultural, technical and professional collaboration between the two countries;

(c)   the provision of scholarships or bursaries in such manner as to enable nationals of each country to undertake or pursue studies, technical training or research work in the other country;

(d)   close co-operation between learned societies and educational and specialist groups of the two countries for the purpose of providing mutual aid in intellectual, artistic, scientific, technical and educational activities and sociological studies and practice;

(e)   the development of holiday courses to be attended by school pupils, students, teachers and academic personnel from the territory of the Contracting Parties.

5.   The Contracting Parties shall consider from time to time what steps should be taken to facilitate the flow of cultural and educational material between their countries.

6.   More particularly each shall examine what measures can be taken to facilitate the transfer to the country of the other of books, scientific and technical instruments, works of art, and any other article likely to further the purposes of the Convention, given, bequeathed, lent to or bought by Universities, public Institutions, libraries, collections, galleries and museums.

APPENDIX B *Agreement between the government of the United Kingdom . . . and the government of the Union of Soviet Socialist Republics on relations in the scientific, educational and cultural fields for 1983–85*

London, 3 March 1983

Treaty Series No. 39 (1983)

Cmnd 8981 (London: HMSO)
(*Reproduced with the permission of Her Majesty's Stationery Office*)

[*Author's Note* This Agreement lays down the visits and exchanges in these three general and also in more specific fields. The difference between this Agreement and the Convention in Appendix A is apparent in its prescriptive provisions and in its reciprocal conception. Programmes of Cultural, Educational and Scientific Exchanges between the United Kingdom and East European countries are also agreed for a two-year period and follow a similar pattern. In view of the length and detail of the Agreement, Article II only is quoted here by way of illustration.]

ARTICLE II

Exchanges in the Field of Science

(1) Both Parties shall facilitate the development of mutually agreed scientific exchanges and co-operation between scientists of the United Kingdom and the USSR on the basis of the Agreement on Scientific Co-operation and the Exchange of Scientists between the Royal Society of London and the Academy of Sciences of the USSR, signed on 21 September 1977, and shall take the necessary steps for the encouragement of such co-operation and exchanges.

(2) In addition, both Parties shall facilitate visits on a basis of reciprocity by scientists and specialists for the purpose of carrying out scientific research and becoming acquainted with the work of

scientific research institutions on the basis that the sending side pays all expenses.

(3)   Both Parties shall facilitate the development of exchanges and co-operation arranged between the British Academy and the Academy of Sciences of the USSR in accordance with the Agreement on Scientific Exchanges in the Humanities and Social Sciences concluded between them which came into force on 1 April 1977.

(4)   Agreement on visits referred to above other than any arranged directly between the Royal Society or the British Academy and the Academy of Sciences of the USSR shall be effected between the British Council and any other appropriate organisations of the United Kingdom on the one hand and the Academy of Sciences of the USSR on the other hand.

(5)   The Royal Society, the British Academy and the British Council on the one hand and the Academy of Sciences of the USSR on the other shall, where possible, facilitate visits of scientists to institutes and scientific research establishments falling outside their jurisdiction.

(6)   Both Parties shall facilitate the invitation of individual scientists from one country to participate in national scientific colloquia, conferences and congresses in the other country and shall inform each other in good time of such events.

(7)   Both Parties shall facilitate visits by scholars who are invited by the Royal Society, the British Academy, the British Council or British universities on the one hand or by the Academy of Sciences or other appropriate Soviet organisations on the other hand to undertake research or to become acquainted with scientific work in the other country. In this context, and in each year of the Agreement, up to ten Soviet scientists may visit the United Kingdom, at the invitation of the British Council, to meet people in similar professions.

(8)   Both Parties shall encourage the establishment and development of scientific co-operation and direct contacts between their institutions and scientists and shall promote the exchanges of scientific publications and information.

APPENDIX C *External broadcasting*

ESTIMATED TOTAL PROGRAMME HOURS PER WEEK OF SOME EXTERNAL BROADCASTERS

	1950	1955	1960	1965	1970	1975	1980	1985
United States of America	497	1,690	1,495	1,832	1,907	2,029	1,901	2,339
USSR	553	656	1,015	1,417	1,908	2,001	2,094	2,211
Chinese People's Republic	66	159	687	1,027	1,267	1,423	1,350	1,446
German Federal Republic	—	105	315	671	779	767	804	795
United Kingdom (BBC)	643	558	589	667	723	719	719	726
Albania	26	47	63	154	487	490	560	581
Egypt	—	100	301	505	540	635	546	560
North Korea	—	53	159	392	330	455	597	535
East Germany	—	9	185	308	274	342	375	413
India	116	117	157	175	271	326	389	408
Cuba	—	—	—	325	320	311	424	379
Australia	181	226	257	299	350	379	333	352
Netherlands	127	120	178	235	335	400	289	336
Nigeria	—	—	—	63	62	61	170	322
Poland	131	359	232	280	334	340	337	320
Iran	12	10	24	118	155	154	175	310
Turkey	40	100	77	91	88	172	199	307
Bulgaria	30	60	117	154	164	197	236	290
Japan	—	91	203	249	259	259	259	287
France	198	191	326	183	200	108	125	272
Czechoslovakia	119	147	196	189	202	253	255	268
Spain	68	98	202	276	251	312	239	252
Israel	—	28	91	92	158	198	210	223

Appendix C – continued

Romania	30	109	159	163	185	190	198	212
South Africa	—	127	63	84	150	141	183	205
Sweden	28	128	114	142	140	154	155	196
Italy	170	185	205	160	165	170	169	173
Canada	85	83	80	81	98	159	134	169
Portugal	46	102	133	273	295	190	214	140
Hungary	76	99	120	121	105	127	127	122
Yugoslavia	80	46	70	78	76	82	72	86

1 USA includes Voice of America (1179 hours per week), Radio Free Europe (558 hours per week), Radio Liberty (497 hours per week) and Radio Marti (105 hours per week). (1985 figures)

2 USSR includes Radio Moscow, Radio Station Peace and Progress and regional stations.

3 German Federal Republic includes Deutsche Welle (542 hours per week) and Deutschlandfunk (253 hours per week). (1985 figures)

4 The list includes fewer than half the world's external broadcasters. Among those excluded are Taiwan, Vietnam, South Korea, and various international commercial and religious stations, as well as clandestine radio stations. Certain countries transmit part of their domestic output externally on shortwaves; these broadcasts are mainly also excluded.

5 All figures are for December or nearest available month.

Source © International Broadcasting and Audience Research, February 1986.

APPENDIX D   *Budgets of Britain and Analogue Countries*

The author's attempt to produce a detailed comparison of expenditure on cultural relations proved abortive, in spite of the help given by government departments and agencies to which he addressed an ambitious questionnaire. The reason for this is not any reluctance on their part to disclose budgets, which are anyway published, but rather the extreme difficulty of establishing common factors in an area where ministerial funding and its allocation to categories of activity are so diverse. In each country different ministries play their part; concepts and nomenclature in national programmes of cultural relations vary so much that detail would be misleading without extensive prior research.

This appendix, therefore, gives only one basis of comparison, namely the funds estimated for 1983 by the principal national ministries for standard cultural relations work. These are normally foreign ministries. Funds specifically for technical co-operation and educational aid are excluded, because this is an obvious source of discrepancy; so are funds for external broadcasting. The French and German budgets include support for schools abroad. The figures for Japan perforce include the Ministry of Education, because of its major role in international exchanges. The US figures are for USIA. For completeness, the great variety of foundations and private organizations should be added, and this would boost the US total, but again much investigation would be required to achieve comparability with other countries.

The following statistics at least yield a certain order of magnitude and are not more misleading than any others available at present:

1983		
	France	258.7 in £ million
	Germany	253.0
	United States	173.7
	Japan	95.0
	Italy	80.8
	Britain	71.5

Source   The British Council

Bibliography

Abshire, D. M. (1979), 'International broadcasting: a new dimension of Western democracy' in D. B. Fascell (ed.) *International News: Freedom under Attack* (London: Sage Publications).

Adams, M. (1958), *Suez and After* (Boston: Beacon Press).

Andenaes, U. (1984), *Presentasjonen av Norge i Utlandet* (Oslo: Universitetsforlaget).

Applebaum, L. and Hébert, J. (co-chairmen) (1982), *Report of the Federal Cultural Review Committee* (Ottawa: Government of Canada).

Archer, C. (1983), *International Organizations* (London: Allen & Unwin).

Ardagh, J. (1982), *France in the 1980s* (London: Penguin).

Arnold, H. (1976), 'Das Buch in der auswärtigen Kulturpolitik', *Zeitschrift für Kulturaustausch*, 1976/3, pp. 3–6.

Arnold, H. (1979), *Foreign Cultural Policy: A Survey from a German Point of View* (London: Oswald Wolff).

Aspen Institute for Humanistic Studies (1984), *Managing East–West Conflict: Statement of the Aspen Institute International Group* (New York: Aspen Institute).

Atkinson, W. C. (1947), 'The British Council in the Field', *Nineteenth Century and After*, vol. cxli, pp. 92–6.

Auswärtiges Amt (1980), *Auswärtige Kulturpolitik im Schulwesen* (Bonn: Auswärtiges Amt).

Ayabe, T. (1977), 'Foreign students as an important channel for cultural change' in *Dialogue, South East Asia and Japan*, symposium on cultural exchange (Tokyo: Japan Foundation).

Barghoorn, F. C. (1960), *The Soviet Cultural Offensive* (Princeton, NJ: Princeton University Press).

Bartlett, F. C. (1942), *Political Propaganda* (Cambridge: Cambridge University Press).

Barton, M. (ed.) (1984), *British Music Yearbook* (London: Classical Music).

Becker, H. (1966), 'Aussenpolitik und Kulturpolitik', in D. Braun (ed.), *Deutsche Kulturpolitik im Ausland, 1955 bis heute* (Munich: Süddeutscher Verlag), pp. 88–102.

Beloff, M. (1965), 'The projection of Britain abroad', *International Affairs*, vol. 41, no. 3, pp. 478–89.

Belyayev, A. (1981), *Who Profits from Telling Lies about the Soviet Union* (Moscow: Novosti).

Berendzen, R. (chairman) (1982), *Foreign Students and Institutional Policy* (Washington, DC: American Council on Education).

Bildung und Wissenschaft (1984), 'Interview with Dr Alois Mertes', no. 5/6(e), pp. 71–6 (Bonn: Internationes).

Borelli, S. (1984), 'The new technologies and the creators', in *Technological Development and Cultural Policy*. Papers presented to the symposium organized by the Council of Europe on 'Technological development and the new challenges of cultural policy' (Strasbourg: Council of Europe).

Boyan, D. R. (ed.) (1984), *Open Doors: 1982/83* (New York: Institute of International Education).

Brandt, W. (chairman) (1980), *North–South. A Programme for Survival* (London: Pan).

Breitenstein, R. *et al.* (eds) (1974), *Twinning, Deutsch–Britische Partnerschaften* (London: Oswald Wolff).

Bretzler, G. (1976), 'Die deutsche Sprache als Bestandteil der auswärtigen Kulturpolitik in Entwicklungsländern', *Zeitschrift für Kulturaustausch*, 1976/2.

British Council (1935), Speeches delivered on the occasion of the inaugural meeting at St James's Palace on 2 July 1935 (London: British Council).

British Council (1936), (London: Public Record Office, BW 40/2).

British Council (1939), (London: Public Record Office, BW 40/9).

British Council (1941), *Annual Report 1940/41* (London: British Council).

British Council (1943a), *Annual Report 1942/43* (London: British Council).

British Council (1943b), (London: Public Record Office, BW 2/95).

British Council (1947), CF/POL/2/A, 20 March 1947 (London: Public Record Office, BW 1/7).

British Council (1982), *Annual Report 1981/82* (London: British Council).

British Council (1983), Correspondence VEN/641/467, 24 May 1983 (London: British Council).

British Council (1985), *Annual Report 1984/85* (London: British Council).

British Council Staff Association (1954), *The Beaverbrook Press and the British Council* (London: BCSA).

Bruézière, M. (1983), *L'Alliance française: Histoire d'une institution* (Paris: Hachette).

Bundestag (1975), *Bericht der Enquete-Kommission Auswärtige Kulturpolitik* (Bonn: Deutscher Bundestag).

Burgh, J. (1984), 'Why Britain needs overseas students', speech at Newcastle University, 19 November 1984 (London: British Council).

Castle, E. W. (1955), *Billions, Blunders and Baloney* (Greenwich, Conn.: Devin-Adair).

Catholic University of Louvain (1985), *University Research on European Integration* (Brussels: EC Commission).

Central Bureau for Educational Visits and Exchanges (1983), *Annual Report 1982/83* (London: CBEVE).

Central Policy Review Staff (1977), *Review of Overseas Representation* (London: HMSO).

Commission of the European Communities (1984), *Television Without Frontiers*, Com (84) 300 final (Luxembourg: European Communities).

Committee on Higher Education (1963), *Higher Education*, Cmnd 2154 (London: HMSO) (The Robbins Report).

Commonwealth Secretariat (1980), *Eighth Commonwealth Education Conference Report* (London: Commonwealth Secretariat).

Conference on Security and Co-operation in Europe (1975), *Final Act (1975)* (London: HMSO).

Coombs, P. H. (1964), *The Fourth Dimension of Foreign Policy, Educational and Cultural Affairs* (New York: Harper and Row).

Crovitz, G. (1984), 'The decline and fall of UNESCO', *Encounter*, December 1984, pp. 9–18.

Crystal, D. (1985), 'How many millions? The statistics of English today', *English Today*, no. 1, pp. 7–9.

D'Abernon, Lord (1930), *Report of the British Economic Mission to South America*, FO371/14178 (London: Public Record Office).

Danckwortt, D. (1973), 'Um die Neuorientierung der auswärtigen Kulturpolitik – Das Beispiel Goethe-Institut', *Zeitschrift für Kulturaustausch*, 1973/1, pp. 39–40.

Daniel, N. (1975), *The Cultural Barrier* (Edinburgh: Edinburgh University Press).

Davy, R. (1975), 'The CSCE Summit', *The World Today*, vol. 31, no. 9, pp. 349–53.

Depaigne, J. (1978), *Cultural Policies in Europe* (Strasbourg: Council of Europe).

Department of Education and Science (1984), *Statistical Bulletin 7/84*, June 1984 (London: DES).

Department of Education and Science (1985), *The Development of Higher Education into the 1990s*, Cmnd 9524 (London: HMSO).

Deutscher Akademischer Austauschdienst (1984), *Tätigkeitsbericht 1983* (Bonn: DAAD).

Direction générale des relations culturelles, scientifiques et techniques (1974), *Bilan 1973* (Paris: DGRCST).

Direction générale des relations culturelles, scientifiques et techniques (1984), *Statistiques 1983–1984* (Paris: DGRCST).

Doka, C. (1956), *Kulturelle Aussenpolitik* (Zürich: Berichthaus Verlag).

Donaldson, F. (1984), *The British Council: The First Fifty Years* (London: Cape).

Drogheda, Lord (chairman) (1954), *Summary of the Report of the Independent Committee of Enquiry into the Overseas Information Services*, Cmnd 9138 (London: HMSO).

Duncan, V. (chairman) (1969), *Report of the Review Committee on Overseas Representation 1968–1969*, Cmnd 4107 (London: HMSO).

Eastment, D. J. (1982), 'The policies and position of the British Council from the outbreak of war to 1950', PhD thesis, University of Leeds.

Efinger, E. (1976), *Politique culturelle et instituts culturels des états membres de la Communauté Européenne* (Brussels: Commission des Communautés Européennes).

Eliot, T. S. (1948), *Notes towards the Definition of Culture* (London: Faber).

Enright, D. J. (1969), *Memoirs of a Mendicant Professor* (London: Chatto and Windus).

Fohrbeck, K. (1981), *Kunstförderung im Internationalen Vergleich* (Cologne: Dumont).

Forbes-Adam, C. (1978), *Life of Lord Lloyd* (London: Macmillan).

Foreign Office (1919), Circular dispatch, FO395/304, 00848 (London: Public Record Office).

Foreign Office (1920a), *Report of the Foreign Office Committee on British Communities Abroad*, Cmnd 67 (London: HMSO).

Foreign Office (1920b), *Memorandum Prepared in the Western Department on French Policy with regard to Propaganda in Foreign Countries*, W 814/814/17 (London: Public Record Office).

Foreign Office (1935a), *Introductory Memorandum, British Cultural Propaganda from 1919 to the Formation of the British Council*, FO 431/1 (London: Public Record Office).

Foreign Office (1935b), P 2512/5/150 (London: Public Record Office).

Foreign Office (1935c), Dispatch from Sir Eric Drummond to Sir Samuel Hoare, P 2512/5/150 (London: Public Record Office).

Foreign Office (1936), *British Cultural Propaganda in the Mediterranean Area*, P 3781/15/150 (London: Public Record Office).

Foreign Office (1937), *Memorandum, Foreign Cultural Propaganda and the Threat to British Interests Abroad*, FO P 823/160/150 (London: Public Record Office).

Foreign Office (1938), *Memorandum on the British Council and the Maintenance of British Influence Abroad*, FO 431/4 (London: Public Record Office).

Foreign Office (1944), *British Council, Memorandum on Future Development*, L 2396/545/410 (London: Public Record Office).

Foreign Office (1946), *Definition of the Work of the British Council*, FO P 802/718/907 (London: Public Record Office).

Foreign and Commonwealth Office (1978), *The United Kingdom's Overseas Representation*, Cmnd 7308 (London: HMSO).

Frank, P. (1982), 'Deutsch-französische Zusammenarbeit – eine politische Notwendigkeit', in R. Picht (ed.) *Das Bündnis im Bündnis* (Berlin: Severin und Siedler).

Frankel, C. (1966), *The Neglected Aspect of Foreign Affairs* (Washington DC: The Brookings Institution).

French Institute, Florence (1962), *Commémoration du cinquantenaire de l'institut français de Florence, 1908–1959* (Grenoble: Université de Grenoble).

German Federal Foreign Office (1978), *Foreign Cultural Policy: Comments of the Government of the Federal Republic of Germany on the Report on Foreign Cultural Policy Submitted by the Commission of Inquiry of the German Bundestag* (Bonn: German Federal Foreign Office).

German Federal Foreign Office (1982), *Zehn Thesen zur Kulturellen Begegnung und Zusammenarbeit mit Ländern der Dritten Welt* (Bonn: Auswärtiges Amt).

German Government (1983), *Bulletin* No. 122 (Bonn: Presse- und Informationsdienst der Bundesregierung).

Goodwin, C. D. and Nacht, M. (1983), *Absence of Decision: Foreign Students in American Colleges and Universities* (New York: Institute of International Education).

Gore-Booth, Lord (ed.) (1979), *Satow's Guide to Diplomatic Practice* (London: Longman).

Greenlees, I. (1979), *The British Institute: Its Origin and History* (Florence).

Grémion, P. and Chenal, O. (1980), *Une culture tamisée* (Paris: Centre national de la recherche scientifique).

Grosser, A. (1974), *Germany in our Time* (London: Penguin).

Haigh, A. (1974), *Cultural Diplomacy in Europe* (Strasbourg: Council of Europe).

Haley, W. (1950), 'Broadcasting as an international force', Montague Burton International Relations lecture at Nottingham University (Nottingham University Library).

Hamm-Brücher, H. (1980), *Kulturbeziehungen Weltweit* (Munich: Carl Hanser Verlag).

Hansard (1938), vol. 331, HC Deb., 5s., 16 February 1938, cols 1929–30 (London: HMSO).

Hansard (1944), vol. 397, HC Deb., 5s., 9 March 1944, cols 2188–9 (London: HMSO).

Hansard (1984), vol. 447, HL Deb., 5s., 25 January 1984, col. 304 (London: HMSO).

Henn, T. R. (1946), 'Interpreting Britain', *The Spectator*, 8 March 1946, no. 6141, pp. 238–9.

Hennessy, P. (1985), 'The firework that fizzled', *New Society*, 3 January 1985.

Herwarth, H. von (1971), *Bericht der Kommission für die Reform des Auswärtigen Amtes* (Bonn: Auswärtiges Amt).

Himmelstrup, P. (1985), *'Det nødvendige kultursamarbejde'*, *Uddannelse*, 4.85, pp. 212–19.

Hitler, A. [1925 and 1928] (1944), *Mein Kampf* (Munich: NSDAP).

Ingberg, H. (1984), *Fourth Conference of European Ministers responsible for Cultural Affairs, Culture and Communications Technology* (Strasbourg: Council of Europe).

Japan Foundation (1983), *Annual Report 1982–83* (Tokyo: The Japan Foundation).

Jenkins, H. M. (ed.) (1983a), *The Role of the Foreign Student in the Process of Development* (Washington: National Association for Foreign Student Affairs).

Jenkins, H. M. *et al.* (1983b), *Educating Students from Other Nations* (Washington DC: Jossey-Bass).

Kadima-Nzuji, M. (1982), 'Le point de vue d'un Africain' in D. Gallet (ed.), *Dialogue pour l'identité culturelle* (Paris: Editions Anthropos).

Kemp, T. (1972), 'The Marxist theory of imperialism', in R. Owen and B. Sutcliffe (eds), *Studies in the Theory of Imperialism* (London: Longman).

King-Hall, S. (1946), 'The British way of life', *The Spectator*, 30 August 1946, no. 6166, pp. 209–10.

Kissinger, H. (1979), *The White House Years* (London: Weidenfeld and Nicolson and Michael Joseph).

Kuhn, G. and Rossbach, U. (1980), *Auswärtige Kulturpolitik der Bundesrepublik Deutschland* (Stuttgart: Institut fur Auslandsbeziehungen).

Laqueur, W. (1970), *Europe Since Hitler* (London: Penguin).

Leeper, R. A. (1934), Correspondence to his father, letter of 8 May 1934.

Leeper, R. A. (1935), 'British culture abroad', *Contemporary Review*, vol. 148, pp. 201–7.

Lendvai, P. (1981), *The Bureaucracy of Truth* (London: Burnett Books).

Liberal Party (1984), *Manifesto for the Arts: The Arts, Artists and the Community* (London: Liberal Party).

Lyche, I. (1974), *Nordic Cultural Cooperation, Joint Ventures 1946–1972* (Oslo: Universitetsforlaget).

Mack Smith, D. (1973), 'Anti-British propaganda in Fascist Italy' in *Inghilterra e Italia nel '900, Atti del Convegno di Bagni di Lucca, ottobre 1972* (Florence: La Nuova Italia).

Maheu, R. (1966), *La civilisation de l'universel* (Paris: Robert Laffont).

McMurry, R. and Lee, M. (1947), *The Cultural Approach: Another Way in International Relations* (Chapel Hill, NC: University of North Carolina Press).

Ministère des relations extérieures (1984), *Le projet culturel extérieur de la France* (Paris: La Documentation Française).

Moore, R. J. (1985), *Third-World Diplomats in Dialogue with the First World* (London: Macmillan).

Mowat, C. L. (1935), *Britain Between the Wars, 1918–1940* (London: Methuen).

Muggeridge, D. (1982), *Why don't we invest in success?* (London: BBC).

Murray, G. (1978), 'The British contribution' in A. Hearnden (ed.) *The British in Germany* (London: Hamish Hamilton).

Myerscough, J. (1984), *Funding the Arts in Europe* (London: Policy Studies Institute).

NAFSA (1983), *Facts about NAFSA* (Washington: National Association for Foreign Student Affairs).

Newland, K. (1984), *The UNU in the Mid-Eighties* (Tokyo: The United Nations University).

Ninkovich, F. A. (1981), *The Diplomacy of Ideas: US Foreign Policy and Cultural Relations* (Cambridge: Cambridge University Press).

Office of Arts and Libraries (1981), *The Arts are your Business* (London: Central Office of Information).

Parsons, A. (1984), 'Vultures and philistines – British attitudes to culture and cultural diplomacy', a lecture given at Chatham House, 24 September 1984 (London: British Council).

Peisert, H. (1978), *Die auswärtige Kulturpolitik der Bundesrepublik Deutschland* (Stuttgart: Klett Cotta).

Pendergast, W. R. (1973), 'The political use of cultural relations', *Il Politico: Rivista di Scienze Politiche*, vol. 38, no. 4, pp. 682–96.

Perry, A. (chairman) (1984), *Review of the BBC External Services* (London: British Broadcasting Corporation).

Rehs, M. (1973), 'Nationale Vorurteile – ein Problem internationaler Verständigung', *Zeitschrift für Kulturaustausch*, 1973/3, pp. 3–9.

Rigaud, J. (1980), *Les relations culturelles extérieures* (Paris: La Documentation Française).

Romano, S. (1982a), Papers given on 'La lingua italiana all'estero' at Urbino in 1981 and Rome in 1982, extracted in *Il Veltro: Rivista della Civiltà Italiana*, Rome, anno XXVI, pp. 3–4.

Romano, S. (1982b), Introduction to report of 'La cooperazione culturale, Francia–Italia', *Il Veltro*, Rome, anno XXVI, pp. 5–6.

Routh, H. V. (1941), *The Diffusion of English Culture outside England: A Problem of Post-War Reconstruction* (Cambridge: Cambridge University Press).

Russo, C. (1982), 'The European Engineering Programme: a joint venture', *European Journal of Education*, vol. 17, no. 1, pp. 59–64.

Salon, A. (1978), *Vocabulaire critique des relations internationales dans les domaines culturel, scientifique et de la coopération technique* (Paris: Maison du Dictionnaire).

Salon, A. (1981), 'L'action culturelle de la France dans le monde', Doctoral thesis, University of Paris 1.

Salon, A. (1983), *L'action culturelle de la France dans le monde* (Paris: Fernand Nathan).

Sartre, J.-P. [1943] (1969), *Being and Nothingness: An Essay on Phenomenological Ontology*, trans. Hazel Barnes (London: Methuen).

Satow (See Gore-Booth).

Schlaginweit, R. (1975), 'Erfolgskontrolle in der auswärtigen Kulturpolitik', *Zeitschrift für Kulturaustausch*, 1975/2, pp. 4–6.

Schulz, K. (1976), 'Vorgeschichte und Vorarbeit des "Deutschen Monats" in London', *Zeitschrift für Kulturaustausch*, 1976/2, pp. 32–41.

Shriver, K. L. (1979), 'American education abroad', *Zeitschrift für Kulturaustausch*, 1979/1, pp. 100–2.

Squires, J. D. (1935), *British Propaganda at Home and in the United States* (Cambridge, Mass.: Harvard University Press).

Stanton, F. (chairman) (1975), *International Information, Education and Cultural Relations, Recommendations for the Future* (Washington, DC: Georgetown University).

Stuart, C. (1920), *Secrets of Crewe House* (London: Hodder and Stoughton).

Tallents, S. (1932), *The Projection of Britain* (London: Faber).

Taylor, A. J. P. (1967), *Introduction to 'The Communist Manifesto'* (London: Penguin).

Taylor, P. M. (1981), *The Projection of Britain, British Overseas Publicity and Propaganda 1919–1939* (Cambridge: Cambridge University Press).

Thibau, J. (1980), *La France colonisée* (Paris: Flammarion).

Thierfelder, F. (1940), *Englischer Kulturimperialismus. Der British Council als Werkzeug der Geistigen Einkreisung Deutschlands* (Berlin: Junker und Dünnhaupt Verlag).

Tilley, J. (chairman) (1920), *Report of the Foreign Office Committee on British Communities Abroad* (London: HMSO).

Tindemans, L. (1976), *European Union* (Luxembourg: European Commission).

Towse, R. (1984), 'Report on the Research Workshop' in R. Myerscough (ed.), *Funding the Arts in Europe* (London: Policy Studies Institute).

Triesch, M. and Deutschmann, A. (1983), *Jeder für sich oder gemeinsam?* (Stuttgart: Institut für Auslandsbeziehungen).

Twardowski, F. (1970), *Anfänge der deutschen Kulturpolitik zum Ausland* (Bonn: Internationes).

UNESCO (1982), *World Conference on Cultural Policies* (Paris: UNESCO).

UNESCO (1983), *Statistical Yearbook* (Paris: UNESCO).

United States Advisory Commission on Public Diplomacy (1983), *1983 Report* (Washington, DC: US Advisory Commission on Public Diplomacy).

Unwin, S. (1960), *The Truth About A Publisher* (London: Allen & Unwin).

USIA (1983), *The United States Information Agency's International Visitor Program* (Washington, DC: USIA).

Wassener, W. (1971), 'Die Auswärtige Kulturpolitik der Bundesrepublik und ihre offiziellen Vertreter' in *Sprache im Technischen Zeitalter*, heft 39–40, pp. 262–79.

Waterfield, L. (1962), *Castle in Italy* (London: Murray).

Weber, R. (1981), *European Cultural Co-operation, Achievements and Prospects* (Strasbourg: Council of Europe).

Werner, P. (1981), Opening address at Third Conference of Ministers with Responsibility for Cultural Affairs (Strasbourg: Council of Europe).

White, A. J. S. (1965), *The British Council: the First 25 Years* (London: The British Council).

Williams, P. (ed.) (1981), *The Overseas Student Question: Studies for a Policy* (London: Heinemann).

Williams, P. (1982), *A Policy for Overseas Students* (London: Overseas Students Trust).

Wisti, F. (ed.) (1981), *Nordic Democracy* (Copenhagen: Det Danske Selskab).

Zapp, F. J. (1979), *Foreign Language Policy in Europe: An Outline of the Problem* (Brussels: European Cooperation Fund).

Zeman, S. A. B. (1973), *Nazi Propaganda* (Oxford: Oxford University Press).

Index